Chongyang Institute for Financial Studies
Renmin University of China (ed.)

# Who Will Govern the New World— the Present and Future of the G20

Chongyang Institute for Financial Studies
Renmin University of China (ed.)


# WHO WILL GOVERN THE NEW WORLD— THE PRESENT AND FUTURE OF THE G20

*ibidem*-Verlag
Stuttgart

**Bibliografische Information der Deutschen Nationalbibliothek**
Die Deutsche Nationalbibliothek verzeichnet diese Publikation in der Deutschen Nationalbibliografie; detaillierte bibliografische Daten sind im Internet über http://dnb.d-nb.de abrufbar.

**Bibliographic information published by the Deutsche Nationalbibliothek**
Die Deutsche Nationalbibliothek lists this publication in the Deutsche Nationalbibliografie; detailed bibliographic data are available in the Internet at http://dnb.d-nb.de.

This edition is an authorized translation from the Chinese-language edition.
Published by arrangement with Social Sciences Academic Press (SSAP).
All rights reserved.

Cover illustration: GDJ / openclipart

∞

Gedruckt auf alterungsbeständigem, säurefreien Papier
Printed on acid-free paper

ISBN-13: 978-3-8382-0925-8

© *ibidem*-Verlag
Stuttgart 2016

Alle Rechte vorbehalten

Das Werk einschließlich aller seiner Teile ist urheberrechtlich geschützt. Jede Verwertung außerhalb der engen Grenzen des Urheberrechtsgesetzes ist ohne Zustimmung des Verlages unzulässig und strafbar. Dies gilt insbesondere für Vervielfältigungen, Übersetzungen, Mikroverfilmungen und elektronische Speicherformen sowie die Einspeicherung und Verarbeitung in elektronischen Systemen.

All rights reserved. No part of this publication may be reproduced, stored in or introduced into a retrieval system, or transmitted, in any form, or by any means (electronical, mechanical, photocopying, recording or otherwise) without the prior written permission of the publisher. Any person who does any unauthorized act in relation to this publication may be liable to criminal prosecution and civil claims for damages.

Printed in the EU

# Contents

*Li Zhaoxing*
All in the Same Boat .................................................................................................. 7

*Chen Yulu*
Building an International "Great Finance, Great Cooperation,
Great Governance" Platform ..................................................................................... 9

*Dr. Robert Mundell*
China will be the World's Largest Economy by 2025 ............................................ 13

*Carlos Magariños*
G20: Innovation of Global Governance in the 21st Century ................................ 17

## Part 1 Global Governance in the Post-Financial Crisis Era .......... 21

*He Weiwen*
Renmin University of China Chongyang Institute
for Financial Studies Research Report on G20 Series No. 2 ................................ 23

*Martin Lees*
First G20 Think Tank Summit (Beijing, August 21–22, 2013) Beyond Economics
and Finance: The Role of the G20 in Promoting a Sustainable and Peaceful World ... 29

*Melanie Hart*
Fine-Tuning the Group of Twenty (G20) for a Post-Crisis Era: Fossil Fuel
Subsidies as a Case Study for Turning Multilateral Consensus into Multilateral Action .. 41

*Christian Dreger*
Managing Globalization through the G20 Forum ................................................. 49

*Du Hyeogn Cha*
G20 and the New Horizon of Global Governance:
Toward a More Collaborative World ...................................................................... 55

*Liliana Alvarado*
G20 Summit 2013: Future Prospects in Economic and Financial Fields .............. 59

*Gabriel Stein*
What is the Point of the G20? .................................................................................. 69

*Zsolt Darvas*
G20: Quo Vadis? ....................................................................................................... 75

*Sung Jin Kang*
G20 from the Perspective of Green Growth and Sustainable Development ........... 87

*Heribert Dieter*
The G20 and the Dilemma of Asymmetric Sovereignty:
Why Multilateralism is Failing in Crisis Prevention .............................................. 95

*Melissa Conley Tyler*
An Australian Perspective on the G20..................................................................101

*Stefano Silvestri*
What about the G20?...........................................................................................111

## Part 2 The Role of Emerging Economies ................................. 115

*José Luis Chicoma and Ana Dávila*
New Kids on the Block—the Growing Power of Emerging Countries in the G20...117

*Edison Benedito da Silva Filho*
Note on the Recent Progress of the G20 and China's Future Role
in the Multilateral Economic Agenda ..................................................................125

*Mohammed Saqib*
G20: Governing Development?............................................................................133

*Jakkie Cilliers*
The Future of the G20 Countires .........................................................................137

*Taher Hamdi Kanaan*
"Great Finance, Great Cooperation, Great Governance"
Statement to the International Think Tank Conference........................................147

*Cafer Sait Okray*
G20 and Turkey...................................................................................................159

## Part 3 China's Development and the G20's Future..................... 163

*Wang Wen and Wang Ruijing*
Interest Camps in the Framework of the G20
and Strategic Space of Emerging Countries .........................................................165

*Carlos Magariños*
G20's Future and China's Role in the G20...........................................................171

*John Kirton*
G20 Governance for the Future:
Performance, Prospects, Possibilities and China's Role ........................................179

## Part 4 G20 Think Tanks: *Joint Statement* ................................ 193

"Great Finance, Great Cooperation, Great Governance"
International Think Tank Conference ..................................................................195

*Wang Wen*
Afterword: Think Tanks, Public Diplomacy and the Chinese Dream......................197

# All in the Same Boat

*Li Zhaoxing*
**Former Foreign Minister of China,
President of the China Public Diplomacy Association**

I am very pleased to be here at the opening ceremony of the "Great Finance, Great Cooperation, Great Governance" International Think Tank Conference. I want to take this opportunity to say congratulations on a job well done. I would also like to extend my heartfelt gratitude to all of our guests representing G20 think tanks.

Personally, I am very excited to be back at the world famous Renmin University of China. My first visit to Renmin University of China was 54 years ago. As a college freshman in the Peking University chorus, I came to sing for the students and professors here. I have much admiration for this university, especially its motto "to seek truth from facts". It is also the only Chinese university to have "Chinese People" as its name, and it is the first university established in the People's Republic of China after China's liberation in 1949. To see Dean Chen Yulu appear here personally today at this conference pleases me a great deal. As Thomas Jefferson, the third President of the United States once said, being President of the United States did not make him happy, but becoming a university president made him happy.

The world is now in a phase of general peace and development, characterized by a multi-polar world order, increasing economic globalization and increasing technological breakthroughs. But the persistence of financial crises and the re-emergence of new interventionism in global politics present enormous challenges. Governments must listen to their people's heartfelt words, put the people first and promote a better life for everyone. This is the common purpose and common interest of every single nation. Second, we must face global problems together. When one considers the threats of financial crises, food and energy security, and climate change, it is clear that no country can develop without the international community. Cooperation is necessary. We must abandon the old zero sum thought process of "I win, you lose, I'm rich and you are poor. "The world needs to take initiatives for shared prosperity. Developed countries have the obligation and responsibility to help the poorest countries develop. Developing countries need to be strong and take initiatives for their own development, including openly and actively entering the global marketplace to utilize their comparative advantage.

Third, reform and innovation are the most effective tools to solve international problems. Over the past 20 years the international order has undergone immense changes. The scope of international trade has increased by fivefold and cross border investment has increased by eightfold. The old international system already cannot keep pace with these changes and needs to adapt. The international monetary system must be reformed, international cooperation must be increased, and the representation and say of developing countries in international financial institutions must be strengthened. In sum, the international financial system must be pushed in the direction of openness and fairness.

Fourth, in order to keep our international promises, we have to cooperate. This will lead to a "win-win" situation in international affairs. Trade protectionism, barriers to trade, restrictions on investment and technology exports, policies that hinder the spread of new technologies, and currency devaluation are all impulses that must be resisted at the international level. The international community must keep its promise to promote sustainable and balanced growth, reject protectionism and move beyond cold war style thinking.

Let's be perfectly clear. In the world today, every country must more vigorously uphold the U.N. Charter and respect the sovereignty of other nations by not interfering in other countries' internal affairs. Interventions from the outside will only lead to even more turmoil and pain for the people inside that country.

Ladies and gentlemen, for the past five years developing countries and emerging markets have led the global economic recovery, contributing over three quarters of new growth and maintaining two thirds of the $10.8 trillion in existing global accumulated foreign exchange reserves. As a developing country, China must remain committed to shrinking the north-south divide by helping other developing countries. Chairman Xi Jinping has said that the Chinese Dream is one of peace, development and mutual gain, the same development dream that is shared by the world. We will continue to push for peaceful development and participate in multilateral affairs, as well as support the role of the G20 and the Shanghai Cooperation Organization.

Congratulations and thanks to you all!

# Building an International "Great Finance, Great Cooperation, Great Governance" Platform

*Chen Yulu*
**President, Renmin University of China, PBOC Monetary Committee Member, Dean, Chongyang Institute for Financial Studies**

"The Great Finance, Great Cooperation, Great Governance" International Think Tank Conference, hosted by Renmin University of China and organized by Chongyang Institute for Financial Studies, welcomes think tanks from over 20 countries comprised of representatives from government, business and academia. Together we strive to plan a better global economic recovery and reform the international financial system. On behalf of Renmin University of China, I extend to you all our warmest welcome.

At present, the global economy is undergoing deep adjustments. The international financial climate is ever more complex. The recovery in developed economies is uncertain, and continued growth in emerging economies has run into many difficulties. The threat of competitive currency devaluations still lingers, and other protectionist measures still reappear.

The deep impact of the financial crisis persists. The path to sustainable international growth will be long and full of difficulties. An important question remains, should the financial crisis that began in the West also be solved under Western leadership? Can the financial storm that occurred under the Bretton Woods framework be resolved under that same framework? How can growth be stimulated to sustain the recovery? These are the root problems that world's 20 major economies must contemplate. It will require a concerted effort to address the pressing challenges we all share.

In an age of deepening global integration, economic systems are ever more complicated. Unilateral measures are not enough to overcome the great problems and challenges facing the global economy and financial system. Similarly, government intervention alone is unsustainable. We must strengthen communication and cooperation among nations, as well as strengthen three-dimensional coordination and dialog between government and nongovernment groups at every level. Open cooperation for mutual gain is the only way the world will make it out of the crisis together.

As a hub that links government and society, think tanks play an increasingly important role in designing policy alternatives. In a world that needs better communication and cooperation, it is important for think tanks from every major economy to strengthen their ties of communication and push toward consensus building. The world needs to create more platforms for think tanks to exchange ideas, especially platforms for exchanges on international financial governance. The "Great Finance,

Great Cooperation, Great Governance" international academic conference hopes to provide such a platform for the world's think tanks.

During the global financial crisis, China gained a great deal of valuable experience and of course learned many lessons. From 2008 to 2012, China contributed on average 44% of global GDP growth. The international system has foolishly gone down the destructive path of financial derivatives while growth in China's real economy is relatively stable. China's most important lesson from the financial crisis is that the development of finance must serve the real economy. Moreover, finance that serves the real economy should become the core value of global economic governance. As a specific policy proposal, we hope to limit the excessive use of financial derivatives to guarantee the flow of capital to the real economy in order to expand production and increase employment. We should promote international cooperation in emerging industries and actively foster new sources of economic growth by taking full advantage of the latent power of technological advancement to pull the world out of the crisis and create common prosperity.

## Please allow me to describe more fully my personal opinions on the matter.

1) "Great Finance" to promote shared prosperity.

It is unrealistic to think that any economy can escape the financial crisis on its own. To make it out of the crisis, the world must create a network to sustain financial coordination. Outside of monetary policy, this financial coordination framework should include macro-economic policy, fiscal policy, and the coordinated supervision and regulation of financial markets. It should also create greater cohesion between financial and industrial policy to better serve the development of the real economy. There should be increased internal communication and coordination within the world's 20 major economies to enable the creation of mutually supportive and mutually complementary policies between countries. This will help policymakers find appropriate solutions to the problems of sovereign debt and risk created by large scale and disorderly cross border financial flows. It will also help control fluctuations in commodity prices and ease global inflationary pressures.

2) "Great Cooperation" to realize shared prosperity.

Promoting a robust recovery is a top concern of the international community. No country is an island in the global economy; no country can develop by itself in the global economy. While pursuing our own national interests, reasonable attention must be paid to conditions within other countries. Competitive currency devaluations are disruptive to international markets, akin to the "beggar-thy-neighbor" policies adopted by economies during the Great Depression—it is a dead end. A more reasoned and just international economic order must show more concern for developing countries and their right to be heard within global institutions. For cooperation on global financial governance to succeed, a full, complete, and consolidated system of international financial regulation is needed. This system of financial regulation should encompass banking, securities, funds, trusts and all financial institutions, accompanied by comprehensive regulations based on a consolidated statistical system. To guarantee the stability of international finance, a global cross border system to monitor financial flows should be created. Through enhanced international cooperation we can strengthen regulation of derivatives trading, commodities trading and other highly speculative markets that impact the stability of the international financial system.

3) "Great Governance" to guarantee shared prosperity.

With the development momentum of the real economy, only a globalized world can escape this crisis. The recovery of the international economy and upgrading of the Chinese economy both rely on innovation as the driving force to bring about high quality and more competitive growth. We can win the future of development by bringing together development and innovation. The greatest bottleneck in global economic development is the inability of developing countries to realize their full potential. Growth in real global demand has not kept pace with growth in production. In the long term, there is an unbalanced distribution of resources, wealth, and development opportunities between developed and developing countries. This gives rise to a downward spiral where the less a country develops, the more backwards a country becomes, and the more backwards a country is, the less able it is to develop, thus stifling sustainable and long lasting growth in the world economy. Speeding up the social and economic development of developing countries and pushing forward the United Nations Millennium Development Goals will in the end enable the world to achieve common prosperity.

There is an old Chinese saying that only after the affairs of the people have been addressed can coordination among the leaders from the various kingdoms become possible, and when this happens, the people of the world will grow closer as a result. Starting from civil society, we can strengthen global cooperation for a global financial governance system, following a path to common prosperity.

# China will be the World's Largest Economy by 2025

*Dr. Robert Mundell*
**Nobel Memorial Prize in Economic Sciences Laureate,
Professor at Columbia University**

I am happy to be back at Renmin University of China because I once taught at this university back in 1995. That was a very happy time for me, so I am happy to be here to meet my old friends Foreign Minister Li Zhaoxing and President Chen Yulu. When I was here in 1995, President Chen was the dean of our department. I am very happy to be able to meet him whenever I come to Beijing.

I must congratulate and thank Renmin University of China Chongyang Institute for Financial Studies for holding this excellent "Great Finance, Great Cooperation, Great Governance" International Think Tank Conference. RDCY is the beginning of a very large and important Chinese research institute. I am honored to be a part of their very first conference.

Of course, at a G20 think tank conference, I must note that the G20 does not have a secretariat. There are many voices for and against the creation of a G20 secretariat, so before the September G20 meeting in Russia is held, it's very important to hold G20 think tank conferences. I remember in the 1980s I held a conference before the meeting of one of the G7 summits. We noted that the G7 had no agenda, and we felt it very difficult to hold a summit meeting without an agenda. During this time I was able to meet President Reagan and Secretary of State Kissinger, so it was a very exciting period.

The international financial system will be part of the G20 agenda in the future. I will be describing the history of the development of the international financial system, and out of this history we will be able to see future developments. In the beginning there was the British Empire. Even though it was not as strong as the United States is today, it was at the time the most powerful country in the world. It established a very large capital market based on the gold standard. After 1792 the United States began its slow rise, eventually the size of its economy surpassed that of England, France and Germany combined. After its rise and England's decline, the United States established its own monetary advantage. But many nations didn't want the Dollar to occupy a hegemonic position in the international monetary system, because as we see today, the Dollar can be devalued. After World War II and the creation of the Bretton Woods system, even though it was not an entirely new system, but rather an improvement of the old system, it was still the only workable system where America was developing and Europe was in decline. Bretton Woods also had its bad side in inflation, arbitrage of gold, and the role of gold was replaced by the Dollar. In 1971 the Bretton Woods system was replaced by the floating exchange rate system, which has persisted until today.

Each country's monetary ability has a relationship to the size of its GDP. Since 1970 the United States has been the world's largest economy, and gradually switched to a system of flexible exchange rates. Oil prices increased by 4 times in this period, and around 1980 the Dollar was extremely weak. After this, the Dollar's rise underscored its important position when flexible exchange rates created a crisis for the world. Countries like Argentina experienced severe inflation. Later, there was the euro area and the rise of the euro.

Germany, France, Italy and England are all very strong economies, but because their currencies had not been united they had no means of acquiring any sort of monetary advantage, and this had a big influence on Europe. The euro has risen to become a new safe haven from risk, but its financial system has been separated into two parts, this is an unfavourable development because it limits the creation of a strong financial system. After the creation of the euro it quickly became the second most important currency in the world. Behind this we can see the Renminbi, but the Renminbi still has a little bit of catching up to do.

There is also the IMF's special drawing rights system (SDR), which is a basket of currencies from over 15 countries. The US Dollar comprises 40% of the basket, and the Euro comprises 30% of the basket, along with the Japanese Yen and the British Pound. In 2007, I proposed that the Renmibi be included in this basket to account for China's large role in international trade and finance. Because the Renminbi is not freely convertible, it is still not included in the SDR system. SDR is still an open system, so if it is willing, I recommend the IMF consider including the Renminbi by 2016.

At a meeting held in March of 2011, then French President Sarkozy pointed out three problems in the global financial system. One is fluctuation in commodity prices, second is unstable exchange rates, and third is dealing with national governance. The first question is fluctuation in commodity prices. For example, in 2008 the price of oil was $50 a barrel, then it shot up to $148 dollars per barrel, and then fell again to $33 dollars per barrel. This is the biggest fluctuation in any commodity price ever.

The second problem is unstable exchange rates. The US Dollar is overvalued, and the Federal Reserve totally overlooked this problem. It is overvalued by 30% against the euro. This severely damaged many of China's export markets. At the G20 summit in Mexico, then President of the European Central Bank Trichet was there, and he mostly spoke about controlling capital flows. I believe that this is a very difficult goal. I think that the G20 should talk about more strategic problems that will affect the international financial system. I think that it is not necessary for the global financial system to maintain only two mainstream currency systems, even though this is very advantageous for the United States and Europe.

By 2025 China will be the world's largest economy, and it will need to create a new financial system. I believe that the SDR system should include the Renminbi, it will then include the currencies of the three largest economies and stabilize the global economy. The goal is to resist powerful fluctuations in exchange rates. If there can be stability in commodity prices, exchange rates and national governance, the global economy will develop and grow more smoothly.

At the G20 we need to talk about the interests of small countries because their competitiveness is rather weak. The protection and security of small countries should be part of what we consider.

# G20: Innovation of Global Governance in the 21st Century

*Carlos Magariños*
**Chairman of Global Alliance of SMEs,**
**Former UNIDO Director General, Argentina**

Good afternoon, ladies and gentlemen! Mr. Chen Yulu, President of Renmin University of China, Mr. Li Zhaoxing, former Foreign Minister of the People's Republic of China, Dr. Robert Mundell, Nobel Memorial Prize in Economics Laureate and Ms. Yi Zhihong, Deputy President of Renmin University of China, and to the all participants, good afternoon. It is a great honor for me to be here, at the International Think Tank Conference hosted by Renmin University of China, and to have this opportunity to speak with all of the experts from Chinese government, institutions and top universities.

Renmin University of China has illustrated its fabulous reputation as one of the nation's top universities by holding this conference and drafting the joint declaration in support of the G20 Summit in Russia. I also appreciate the professionalism of Chongyang Institute for Financial Studies for preparing the related materials and organizing the conference. Their contribution has been quite impressive. I now serve as the Chairman of the Global Alliance of SMEs and this conference will definitely provide a remarkable platform for strengthening the provision of public goods. Now we all agree on the idea that specific public goods should be provided together at the national level in order to promote economic competitiveness.

From my standpoint, it is necessary to offer public goods for the global society. Provision of public goods can ensure an increasing integration of the international society, especially in the global economy. The significance of procuring international public goods is that it is just as important as guaranteeing stability in global finance. In the past few years we have experienced both real and latent economic losses due to the lack of public goods. In this context there are some challenges, such as decreasing demand for products, payment delays and weakened liquidity for SMEs. Besides these issues, reduction of liquidity, tightening of credit and augmentation of financial costs will in no doubt lead to the bankruptcy of SMEs at a worldwide level.

There is considerable literature on the efficient provision of Global Public Goods, and their contribution to development and prosperity. At the national level, the work to provide public goods is obviously done by local governments. At the international level, however, we can only rely on a patchwork of institutions created more than half century ago. The contribution of the G20 alters the structure of multilateral financial systems, provides a new balancing mechanism for the coordination and implementation of policies, and makes more space for institutions in charge of regulation, renewing loans and responsibility.

Working as a Board of Directors or—as some have said—a "Council of Governors" for the global economy, G20 countries can claim some reasonable success in building consensus around a common set of actions to bring the international financial crisis under control, preventing further damage and minimizing its social costs. To achieve the above targets, the Group expands on its original design. We have to reflect on the situation facing the G7 meeting in 1999, when it was first created. It defined the G20 as a meeting to be attended by finance ministers and presidents of central banks, a new mechanism that is to enhance dialog on financial and economic policies for systemically significant economies. After its emergence at the G7 in 1999, global financial crises completely altered many established patterns. Between November 2008 and November 2010 (running from the first meeting of G20 Leaders in Washington to its fifth meeting in Toronto), the Heads of State and Government of the G20 have met five times.

This series of meetings marked the transformation of the G20 from a deliberative body into a decision-making forum, a centre for world economic development to find its way out of the worst financial crisis in almost a century. On the basis of its previous successes, the G20 will undergo another vital turn as it moves into the role of a strategic planning body. It is well known that the G20 agenda has three primary aspects. One is to serve as the framework for strong, sustainable and balanced growth. Second is to reform the architecture of international finance. Third is to strengthen financial regulation. The above goals were mentioned at the original meetings, with development for all appearing in the fourth agenda. The 2012 Mexico Summit expanded the agenda again to include food security and innovation, extended dialog with non-G20 member states, and the evolution of Y20 (Youth20) and B20 (Business20). Business 20 was initially hosted in Toronto. New items on the G20 Leaders' Summit agenda will include energy security, C20 (Civil Society 20) and G20 Labor Minister Meetings.

These various meetings and approaches will provide sources of much needed legitimacy and transparency to promote and deepen the G20 decision-making process. Holistic solutions and strategic planning on substantive long-term challenges are needed in systemic crises. At the same time, it places a challenge on the G20 working mechanisms. Those routines and mechanisms seem to work reasonably well for decision making to confront concrete and immediate problems. It remains to be seen yet how well they would do for strategic planning to address longer term challenges, such as those posed by food or energy security, the environment or development for all.

Given the certain vacuum in multilateralism, one could find it reasonable for the G20 to fill the space. The real challenge, however, would be to keep the focus and dynamism of the G20 while avoiding the temptation to address all the problems at once, discerning clearly where there is room for consensus and collective action producing significant results in reasonable period of time, and where it is necessary to refrain from overlapping with existing multilateral mechanisms. This balance is important for the world economy that still calls for clear leadership and strong decision making.

The global economy will confront enormous challenges. In such a context, the advanced economies need to sustain a macroeconomic setting to support industrial activity while simultaneously devising appropriate measures to ensure debt sustainability. Those countries also need to stabilize company balance sheets and restore credit channels. Although vulnerability varies across emerging markets and developing economies, they all must have a balanced emphasis on reinvigorating economic activity with policies to contain capital outflows, probably through the implementation of structural reforms and prudent macroeconomic policies, according to the different stages in their economic cycles.

Should forecasts for reduced volatility in the coming months (due to monetary and financial changes in the US) not materialize or take longer than expected, emerging economies should be ready to handle further investment portfolio shifts through macroeconomic policies, especially regarding monetary easing policies, to achieve satisfactory results. We will just wait and see.

The leaders of the G20 must concentrate on the current agenda to implement the G20 decisions. To provide global financial stability and global public goods, it needs further coordination of macroeconomic policies and structural reform on global financial regulation systems for the purpose of bolstering and intensifying the voices of emerging economies. We have to review the IMF's quota system in its new revision that starts in January 2014. It is necessary to do more work and strengthen cooperation with the IMF and foster regional finance coordination.

One of major tasks for the G20 is to support the FSB (Financial Stability Board), reinforce financial management, facilitate the institutionalization process of the FSB, design its regulatory framework, and carry out peer reviews. Simultaneously, it is necessary to take prudent and systematic measures to tighten supervision of shadow banks and counter derivatives (OTC).

To better utilize global financial stability, the Global Alliance of SMEs suggests that more research be conducted on global value chains so as to learn more about the relationship between global financial value chains and trade, employment and investment in order to reduce financing obstacles in the real economy.

As the most crucial innovation of global governance in the 21st century, I believe that protecting the G20 at most requires a focus on an effective agenda to overcome financial crises and accomplish its given mission.

Thank you!

# Part I
# Global Governance in the Post-Financial Crisis Era

After the 2008 global financial crisis, the international landscape underwent drastic changes and adjustments. While reflecting on the crisis, nations have been continuously searching for paths that are suitable to their development and that avoid repeating the mistakes made during the process of globalization. After the world entered the "Post-Financial Crises Era", the developed economies recovered slowly, while growth in major developing economies began to slip. The global economy is now situated in a period of unbalanced recovery. In a new era full of challenges and opportunities, how will the international economy, political structures, and international relations change, and how can the members of the G20 better serve as a part of global governance?

# Renmin University of China Chongyang Institute for Financial Studies Research Report on G20 Series No. 2

## Analysis of G20 Conferences and Recommendations for the 2013 Leaders' Summit

*He Weiwen*
Former Economic and Commercial Counselor, Chinese Consulates General San Francisco and New York, Senior Fellow, Renmin University of China, Chongyang Institute for Financial Studies

The emergence of the G20 Finance Ministers and Central Bank Governors' Meeting in 1999 was intended to tackle the Asian financial crisis. After the global financial crisis in 2008, it then became the major international dialog platform for multilateral economic strategy. On September 5th and 6th, the eighth meeting of the G20 Leaders' Summit will be held in St. Petersburg, Russia. The Russia Summit carries great global and strategic significance, and will offer a crucial opportunity for China's participation in world economic governance. China must make good use of it. An overall evaluation of the status and role of the G20 follows:

## I. As a multilateral platform for global strategic economic dialog, the G20 exceeds any other international system or platform. The G20 Finance Ministers and Central Bank Governors' Meeting has the following characteristics:

1. The number of countries participating in the G20 is adequate for emerging and developing economies to participate jointly. G20 countries (including the EU) are home to 60% of the world's population and represent 80% of the world's economy and 90% of its trade volume. Unlike the traditional G7+1 developed nations' club, there are 10 emerging economies and developing countries in the G20, exactly 50%. Therefore the G20 is authoritative and global. Although APEC, the East Asian Summit (EAS) and Asia-Europe Meeting (ASEM) are all essential, they are regional summits, not global forums.
2. The dialog covers almost all economic and financial areas. Topics include the usual G7 macroeconomic coordination, the international financial system under the management of the IMF and World Bank, stability, governance and reform, the UN Millennium Development Goals, trade and investment liberalization in the WTO, climate change and green development within the UN Climate Conference.

3. Operation of the G20 combines flexibility with execution. The G20 is an unofficial conference, but since it is attended by the leaders of its member countries and has an operational level that includes finance ministers and central bank governors, it also possesses great power of execution. The G20 also includes Business 20, Youth 20, Labor 20, and Think Tank 20.

## II. The G20's weakened role in coordinating countries to stabilize the world economy and financial markets

Previous Leaders' Summits and series summits have contributed to overcoming the global financial crisis by coordinating national efforts, supervising the turmoil in financial markets, and promoting the revival of the world economy and reform of the global financial system. In the period between 2009 and 2010, when the shock of the financial crisis was severe, the summits had a fairly good effect. With the gradual recovery of the world economy, diverging interests have become more apparent and the role of the G20 has diminished. The 2011 European Credit Crisis dragged down the world economy and increased risk. To solve the issue, G20 central banks individually adopted quantitative easing policies independent of one another. The G20's future coordination effect will pale in comparison to what existed during the 2009–2010 period.

## III. The past achievements of the G20 are generally in line with China's proposals

1. China's top leadership, finance ministers and central bank governors have attended previous G20 conferences. They directly participated in global cooperation after the financial crisis, helping to conquer the crisis through a no-effort-spared approach to enhance recovery and governance in the financial system. This kind of coordination is fully supported by China's policies and proposals. Many of China's policies and proposals have been received favourably by the G20. For example, China has proposed the increase of voting shares and status for developing countries in the IMF, promoting domestic demand stimulus during the global economic recovery, promoting free trade, anti-protectionism and stability in world exchange markets, enhancing energy conservation and emissions reduction in response to climate change, and measures related to world food security.
2. The final outcomes of past G20 summits, including the outcomes outlined in Leaders' Statements, are essentially consistent with China's thinking and proposals. A good example is the 2012 Los Cabos Summit Leaders Statement, which included the "Los Cabos Growth and Jobs Action Plan". The focus of this plan was on supporting growth, financial stability and global recovery through reform of the international financial system, reform of IMF voting rights and funding sources to strengthen the status of emerging economies. This plan also supported the WTO's core role in anti-protectionism, supported the completion of the

Doha Round, endeavored to guarantee food security to deal with fluctuations of commodity prices, highlighted poverty relief as a core of the development agenda, and advocated for green growth. China has more channels to elaborate its views in all of these fields and establish meaningful relations with other countries through the G20.

3. During the post-financial crises period, significant developments in the Chinese economy have greatly elevated and expanded China's influence in the world. Successful experiences in vital areas have set positive examples for the G20. For example, at the fifth BRICS Summit in South Africa, President Xi Jinping confirmed a plan to create a Development Bank for BRICS. This plan has made it into the Russia Summit Outline (the foundational infrastructure for multilateral banks).

4. G20 announcements and initiatives unfavorable to China have been relatively mild, and also have greatly differed from unfavorable statements against China made by the United States. With respect to the RMB exchange rate, China has been encouraged to adopt market mechanism reform. With respect to trade rebalancing, the G20 has made general statements about the distinct needs of deficit countries and surplus countries without blaming China. Though China does not entirely agree with the G20's conclusion on rebalancing, it takes an inclusive attitude.

## Limitations of the G20: While the G20 has played an important and irreplaceable role, it also has significant limitations

### I. The G20 does not play a decisive role in any of the fields in which it is involved

1. Cooperation on macro-policies for economic and job growth is the internal responsibility of each country. Countries only take action at their own discretion after signing an agreement. The Los Cabos Leaders' Statement has warned against the "spillover effect" of macro-policies. The Federal Reserve started QE3 two months after the close of the Summit, and announced an orderly exit last month. The announcement shook the stock and currency exchange markets as well as the price of gold, causing enormous amounts of capital to flow back to the US from emerging economies. According to June data from a Boston consulting firm that tracked 45,000 management funds (with a total value of $17.5 trillion), the capital outflow from emerging economies amounted to $19.86 billion, with $5.6 billion dollars just in the last week. This is the largest sum recorded since the firm started its tracking in 1995. From January to May, the net inflow was $18.1 billion. Net outflow reached $1.7 billion dollars at the end of June. Negotiations within the G20 were completely ignored.

2. The IMF plays a more direct role in stabilizing the financial market. The annual meeting held by the IMF and World Bank did not consider the quantitative easing monetary policies of the central banks in the US, Japan, EU and UK as a huge risk. Japan has gone even further with its quantitative easing.
3. Even the IMF and BIS cannot limit government policy. The Global Finance Stability Report issued by the IMF in April pointed out that quantitative easing policies would be beneficial in the short term but the risks would add up in the medium term. The BIS annual report published on June 23rd recommended that central banks quit their easing policies to avoid impeding the growth of world economy. However, UK and EU central banks persisted in easing while Japan accelerated the process.
4. Quota reform in the IMF is not driven by the G20 but by the IMF itself. G20 supports this reform, but it is national governments that play the decisive role. These reform initiatives have not been authorized by the US and other crucial members, so the end result is still pending.
5. Before the ink was dry on the Los Cabos G20 Summit Leaders' Statement in support of the Doha Round, the US and EU respectively launched the Trans-Pacific Partnership (TPP) and Trans-Atlantic Trade and Investment Partnership (TTIP) negotiations, effectively ignoring the Doha Round.
6. The principle platform for dealing with climate change remains the UN Climate Change Conference, which is struggling to achieve results. In this area, the G20 is just a talk shop.

## II. The G20 overlaps with other multilateral systems.

Every area in which the G20 is involved already has an alternative existing mechanism. These mechanisms are decisive in solving problems and should be utilized. With a G20 Leaders' consensus it would be easy to take actions within the relevant systems. The G20's role is limited by its redundancy, and its inability to reach a consensus and concrete decisions on difficult projects.

## III. The G20 does not represent the interests of the most disadvantaged groups in the world

The G20 consists of major economies, yet the majority of the world is made up of small and poor countries. Although these states account for just a small proportion of the world economy, they represent the majority of the sovereign states. Moreover, they are at the frontlines with respect to the challenges facing the world economy, including the realization of the UN Millennium Development Goals, food security, poverty relief, and climate change. G20 conferences fail to adequately address these pressing matters.

## I. The impact of the G20 is increasing in strength. The main reasons for this are as follows:

1. The evolving "fourth phase" of globalization is the economic foundation of the G20. Under this phase, the information and communications technology base of modern, large scale production will undergo dramatic changes. The "economic boundaries" of countries will become increasingly blurred, and the production chains between developed countries and emerging economies will be homogenized. Coexistence and cooperation among countries will also increase.
2. The most vital factor governing the global economy is still finance. The operation of world financial systems is strongly related to daily coordination and risk. World financial governance will be a focus for quite some time.
3. Climate change and food security threaten the interests of all humanity. UN systems are huge and inefficient, demanding the creation of platforms among major nations to coordinate actions. These platforms act as a bridge linking the UN with respective nations.

## II. Recommendations for China's Participation in the G20

1. Maintain a low profile and be pragmatic. China does not need to advertise to get the attention of the world, but it should recognize that most of the world's economic administrative power and speaking rights will continue to reside in the hands of the United States and other developed countries for a long time. China should work to realize the goal of strong, balanced, and sustainable growth in the global economy.
2. Attend all G20 activities to the greatest extent possible. This means gaining an understanding and knowledge of the world and the main trends in national economic development. Through participation in G20 activities, China can learn how to manage risk, enhance its familiarity with and monitoring of economic governance, and improve its national position. In addition to attending all the G20 Finance Ministers and Central Bank Governors' Meetings, Business 20, Youth 20, Labor 20, and Think Tank 20 meetings, China should promote a "G20 Plus" that includes consultations on important issues at the working think tank level within the G20 framework.
3. China should propose realistic policies and programmes and take a leading role in the process. China could advocate for the foundation of a G20 infrastructure information platform and a G20 secretariat.
4. Take advantage of IMF voting share reform and IMF management systems. China should promote reform of the SDR, while pushing the RMB toward the status of an international reserve currency.

# First G20 Think Tank Summit (Beijing, August 21–22, 2013) Beyond Economics and Finance: The Role of the G20 in Promoting a Sustainable and Peaceful World

*Martin Lees*

In preparation for the first G20 Think Tank Summit, which is intended "to provide G20 Leaders with insights into international issues and relationships", the participants are asked to include their views on three specific subjects: 1) their opinion on the G20; 2) the G20's future prospects, especially in economic and financial fields; and 3) China's role in the G20. To provide a basis for responding to these important questions, I will first briefly outline the characteristics of 21st century challenges to which the G20 and the wider world community must respond. This will help to clarify the potential role of the G20 in promoting a sustainable and peaceful world at this critical time in international affairs.

As the expertise and priorities of the G20 itself and of the Think Tank Summit are dominated by economic and financial concerns, I will focus on two of the four stated Summit objectives: 1) "explore new ways to promote the stable development of the global economy" and 2) "provide helpful advice on economic governance for the world leaders."

## Characteristics of 21st Century Challenges

Economic growth has generated enormous progress for hundreds of millions of people across the world who today enjoy a standard of living unprecedented in human history. Millions have emerged from poverty and life expectancy, literacy and health have greatly improved. In overall terms, substantial progress has been made towards achieving the United Nations Millennium Development Goals established by the leaders of the world in 2000.

However, this progress has been achieved at the high cost of environmental devastation and at the expense of the millions of people who remain mired in poverty and deprivation, excluded from the benefits and opportunities of the modern world. With the world population projected to exceed 9 billion people by 2050 and the pressure increasing on our fragile planet's ecological and environmental systems as a result of swelling consumption by the world's growing middle class, continued progress is by no means assured. In the absence of innovative and effective strategies, this progress may indeed be reversed.

The global community today faces an array of interconnected social, economic, environmental and security issues that will determine the prospects for progress and peace. Among the most critical challenges include demographic change, entrenched poverty and deprivation, rising inequality and unemployment, resource scarcity and overuse, intensifying competition for vital resources, ecological degradation, ocean acidification and the rising risk of irreversible destabilization of the global climate.

These powerful, underlying and rapidly transforming realities will determine the prospects and vulnerabilities of the world economy. In effect, the stable development of the world economy in coming decades—which is the exact focus of the G20 Think Tank Summit—will be shaped and determined by issues beyond the economic arena, such as the tightening constraints on resources, the environment and climate, which in turn have consequences for poverty, exclusion, human security and development and thus for world peace.

In order to consider how the G20 can play an effective role in future world governance, we must first clarify the characteristics of the emerging challenges that face the world community. The issues facing the global community are unprecedented in scale: we live in the "anthropogenic age," where human activities now impact the behavior of the ecological and physical systems of the planet. The projected increases in population and consumption by the middle of the 21st century will have an intensifying impact on the environment and climate. This underscores the need to develop more responsible strategies for growth and development.

The challenges across different fields are essentially interconnected, although we insist on treating them separately. For example, to meet the needs of 9 billion people, energy output needs to double by 2050. However, climate emissions must be severely cut, by as much as 50 to 80 percent, if the rise in global average temperature is to be held below the 2°C change considered to be safe. We need coherent strategies that integrate the economic, social, environmental and security facets of policy.

The issues we face are systemic. We need new models, new patterns of cooperation and new forms of governance—along with carefully considered and coherent strategies—to understand and manage the behavior of the complex systems of the modern world. Today's disconnected, national, sectoral, and short-term interventions are insufficient to assure the stability of the world financial, economic and climate systems. The issues described above are in a process of rapid and dynamic change and do not progress linearly. We must expect sudden shocks, not gradual change. Ecosystems—and governments—do suddenly collapse under sustained stress. It is an illusion to believe that we face a gradual process of global warming with time to deliberate and delay. Unless we act soon, we will have passed the threshold into irreversible climate destabilization. Despite 20 years of inconclusive negotiations, emissions continue to rise and we remain on a path to dangerous climate change.

The issues are also increasingly high-risk, demanding timely, precautionary action to avert breakdown. For example, the "positive feedback processes" which will drive climate change beyond our control are starting up. We need to anticipate change and to create the capability and the flexibility to make decisions and act rapidly. This constitutes a major challenge to policy because action may have to be taken before the issues are clear to the public; by the time they become evident, it may be too late for action to be effective.

The issues of the modern world are in many aspects truly global, demanding solidarity and cooperation to assure fairness in the allocation of the costs and benefits of a globalized and interdependent world.

## I. New models, policies and priorities for growth

The prospects and the role of the G20 must be assessed in relation to the key characteristics of the challenges that we face today and that, more importantly, will intensify in coming years. As Einstein once said, "it is not the consciousness that created the problems that will solve them." We need new ideas and new patterns of governance and cooperation to manage the interconnected challenges of the modern world; we simply cannot manage the issues of the 21st Century with the policies and tools of the 20th.

At this juncture, and significant opportunity, in world affairs, the overriding challenge for the G20 is to lead the world towards a new path of inclusive and responsible growth and globalization: to make economic progress sustainable in human, social and environmental terms. Yet today's policies for recovery and growth are still founded on the implicit assumption that the world economy will grow indefinitely on the present basis, and therefore consumption, together with the accompanying pollution, emissions and waste, can double by around 2030. But both science and evidence from around the world reject this assumption.

The human population is currently overusing the biosphere's ecological resources by more than 50%. All regions of the world are already experiencing the impacts of climate change driven by the rise in global temperature of "only" 0.8°C since 1750. The present business-as-usual path of fossil-fuel-based growth would lead to a rise of around 5°-6°C by 2100, with devastating consequences. It is in fact an illusion to believe that a stable and productive world economy can be preserved if the fundamental social, resource, environmental and ecological issues are not properly resolved.

The G20 has generally been concerned about containing deep imbalances in the world economy. But the greatest and most dangerous imbalance we face today, and which will have a large impact on the future, is the escalating imbalance between human activity and the capacities of the natural world. The Club of Rome made this simple but central point over 40 years ago; exponential growth in consumption, pollution and waste cannot continue indefinitely on a finite and fragile planet. If this issue is not addressed and resolved, the stable development of the world economy will not be attainable. These concerns are well understood in the security sector in many major countries, where they are recognized as "non-traditional" threats to peace.

Indeed we face complex and intensifying problems, yet we have enormous human, scientific, technological, organizational and financial capacities to resolve them if we choose to do so and if we assign them top priority. We have seen vast financial resources deployed in just a few years to preserve the banking system from the consequences of its self-inflicted crisis. We must assign high priority to preserving a viable environment and a stable climate if we are to sustain growth and to preserve world peace.

There is also a remarkable opportunity to lay the foundations for the sustainable, productive and employment-generating economies of the future by focusing not only on the quantity of growth as measured by GDP, but on the quality or content of growth. This will require a major shift in priorities from the present approach, in which policies for economic growth and financial stability have been given highest priority while human, employment, social and environmental considerations have been subsidiary. This approach is based on the grounds that, once growth resumes, social, employment and environmental issues can gradually be resolved. This strategy is, however, failing in many countries as rising inequality, entrenched poverty and unemployment now coexist with growth in aggregate as measured by GDP.

Our present model of growth is failing. A new growth strategy must be implemented that places higher priority on the human, social and employment goals of policy in harmony with the real constraints and capacities of the natural world. This new growth strategy must be carefully articulated with the instrumental financial and economic policies required to achieve them. This may seem an unrealistic hope, but a number of countries across the world, China in particular, are moving in this direction, recognizing two key points: 1) a business-as-usual strategy for economic growth is not viable in the new conditions of the modern world of today and tomorrow; and 2) a new environmentally and socially responsible growth strategy can bring great benefits in terms of human welfare, competitiveness and economic opportunity.

It is an important and delicate task for think tanks to question the implicit assumptions on which the "conventional wisdom" underlying policy is based. From the above brief analysis, three fundamental questions arise which are directly relevant to the future role of the G20 in world affairs.

Is it realistic to base economic strategy on the assumption that growth in consumption, pollution and waste can continue indefinitely on a finite planet? Is it the most appropriate response to the economic crisis to stimulate further demand for consumption? Should economic and financial considerations take primacy in national and international policies when the critical issues determining the future are inequality, exclusion, unemployment and the preservation of a viable environment and a stable climate? Is it not clear that we need a new level of intelligent forward planning and concerted international action to master the dangerous systemic challenges which threaten the future in the limited time now available?

This brief overview of the issues of the 21st Century, to which the G20 must respond, can be summarized under the following five points:

1. The present strategy for economic recovery is to resume growth as soon as possible by stimulating consumption and thus increasing the use of fossil fuels and resources. However, this strategy would have devastating consequences for the ecology and environment as it threatens the natural capital of the planet and the global climate on which humanity and all other species depend. The science and analysis are clear: the scale of human activities has reached the point where the business-as-usual model of growth is no longer viable in the long term. Indeed, the more rapidly we return to this established trajectory of growth, the more devastating the longer-term consequences will be. Therefore, to assure stable and sustainable progress in the future, we must urgently restructure national economies and energy systems to become resource-efficient, inclusive and sustainable. We are increasingly living at the ecological and financial expense of future generations.
2. There are many examples across the world that demonstrate the immense opportunities to build productive, low-carbon, sustainable, healthy and inclusive societies and economies of the future that fulfil the needs and aspirations of more than 9 billion people within the constraints of a viable environment and a stable climate. Moreover, many practical examples in nations, states, cities, communities and enterprises show that the benefits far outweigh the costs of transition, and that early action is cheaper than action delayed. There is a choice fora better future.
3. In most areas of policy, a wide array of new approaches is available using proven, existing technologies and methods. There is ample knowledge about what needs to be done: restructuring energy and productive systems, cutting emissions and improving energy efficiency, reducing resource intensity, restoring degraded lands and generating employment and opportunity. It is not a lack of knowledge which restrains action.
4. Humanity has never had a greater range of capabilities to master such problems: human creativity and energy; knowledge and expertise; technological solutions and organizational capabilities could be mobilized and focused at every level to tackle the problems we face.
5. However, we seem unable to recognize the looming threats to our civilization and to overcome our differences to agree on action to avert them. This is the tragedy of the human condition, and has been the fate of previous civilizations, whose downfall was caused by the lack of vision and commitment and obstruction by

powerful vested interests that prevented essential action in time to prevent breakdown. A series of inconclusive and failed negotiations on critical global issues simply underlines this incapacity to agree and act so as to preserve a decent, safe and prosperous world for future generations.

We are at a critical juncture in world affairs where incremental, partial and slow adjustments to established institutions and entrenched ideas will no longer be sufficient to master the scale and intensity of the systemic challenges we face. Transformational change in ideas, strategies, partnerships and institutions is essential. Fortunately, the certainties of market fundamentalism have weakened and there is now an opportunity to advance new ideas. The public, unsettled by evidence of the deep problems and vulnerabilities of the modern world and the growing risks and threats to the future, is increasingly calling on governments for action and effective policy.

From this perspective, the debate on the future role of the G20 takes on a real and urgent importance. We have the capability to resolve our problems if we can find the will and the solidarity to do so. But the established system for world governance is proving inadequate. The G20, as a new, innovative element in the framework of global governance has the potential to provide a constructive vision and guidance to a rudderless, divided and confused world, and to propose a new path for world development to salvage the future.

## The Future Role and Potential of the G20

### I. My opinion of the G20

From the analysis above, it is clear that the world needs new patterns of governance and cooperative leadership to manage the new constellation of issues and the changing structures of power, interest and influence. Many of us have followed with close attention the evolution of the G20 from its origins as a group of finance ministers and its growth from the G7 to the G8, to the G8 + 5, and finally to the G20 of today.

The G20 clearly has the potential to foster economic growth and stability and a more effective and secure world financial system. It could also extend its role to address the underlying drivers of the global risks, threats and imbalances sketched above, and thereby lead the world towards a more sustainable and just path of development based on solidarity and cooperation. However, perhaps because of its origins, a number of weaknesses will have to be corrected if the G20 is to play a significant leadership role in world affairs.

- The G20 brings together an important but small group of key countries. This naturally implies the exclusion of a large majority of the world's countries. In order to strengthen the legitimacy of its positions, the G20 must reach out to effec-

tively engage a wider range of concerned countries in its deliberations. In particular, the interests and concerns of the poorer and disadvantaged countries who suffer the consequences of global change must be taken properly into account.
- The dominance of economic and financial policy issues in the work of the G20 has limited the time available for serious consideration of wider, more fundamental issues, such as the social, resource and environmental issues outlined above. These issues are often viewed as externalities or second order priorities. This distorted approach is inadequate to achieve sustained economic growth and stability and a prosperous and secure world.
- The strong focus on the management of crises, imbalances and vulnerabilities in global financial and economic systems has limited the attention and time devoted to fundamental structural problems and to crucial emerging longer-term threats and challenges.
- The diversity of interests and views within the G20 can be a great source of strength if they can be processed towards a constructive consensus. However, in the absence of a strong process of collaboration and preparation, these differences can inhibit agreement by the G20 as a group and thus obstruct effective action.
- Finally, as the preparation of each Summit Meeting is the responsibility of the convening nation, it is difficult to achieve consistency in the preparation of the discussions and effective follow-up of the agreements reached. Substantial financial expenditures and intense organizational efforts are required to bring the most influential national leaders together at each Summit. Although the summits attract intense media attention, for all the above reasons, the relevance and effectiveness of the decisions made by the G20, and the role of the G20 itself in world affairs, are not clear to the public.

## II. The Future Prospects of the G20

The G20 has the potential, the opportunity and the responsibility to develop a new style of cooperative leadership at this critical time in world affairs. In the past, major innovation in the framework of institutions for international cooperation has come about as the consequence of war. The catastrophe of two world wars triggered the creation of the United Nations System and the Bretton Woods institutions so as to manage global issues to avoid the disastrous errors of the past and lay the foundations for a prosperous and peaceful world. Similarly, the European Community was established explicitly to avert the threats of another European conflict by building economic interdependence and cooperation. In both of these cases, the community of nations felt compelled to act in the face of perceived threats, overriding common challenges in the pursuit of opportunity.

We are now at a turning point in international relations where innovation in governance and policy is clearly needed to address the intensifying threats to the common future of all nations. We are obliged to act before the situation becomes unmanageable. The G20 could rise to this historic challenge by recognizing the scale, the intensity and the urgency of the emerging threats to progress and peace, by defining a positive vision of opportunities and hope, and by building international consensus and motivating public support for action.

In effect, the future prospects of the G20 depend on a fundamental political choice. It can choose to remain predominantly focused on economic and financial issues, seeking to reduce imbalances, vulnerabilities and risks and to improve supervision and regulation to assure stable and open economic and financial systems. These are essential and urgent tasks, as sustained and stable economic growth is a precondition for poverty reduction and world development, and underlies the means to generate the investment resources needed to meet the needs of a growing world population.

The G20 could, however, decide to extend its role in world affairs beyond this focus on economics and finance so as to enhance coherence, vision and leadership in managing the critical issues of the 21st Century as outlined above. It would thus become the unique responsibility of heads of state and heads of government to advance the overall goals of equitable and sustainable world development at G20 meetings, rising above the individual sectoral competences of ministers. This would fill a crucial gap in the framework of global governance, providing a focus and an impulse for vision, strategy and concerted action to avert dangerous risks and to achieve a just, sustainable and peaceful world for present and future generations.

Briefly, a decision to extend the role of the G20 to provide clear and progressive leadership in world affairs would, in my view, imply the following:

1. Cross-sectoral integration of policy:
   The three critical facets of policy—resources, environment and climate, social and employment issues and economics and finance-should be properly balanced and integrated within a coherent overall strategy and in the preparations and deliberations of each summit. With adequate preparation, this would enable world leaders to recognize and cooperate on the fundamental systemic issues which, beyond the economic arena, will determine the future of humanity. In particular, both scientific and real-world evidence together demonstrate that the scale and the global nature of the climate challenge demand a new level of statesmanship, new vision and urgent international action. The G20 could provide the needed leadership to accomplish the following: mobilize a powerful movement of concerted international action to address this existential threat to humanity; explain to the global public why strong climate action must be taken before it is too late; and communicate how low-carbon, resource-efficient societies of the future will offer immense benefits in human welfare and security.

2. Anticipation and forward thinking:
   Greater forward-thinking and analysis by the G20 is needed to develop a positive vision of the future with new longer-term strategies for sustainable and inclusive growth to promote a more stable and equitable distribution of the costs and benefits of globalization. Each Summit agenda should ensure the consideration of fundamental issues and effective time management should be imposed so that these issues are not pushed aside by the pressures of crisis management.

3. Innovation in international governance:
   The G20 could initiate an international debate on how to reform the established framework of international governance to respond to the systemic, connected and rapidly developing challenges and risks of the modern world. It could also revive a global dialog on strategies to avert the intensifying threats to humanity and to build productive, sustainable and equitable societies of the future, based on the current resources available.

4. Accounting for wider interests:
   Building on the processes already implemented by the Russian Federation in its preparations for the St. Petersburg Summit, the G20 could also reach out more systematically to engage major interests and sources of expertise. In particular, the G20 must visibly and systematically respect and consider the interests and concerns of the billions of impoverished people who are largely excluded from the processes of international decision making. The legitimacy and the successful implementation of policies elaborated by the G20 will largely depend on whether they are considered to be fair and constructive by the wider world community.

5. Independent scientific advice:
   The G20 could benefit immensely from the provision of balanced scientific advice to inform its deliberations. Critical global issues cannot be properly understood and resolved and future risks cannot be properly assessed, without the knowledge and insights derived from careful and objective scientific analysis informing the policy process. Such changes in focus and process would enable the leaders of the G20 to take proper account of the scale, intensity and complexity of the emerging challenges and the deep transformations in progress which will determine the future. On this basis, the G20 has the potential to enhance global cooperation and concerted action to avert the common threats to the future of humanity and to build a just, productive and sustainable world.

## III. China's Role in the G20

Over the past thirty years, the policies of "reform and opening-up" have transformed China from a poor and struggling country to a major economic power. In spite of evident domestic and international challenges, rapid growth will continue in China and in Asia as a whole. In contrast, the major existing powers—the United States, Europe and Japan—will continue to struggle against intractable problems as they seek to return to sustainable and balanced economic growth, reduce levels of inequality and unemployment and restore financial stability. The scale of the Chinese economy, its financial power and its full interdependence with global economic, financial and trading systems imply that China can play an increasingly important role in the future of world governance and the future of the G20. The issues of economic growth, social cohesion, environment and development highlighted in this chapter are similar to those that confront the leadership of China in determining the future path of China's development. The commitment to further reduce poverty and to improve the lives and opportunities of the Chinese people remains paramount, with very evident consequences for energy and resource overuse and environmental degradation at this stage of the development process. Over the past 20 years, Chinese leadership has carefully considered and taken actions to reorient the trajectory of the Chinese economy toward a new development path that is less environmentally damaging, targeted at reducing poverty and inequality, and more regionally balanced. For example:

- The goals of the Twelfth Five Year Plan include major expenditures on education, science, research and development, green technologies and infrastructure. These areas are intended to lay the foundations for a low-carbon, resource-efficient, innovative and competitive economy of the future.
- The Xiao Kang Programme proposes a new strategy for development to achieve an "all around prosperous society".
- The China Council for International Cooperation on Environment and Development, established in 1992, directly provides Chinese leaders with balanced advice on how to integrate economic growth with environmental protection. It engages senior Chinese and international experts and officials in developing specific policy recommendations on priority issues based on sound scientific preparation. It also explores key policy options in relation to their risks and longer-term implications.

Many statements show that the new leadership in China is fully aware of the reality of the social, economic, environmental and international challenges to China's longer-term development. Moreover, they intend to act strongly in response. Over the past thirty years, China has in fact demonstrated a constructive role in addressing these challenges through thoughtful policy analysis, careful experimentation, learning from wide international experience, and longer-term indicative planning and policies to guide the future of 1.3 billion people, 22% of the world's population. China is strongly positioned to contribute ideas, insights and experience to the debate on new strategies for world development in the 21st Century, which will be of particular relevance to other developing countries. Furthermore, China can play an important role in the evolution of the new approaches, policies and partnerships that the G20 can adopt to advance stable and peaceful world development.

# Fine-Tuning the Group of Twenty (G20) for a Post-Crisis Era: Fossil Fuel Subsidies as a Case Study for Turning Multilateral Consensus into Multilateral Action

*Melanie Hart*
**Centre for American Progress, Washington, DC**
**Renmin University Chongyang Institute for Financial Studies**
**G20 Think Tank Forum**
**August 2013, Beijing, P. R. China**

The global economy is moving through a major inflection point. For the first time in over two hundred years, the economic balance of power is shifting from the developed to the developing world. As of 2013, emerging economies now account for over half of our global economic growth, and their lead is expected to widen over the coming decades.[1]

China, in particular, is taking on a larger role in this new global economy. Over the next five years, the emerging world is projected to provide around 74 percent of overall global growth, with China accounting for around 33 percent, almost half of the emerging market total.[2]

This new economic constellation creates new opportunities but also new challenges. When global economic growth was concentrated among a small number of western developed nations, concerted action among that small group of nations was enough to impact the global market. Multilateral organizations such as the Group of Seven (G7) and the Organization for Economic Co-operation and Development (OECD) reflected that small-group mentality. Emerging markets did not have a seat at the table in those organizations because it was assumed that adding more seats at the table would simply slow consensus-building without increasing group impact.

Now global economic power is increasingly diffuse. Growth is shifting from developed to emerging markets, and western developed nations no longer have the economic influence they once did. Adding more seats to the table is now seen as the only way to be truly effective, particularly on global economic issues.

The Group of Twenty (G20) was launched to address this new reality, and the initial launch of the G20 Leaders' Summits, in particular, was wildly successful. Since the first summit meeting in 2008, the economic balance of power has continued to

---

[1] Chris Giles and Kate Allen, "Southeastern Shift: the New Leaders of Global Economic Growth", *Financial Times*, June 4, 2013, http://www.ft.com/intl/cms/s/0/b0bd38b0-ccfc-11e2-9efe-00144fe ab7de.html#axzz2axQY7CVw.
[2] Ibid.

shift toward emerging markets. One would therefore expect the G20 to become an increasingly important and impactful forum.

Unfortunately, the opposite appears to be happening. After the immediate 2008–2009 crisis faded, the G20 momentum appears to have stalled. G20 leaders are still releasing joint communiqués, but those promises are not leading to the type of joint action that once pulled the global market out of a downward spiral.

Now, as the G20 leadership summits approach their 5th anniversary (and their 8th high level meeting) since the first gathering in Washington, D.C., one of the biggest questions facing this institution is how to reform the G20 architecture for a post-crisis era.[3] It is clear that coordinated action across established and emerging markets is still sorely needed. The question that has not yet been answered, however, is how to make that work when the end goal is forward-looking policy reform rather than emergency response.

The G20 commitment to reduce inefficient fossil fuel subsidies is the perfect test case. That commitment, like many others, has stalled due to a lack of good G20 mechanisms for implementation. At the last leadership summit in 2012, G20 leaders called on their finance ministers to develop proposals for improving the transparency and accountability of that commitment. Common implementation standards are difficult to develop on the subsidies issue due to the variation in energy policy contexts across borders, so the G20 nations are considering a peer-review process. That option has worked well for energy policy issues in other multilateral organizations such as the Asia-Pacific Economic Cooperation (APEC) forum.

The G20 nations should pay close attention to the peer-review discussions in St. Petersburg. China, in particular, should consider playing a stronger leadership role in the fossil fuel subsidy reform discussions currently underway within the G20. As the world's largest energy consumer, China has a natural interest in the outcome of this process. Yet, China did not opt to include any of its fossil fuel subsidies in the G20 reform programme, and is therefore watching this process from the side-lines.

This report will identify the institutional features of the G20 that make consensus building possible on complex issues such as fossil fuel subsidies, and the areas where more progress is needed to move from consensus-building to real market action. Efforts are already underway on the latter. If those efforts can move the fossil fuel subsidies commitment forward in St. Petersburg, that success could provide a good roadmap for other problematic energy issue areas, and a good roadmap for G20 reform more broadly.

---

[3] "US-China Study Group on G20 Reform: Final Report, " Joint Report by the China Institutes of Contemporary International Relations, the Centre for American Progress, and the Stanley Foundation, February 13, 2013, http://www.americanprogress.org/issues/china/report/2013/02/13/52548/us-china-study-group-on-g-20-reform-final-report/.

## Comparative advantages can be a double-edged sword

Going forward, as we seek new roadmaps for how best to take this institution beyond the initial moment of crisis, we should aim to protect and build on the unique comparative advantages that this institution offers. Those advantages are three-fold: direct leadership involvement at the highest levels, an informal decision-making process, and a balanced composition that includes both established and emerging market economies.

First, direct involvement by world leaders at the highest level has been essential for pushing the G20 nations beyond the lowest-common-denominator policymaking that can plague other multilateral institutions. Bringing top leaders together for in-person dialog enables them to move beyond historical divides and identify new opportunities for consensus. Direct leadership involvement also puts personal political capitol behind G20 commitments, and that increases the likelihood that the individual G20 nations will follow through on their promises once the leaders return home.

Second, the informal nature of the G20 provides a relaxed environment for consensus building, and that has enabled G20 leaders to move beyond their comfort zones and wade into difficult policy issues. If G20 commitments were legally-binding, or if the leadership discussions occurred via a more formal process, it is likely that the G20 leaders would approach those discussions more cautiously. When leaders know their commitments are not binding, that makes it much easier to think outside the box.

Third, compared to earlier organizations such as the G7 or the OECD, the G20 is more inclusive, and the membership is more reflective of how power is actually distributed in our current global economy. On inclusiveness, the G20 certainly is not perfect. Twenty nations are still a small group when compared to larger organizations such as the UN, and that has triggered some complaints from non-members who do not believe their views are adequately represented. The focus of the G20, however, is to facilitate dialog among the world's most powerful economies, not among all economies regardless of size. Keeping the group to a dinner-party scale facilitates communication and reduces the incentive to align in interest-group blocs, which we too often see in larger summits such as the United Nations Framework Convention on Climate Change (UNFCCC).

This combination of attributes—leadership involvement, a flexible decision-making atmosphere, and an inclusive composition of manageable size—provides new consensus building opportunities that do not exist in other institutions. The G20 architecture is not perfect, however. One major problem that has become apparent over the past few years is the fact that the same mechanisms that enable coordination actually hinder implementation. In particular, the fact that G20 commitments are non-binding may enable leaders to forge deals that might not be possible in a more formal institutional setting, but when it comes time to implement those deals, there is often no clear pathway forward.

The biggest weakness undermining the G20 today is the difficulty moving from multilateral consensus to multilateral action. The G20's response to the global financial crisis was impactful because G20 leaders not only reached new agreements but also acted on them, and their concerted national action had a real impact on the global market. As we seek new ideas for applying that model in a post-crisis era, the biggest risk we face is that without the immediacy of a major international crisis, the G20 may turn into a forum that issues empty promises with no real follow-through. One initiative that has triggered these implementation concerns is the G20 commitment to reduce inefficient fossil fuel subsidies.

## Fossil fuel subsidy commitment demonstrates need for transparency and accountability

The biggest energy commitment to come out of the G20 Leaders' Summits thus far was the 2009 promise to address fossil fuel subsidies. At the Pittsburgh summit in September 2009, G20 leaders jointly acknowledged that "inefficient fossil fuel subsidies encourage wasteful consumption, reduce our energy security, impede investment in clean energy resources and undermine efforts to deal with the threat of climate change."[4] To address those problems, the G20 nations jointly promised to "phase out and rationalize over the medium term inefficient fossil fuel subsidies."[5]

By any measures, this is a ground-breaking commitment. The International Energy Agency (IEA) estimates that global energy subsidies totaled at least $523 billion in 2011, with over half of those funds going to the oil industry.[6] Those subsidies included grants, tax exemptions, and other government policies designed to artificially decrease production costs, artificially increase the prices paid to energy producers, or artificially decrease the prices paid by consumers.[7] We know that reducing the amount of money spent on those market-distorting programmes makes economic sense. Subsidizing fossil fuels keeps our economies addicted to the technologies of the past and makes it harder for new, more efficient clean energy technologies to gain a foothold.[8] The latter is particularly important because next-generation technologies are more

---

[4] G20 Leaders' Statement, the Pittsburgh Summit, September 24-25, 2009, available at http://www.treasury.gov/resource-centre/international/g7-g20/Documents/pittsburgh_summit_leaders_statement_250909.pdf.
[5] Ibid.
[6] International Energy Agency (IEA) World Energy Outlook 2012, Energy Subsidies, http://www.worldenergyoutlook.org/resources/energysubsidies/.
[7] "Carrots and Sticks: Taxing and Subsidizing Energy" International Energy Agency, 17 January 2006, https://www.iea.org/publications/freepublications/publication/oil_subsidies.pdf.
[8] "Analysis of the Scope of Energy Subsidies and Suggestions for the G-20 Initiative," IEA, OPEC, OECD, World Bank Joint Report, Prepared for Submission to the G-20 Summit Meeting in Toronto, 26-27 June 2010, http://www.worldenergyoutlook.org/media/weowebsite/energysubsidies/G20_Subsidy_Joint_Report.pdf.

likely to generate new growth, make our economies run more efficiently, and put the G20 nations on a firm path to post-crisis stability.

Fossil fuel subsidies also tend to benefit the rich at the expense of the poor. The IEA estimates that, on average, only 8 percent of the money spent on fossil fuel subsidies in 2010 went to the poorest 20 percent, which is not an efficient allocation of resources if your goal is to help the poor.[9] Since one of the core goals of the G20 is to address the systemic causes of economic stagnation and income inequality, the fact that G20 nations are spending billions of dollars every year on programmes that distort markets and disadvantage the poor certainly makes those programmes a worthy focus for coordinated action. The problem is, once these subsidy programmes are established, they can be hard to walk back. Inefficient subsidies may not benefit the economy as a whole, but they do benefit powerful interest groups, and that makes phasing down those programmes a contentious issue within most subsidizing nations. Policy consensus is even harder to achieve at the multilateral level, particularly when combining nations with different income levels and different economic orientations (such as fossil-fuel-producing and fossil-fuel-consuming nations).

The fact that the G20 nations managed to reach consensus on the language in the 2009 commitment is, in itself, an impressive feat. That statement alone was enough to trigger similar action in other forums. At the November 2009 Asia Pacific Economic Cooperation (APEC) leadership summit in Singapore, for example, APEC member nations put a nearly identical commitment into their own communiqué, thus extending the potential impact beyond the Group of Twenty.[10]

The problem is that four years after the G20 fossil fuel subsidy commitment was issued, global subsidies are still going up.[11] The 2009 commitment was an important turning point, but the next step is to follow through with some type of coordinated policy action, and that is proving more difficult to achieve. Many of those difficulties can be traced to the wording of the commitment itself, which leaves too much leeway for discretionary interpretation. Particularly:

1. There is no common standard for distinguishing between subsidies that should be phased down because they are "inefficient" and "cause wasteful consumption" versus market-appropriate subsidies that should be maintained to support growth. The lack of clear definition for what exactly the G20 nations should be phasing down makes it hard to standardize reporting. Eight out of the twenty G20 nations submitted reports claiming that they had no inefficient and wasteful fossil fuel

---

[9] World Energy Outlook 2011 Factsheet, International Energy Agency, http://www.worldenergyoutlook.org/media/weowebsite/2011/factsheets.pdf.

[10] 2009 Leaders' Declaration, Asia Pacific Economic Cooperation (APEC), Singapore, 14-15 November 2009, http://www.apec.org/Meeting-Papers/Leaders-Declarations/2009/2009_aelm.aspx.

[11] "Energy Subsidy Reform, Lessons and Implications," International Monetary Fund, January 28, 2013, http://www.imf.org/external/np/pp/eng/2013/012813.pdf.

subsidies and therefore did not need to enact any phase-downs to meet the 2009 commitment. Many of those claims do not hold water when compared to actual market data, but since there is no common standard, individual countries can define subsidies as they see fit.

2. There is no clear time line. The G20 nations promised to take action "over the medium term," but that can be interpreted to mean any number of years.

3. To the extent that some G20 nations actually do admit to having inefficient and wasteful fossil fuel subsidies, there are no common standards for the actions those nations should take to "phase out and rationalize" those policies. Individual nations can easily define that goal to reflect policy changes they were planning to roll out anyway. There is no pressure to do anything new, no pressure to move the G20 nations beyond a business-as-usual scenario.

4. There are no incentives for individual nations to take on a leadership role. In 2009, when the G20 nations were aiming to expand International Monetary Fund (IMF) resources, Japan was widely praised for stepping forward to make the first lending commitment, which spurred additional lending commitments from other nations.[12] On the fossil fuel subsidy issue, since there are no clear definitions or metrics for what these nations should actually be doing, it is difficult for any nation to take ambitious action on its own and expect others to follow suit.

The G20 was never meant to serve a policy enforcement role, but the outcomes of these summits do need to result in some degree of real policy action. Without action, the leaders' commitments will not have a strong market impact, and the G20 was formed to actually impact markets, not to release vague communiqués.

We clearly need better mechanisms for action on the fossil fuel subsidies issue, but itis important to note that those mechanisms need not be formal or punitive. It is entirely possible to facilitate implementation while simultaneously respecting the institutional informality that got the G20 nations to the bargaining table on this issue. The fossil fuel subsidies programme can be an excellent system for sharing best practices and for using positive peer pressure to encourage progressive reform, even without rigid and enforceable commitments. To do that, however, we will at least need some sort of mechanisms for comparing fossil fuel subsidy policies across borders and identifying which nations are good sources of "best practices" that others should follow. We do not have such mechanisms, however, and that is where we should focus our efforts.

The G20 nations are already moving in that direction. At the 2012 meeting in Los Cabos, the G20 leaders restated their commitment to phase down fossil fuel subsidies and called for each nation's "Finance Ministers to report back by the next summit on

---

[12] "IMF Gains New Funding, Puts Focus on Bank Clean Up," *IMF Survey Magazine*, February 14, 2009, http://www.imf.org/external/pubs/ft/survey/so/2009/new021409a.htm.

progress made, and acknowledging the relevance of accountability and transparency, to explore options for a voluntary peer-review process for G20 members by their next meeting".[13]

The "voluntary peer-review process" will be a big topic at the St. Petersburg summit next month. The G20 energy working group has been weighing ideas for how best to structure that type of process, and the working group will provide recommendations in St. Petersburg on various design issues. Questions on the table include how to divide G20 nations into groups for peer review, whether to involve third-party experts in the review process, how formal that process should be, and whether the results of that process should be public or private.

The G20 nations should implement a peer review process for fossil fuel subsidies without delay. The United States is prepared to serve as a voluntary participant in that process, and other nations are certain to follow suit.[14] Once these reviews commence, the lessons learned could have implications that go far beyond the energy realm.

## Applying lessons learned to develop a roadmap for broader G20 reform

The campaign to implement the G20 fossil fuel subsidies commitment raises two important questions that underlie the difficulties involved in G20 reform.

First, how can the G20 develop useful standards for common action when policy contexts vary so greatly across national borders? The G20 aims to improve the global economy via concerted national action, which is driven by common voluntary commitments among the G20 nations. Even when a group of nations makes a common commitment, however, it can be hard to translate that commitment into a blueprint for action within individual nations, particularly when the wording of the commitment is extremely vague.

Second, how can the G20 balance greater accountability among nations with the informality that is often critical for getting leaders to the bargaining table on contentious issues such as fossil fuel subsidies? Even when commitments are voluntary, we still want to know whether individual nations are meeting those commitments. That information can generate peer pressure and stronger incentives to actually follow through with implementation.

The peer review procedures under consideration for fossil fuel subsidies offer a flexible answer to both of these questions. To address variation across borders, the

---

13  "G20 Leaders' Declaration", Los Cabos Summit, 18-19 June 2012, available at http://www.treasury.gov/resource-centre/international/g7-g20/Documents/Los%20Cabos%20Leaders%27%20Declaration.pdf.

14  "Friends of Fossil Fuel Subsidy Reform" Roundtable for G20 Countries on Recent Progress and Peer Review of Fossil-fuel Subsidy Reform, Summary Record, 18 April 2013, http://www.mfat.govt.nz/fffsr/docs/FFFSR-G20%20Roundtable%20April%202013%20Summary%20Record.pdf.

G20 can group nations based on policy context and conduct the reviews within those groups. To allow for both accountability and informality, peer reviews can produce country-specific blueprints for progressive reform rather than a name-and-shame tallying of problems. Positive peer pressure could then be deployed to encourage G20 nations to implement at least some of the reform suggestions generated through this process. If those initial reforms generate good outcomes, that positive experience could then trigger a race to the top on energy subsidies within the G20. That could have far reaching implications for other energy policy issues and for G20 reform debates more broadly.

# Managing Globalization through the G20 Forum

*Christian Dreger*

The G20 is the premier forum to address key economic challenges in a timely manner at the level of world leaders. It is an instrument to manage the ongoing process of economic globalization and designated to encourage the informal exchange of views between industrial and emerging countries. To maintain sustainable and balanced growth in the post-crisis period, it is of vital importance that the G20 becomes more effective. To raise its efficacy, the participants should develop a clearer understanding about their shared interests and need to be more accountable on their commitments. Being a large and heterogeneous group of 20 countries, the focus should be on what the members have in common rather than on areas where they have different opinions. Due to tighter trade and financial relations, the development in one country can affect other countries to a high extent. Thus, it would be beneficial if economic policies could be implemented in a more coordinated way. A framework to ensure sustainable and balanced economic growth should be the main focus of the G20. In an improved system of global governance, the G20 can eventually concentrate on its role as a steering board, while other institutions such as the IMF and the WTO could focus on the implementation and better enforcement of rules.

The G20 is the specific forum to discuss changes in the international economy, as it comprises the relevant factors, including both industrial and emerging market economies. The G20 countries account for 65 percent of the world's population, 75 percent of GDP and 80 percent of global trade. Over the past decades, the globalization of markets has established additional major players in the world economy that need to be incorporated in international decision making. The increasing role of emerging countries is particularly striking and visible, for example, in terms of their output and trade shares. After the financial crisis, the emerging markets have been the main driver of global economic growth. The G20 is more representative than other organizations, such as the G7, as the latter comprises only industrial countries, with a declining share in production. However, this comes at the cost of higher divergence of values and interests. Members have different political and economic systems and cultural traditions. Therefore, agreements might be harder to obtain, but are nonetheless indispensable for better global governance. Issues of interest include the further promotion of world trade, the challenge for economic growth under the pressure of fiscal consolidation, the future design of monetary policy and financial market reforms, and the increasing weight of China in the world economy. These topics are briefly discussed in turn.

## G20 and the opening of markets

While liberalization of foreign trade can provide large dividends with respect to higher output growth and employment, the risk of protectionism increased after the financial crisis. Tariffs and non-tariff barriers to trade can trigger losses in global welfare, as a suboptimal allocation of resources is involved. Comparative advantages arising from higher specialization are not fully exploited. Incentives for firms to compete and innovate are reduced in such an environment, and trend productivity will expand at a lower path.

Compared to the development in the pre-crisis period, net exports become more important as drivers of growth in industrial countries. This may raise the risk of depreciation between the major currencies, with subsequent disintegration effects to the world economy. It should be noted that both protectionism and competitive devaluations of currencies are not appropriate instruments, as they can harm the evolution in other countries and cannot compensate for the implementation of structural reforms in the respective economies. In addition, direct investment decreased in many regions because of higher risk perceptions of international investors. As these flows are particularly relevant for developing countries to modernize their economies, a ruinous competition can emerge. Governments might try to attract investments by introducing dumping practices, and the G20 should provide a forum to set the rules.

The G20 should accelerate the further opening of markets and undertake efforts to finish the Doha round of trade negotiations. There is a serious risk that multilateral trade agreements lose their relevance, if they are not successful. Regional preferential trade agreements can lead to a higher segmentation of product and labor markets, as they might not be consistent with WTO rules of no discrimination. Sluggish negotiations at the global scale might act as a catalyst for the formation of these agreements. While they promote trade between partners, countries not embedded will often experience a decline in trade with the participants. In addition, a variety of regulation regimes can act as an obstacle for firms included in international supply chains. Although lower transportation and communication costs contributed to a higher fragmentation of production, world trade expanded at lower rates compared to the period before the financial crisis. This pattern might be related to austerity measures particularly in the euro area, but the slowdown could also indicate impediments towards further globalization. Liberalization of markets should not refer only to trade flows, but should also include a broader set of topics, such as investment protection and competition policies.

## Maintenance of economic growth in periods of fiscal consolidation

During the financial crisis, public deficits increased because of the response of automatic fiscal stabilizers and the launch of fiscal stimulus packages. The strong commitment of governments to assist distressed systemic banks pushed the risk of sovereign default.

Solvency ratings worsened in many countries. Japan's debt-to-GDP of about 250 percent has been one of the biggest in the world, while the US debt-to-GDP ratio reached100 percent. The prime example in Europe is Greece, which has a ratio of roughly 150 percent. Projections of government debt-to-GDP ratios look even worse, especially if demographic trends are taken into account. Ageing populations will likely imply a decrease in potential output growth and an increase in expenditures related to the health and pension systems in many countries. The debt burden is not limited to industrial states, but also relevant for emerging markets. For instance, the higher indebtedness of many Chinese provinces since the financial crisis can pose a serious risk on further growth.

According to the Reinhart and Rogoff (2009, 2010) analysis, the impact of debt is rather weak for debt to GDP ratios below a threshold of 90 percent. If debt ratios exceed this level, median growth falls by one percentage point, and average growth falls considerably more. Periods of excessive debt are often long lasting with an average duration of more than 20 years. This suggests that the cumulative shortfall in output resulting from a debt overhang can be potentially massive. While fiscal consolidation and structural reforms are important to foster competitiveness and potential output growth, their short run effects could impair the economic development. As the long run inevitably results from a sequence of short run decisions, they can undermine the prospects for high speed and sustainable growth. Austerity measures have deepened the recession particularly in the Southern member states of the euro area. Therefore, the current policy responses bear the risk of a longer period of low economic growth, with poor employment perspectives especially for the young.

The G20 should discuss the prospects of a more balanced mixture between fiscal consolidation in the long run and measures to activate output growth in the short run. Adjustment will take place in a period where most countries are required to redefine the sources of growth. In China, for example, rising social expenditures and probably higher interest rates will be triggers to support the economic transformation towards a stronger consumption pillar of output growth. In contrast, US consumption will no longer constitute one of the major sources of growth for the world economy. Embedded in a coordinated approach, large surplus countries should do more to boost domestic growth.

For example, a strategy towards higher firm investment might be appropriate for Germany, as the investment share in output is relatively small. In contrast, countries with huge deficits should implement measures directed to improve competitiveness in international markets.

## Monetary policy and financial market reforms

Due to aggressive cuts in the financial crisis, policy interest rates reached quickly zero lower bounds, and central banks had to switch to unconventional measures to further stimulate the economy. Since fiscal policies are trapped by high government debt and consolidation efforts, monetary policy plays an even more crucial role in the adjustment process. The unconventional measures led to a substantial increase in the monetary base, with long run inflation potential. For example, monetary multipliers are about 20 percent below the pre-crisis levels in the euro area. A return to normality can imply a huge monetary overhang if the measures are not sterilized in an appropriate way. From the perspective of some governments, higher inflation may be also seen as an instrument to reduce the real burden of debt. The expansionary monetary policy stance might contribute to the re-emergence of bubbles in asset markets, including price distortions for food, oil and other raw materials. Currencies of industrial countries are expected to depreciate in response to higher inflation pressures. However, this implies an appreciation of the currencies of emerging market countries, with subsequent losses in price competitiveness and a risk of a slowdown in the catching up process. An exit from low interest rates and unconventional monetary policies should be implemented carefully and in a coordinated way across central banks.

The G20 is also the appropriate forum to discuss realignments of exchange rates. This might include efforts towards a greater flexibility and the internationalization of the Renminbi. While China accounts for a substantial share in world trade, its currency is still highly under-utilized. In contrast, the US Dollar or the Euro are used far beyond the shares of these countries in the international payment system. A third-world currency, especially an Asian currency, can be beneficial to underpin the changes in the global economy. However, if the Renminbi becomes fully convertible, it can be subject to speculative capital flows.

Therefore, a closer coordination of exchange rates might be desirable. In general, exchange rates should be determined by market forces based on fundamental economic conditions, as embedded, among others, in output growth and inflation perspectives. Countries should refrain from manipulating their currencies towards levels putatively supportive for their economies. While depreciations can boost exports in the short run, they can harm other countries. And they cannot be considered as a substitute for structural reforms.

During the recent crisis, the importance of financial markets to the real economic evolution has become evident. As financial markets are highly globalized, a consistent framework for their operations is required. Basel III provides new world standards under which banks and banking systems should be more resilient against shocks. The reforms foster micro prudential regulation, i.e. regulation at the bank level, which will help to raise the resilience of individual financial institutions in periods of financial stress. The focus is on capital adequacy and liquidity regulations. The macro prudential dimension addresses system-wide risks that can build up through the banking sector and the pro-cyclical amplification of these risks. Confidence in the long-term stability of the financial system can improve, as banks are better capitalized and more liquid. These benefits might outweigh short term losses related to tighter lending constraints, as banks will eventually pass the higher costs to borrowers, with adverse effects on the real economy. The work of national authorities and regional efforts such as the introduction of a banking union in the euro area should be coordinated by the Financial Stability Board established by the G20 as a reaction to the crisis. The aim is to further develop and promote the implementation of effective regulatory, supervisory and other financial sector policies in the interest of financial stability.

## Increasing role of China in the G20 forum

The integration of China into the world economy is one of the most spectacular events in recent economic history. Over the past two decades, China maintained an annual output growth rate of more than 8 percent. China transformed from a closed and agricultural country to the second largest economy in the world, with a share exceeding 15 percent of global GDP in PPPs. According to many analysts, China will overtake the US in a few years. This reinforces the need for an internationalization of its currency. The industrial countries have largely benefitted from the development due to manufactured and intermediate products at lower costs and the creation of new markets to sell their products.

China absorbs more than 10 percent of exports from the advanced economies, after 5 percent at the turn of the century. More than 40 percent of the overall increase of Japanese exports over the past 5 years has been delivered to China. The shares are 16 percent for the US and 8 percent for the Euro area, respectively. At the same time, however, concerns have risen in the industrialized world, as manufacturing and labor intensive industries have come under higher competitive pressure. These reservations became even more relevant because of the decline in growth in many countries during the financial crisis.

Over the next years, competition will likely intensify for high-skilled products. As China approaches the technological frontier, the potential for acquiring and applying knowledge and technology from abroad will be gradually exhausted. To manage the next steps in its transformation process, China's growth will become more innovation based. Otherwise, the country may get stuck in a middle income trap, with rising wages and declining cost competitiveness. To exploit the benefits from open markets, fair trade and knowledge exchange for all sides and the changes in the international division of labor require further agreements at the international level.

The rising power of China already affects economic performance in industrial countries. For example, many observers have argued that the integration of China into the world economy can help prevent global recessions caused by crises in industrial states. While China's impact on output growth in advanced economies is indeed substantial for the Asian region, the spill overs for the US and the euro area have been much lower up to now.

Evidence supporting this view can be inferred when the recent fiscal stimulus programme is considered. In contrast, China is highly vulnerable to shocks arising in industrial states, including the debt crisis. The high exposure to evolution in advanced countries is a major factor behind the current slowdown of Chinese output growth.

The Chinese growth miracle is not without risk for a smooth development of the world economy. High growth rates in recent years are probably unsustainable, since they have been driven by increasing imbalances, at least in part. To avoid a slowdown of output growth caused by a reduction of exports to industrial countries, the Chinese government has raised expenditures for infrastructure. The huge state owned banks supported the fiscal stimulus measures, as access to credit improved particularly for state owned enterprises, no matter whether they have been efficient or not. Investments may have led to overcapacity in many areas. As lending has often been motivated by political and not by economic arguments, the amount of non-performing loans at the banks can be substantial.

Government debt is on a rising trend, especially at the level of provinces. At the same time, China needs to make progress with respect to the deregulation of financial markets to further support the transformation of its economy, including a larger role of the private sector. It is not clear whether all these challenges can be properly addressed.

# G20 and the New Horizon of Global Governance: Toward a More Collaborative World

*Du Hyeogn Cha*
The Korea Foundation

## G20 Meetings:
## Accomplishments, Constraints, and Future Potential

While the concept of the "G20" launched in 1999 with the inaugural meeting of finance ministers from twenty countries, it was not until the global financial crisis in 2008 that this forum emerged as a meaningful cooperative mechanism to address concerns on various global economic issues. The importance of interstate economic cooperation for the stability of the world economy, however, has loomed larger than ever before since the Global Financial Crisis of 2008. One of the key lessons the global community has learned from the analysis of causes and consequences of the "crisis" is that the stability of the world economy requires not only the active cooperation of advanced countries, it also depends on the development of a new framework that encourages the strong participation of emerging economies who have garnered increasing economic clout in a deeply interconnected world economic system. In this context, the G20 Summit was launched in 2008 as one of the most prestigious global economic forums for effective management of the world economy that bridges advanced and emerging economies.

While the G20 has produced some progress in thinking about how to address various global economic issues over the last five years, it has yet to come up with concrete measures to meet daunting challenges facing the world economy. For example, the G20 still needs to work out a clear vision and solutions for sustainable economic growth and development of developing countries, construction of new rules and a safety net for the global financial system, structural reform of international financial institutions, and addressing the global imbalance of macroeconomic management. In addition to these challenges, the G20 has committed to effectively dealing with potentially divisive issues like climate change and global competition of energy resources in its efforts to ensure sustainable and mutually beneficial development of the world economy. Although it is too premature to tell whether the G20 will be able to institutionalize an effective global mechanism or measure to cope with various challenging issues at global level, it has shown a glimmer of potential in establishing a new multi-national and multi-dimensional global governance system.

The G20's management of the global financial crisis has accumulated meaningful lessons that can be applied in resolving other issues: It has developed collaborative dialogs based on common perceptions rather than contending thoughts in dealing with economic agendas of countries that are the most closely interrelated and interdependent. G20 meetings focus on identifying issues and discussing alternatives rather than inducing binding commitments. These lessons can be applied in the evolution of the G20.

## Why should the G20 evolve?

The G20 has yet to resolve various economic issues, including the following: 1) Institutional reform for international economic cooperation: how to structurally reform the IMF and the World Bank? 2) International coordination of macroeconomic management: how to resolve the global imbalance? 3) Overcoming national differences: exploring shared ideas and mutual interests.

Moreover, given the implications of the meetings, the G20 also needs to consider new roles beyond the economic realm in the mid- and long-term. Many of the global issues demand collaborative assessment and countermeasures by both major and middle power countries. Among them, transnational and non-traditional threats have emerged since the end of the 20th century that are especially remarkable. These comprehensive and supranational threats that have risen upon the dissolution of the Cold War are a common denominator of concern for all countries in the world.

Very few countries are immune to the non-traditional threats of the post-Cold War, such as terrorism, piracy, narcotics trafficking, international crime, environmental destruction, weaponization of resources, environmental pollution, and threats to major sea lanes. On the positive side, the increased visibility of the arms race between major countries in the 21st century has paradoxically aided in reducing the chances for warfare and military confrontation (although the aftermath of such eruption is a separate matter). Hence, it is likely that states will be deterred from resolving issues through military force and direct conflict given the immense burden and costs of that choice. On the flip side, this means that risks from non-traditional and non-military threats will most probably be larger in the future.

An issue acquiring attention on this front is "new terrorism." For most of the 19th and 20th centuries, terrorism was extensively used by political activists as a tool of resistance. The term "new terrorism" was born after the 1990s, when the scope and profile of victims expanded beyond mere psychological terror against particular governments or officials. According to a 2006 report on terrorism by the Congressional Research Service (CRS), "New terrorism" has evolved over the years to display the following five characteristics. First, the faces behind initiators of terror have become increasingly diverse. Unlike the early post-Cold War period, the modern form of terrorism is not instigated by large groups but rather is perpetrated by small autonomous cells and even individuals funded by an umbrella organization. Second, boosted by access to information, funds, and ideas, the methods and weapons used to carry out terrorism activities have become more sophisticated. Third, there is growing overlap between terrorism and international crime such as narcotics or money laundering. Fourth, in correlation to U.S. activities in Iraq, international terrorism and attacks by suicide bombers have increased. Fifth, there has been a decline in state-sponsored terrorism.

The most lethal facet of "new terrorism" is its increased capacity for fatalities. Terrorism in the past was typically able to garner a limited support base because its aim and target was restricted to a particular government or leaders, along with military targets governed by the said regime or head. However, the lethality of new terrorism is non-discriminatory nature, and is no longer considered a last resort by the weak and marginalized players in society and politics. When one thinks of a large-scale incident of terrorism, most would think back to the devastating image of New York after 9/11 in 2001. Yet the accumulative damages incurred by various acts of terrorism since the start of the 21st century actually surpass this fatal attack. In fact, casualties from terrorist acts since 2000 are typically in the hundreds of people. The lives lost during the 9/11 attacks stand at around 3,000; a total of 202 people died and 300 were wounded from the 2002 Bali bombings; 199 died and 1,463 were wounded from the March 2004 Madrid train bombings; also in 2004, roughly 1,000 people were wounded in North-Osetia during the Beslan hostage crisis; and there were 56 deaths and approximately 700 casualties from the 2005 carnage in the London subway. Actual wars on the battlefield that are even comparable to such human casualties in the post-Cold War era are few and far between. The wars in Bosnia, Somalia, and Kosovo are perhaps the sole cases.

According to the 2006 Report on Terrorist Incidents issued by the U.S. National Counter-Terrorism Centre, 14,000 incidences of terrorism were recorded in 2006, with a total human cost of 20,000. Compared to the previous year of 2005, this represents a 25% jump (3,000 cases) in incidents and a 40% increase in human lives (5,800). This increase was particularly visible in the Near East and South Asia, with attacks against non-combatants also on the rise. Moreover, terrorist groups actively used methods such as killing, injuring, and hostage-taking as propaganda or promotional tools.

Another facet of "new terrorism" is that it transcends particular regions and cultures to reach a global audience (or target). The 2006 Country Report on Terrorism released by the Office of the Coordinator for Counterterrorism under the U.S. State Department underscores the transformation in terrorist acts. In the past, terrorist acts revolved around "expeditionary" plots by groups such as al-Qaeda, in which a team is sent abroad to carry out an assault. Today, terrorist acts are committed in a "guerrilla-like" fashion by local recruits. Additionally, many terrorist groups have expansive networks for both information and funds. Thus, unlike the case of the arms race, non-traditional threats require a solid comprehensive cooperative effort on part of the global actors.

On the one hand, these non-traditional threats are basically security issues. On the other hand, however, they are directly or indirectly related to economic prosperity. For example, an international criminal organization that engages in smuggling or illegal migration could influence a nation's domestic economy by disturbing the labor market or distorting market prices. Given capacity limitations to cope with these issues through existing governance mechanisms (such as the United Nations or other international organizations), we need to consider additional countermeasures. Furthermore, other emerging issues need cooperative and common global approaches, including urbanization, migration, acceleration of aging populations, informatization and cyber security, a widening generation gap, etc.

## How to manage global issues through the G20?

As mentioned, the 21st century post-Cold War period requires a trustworthy mechanism for resolving issues related to global security and the economic environment. Evolution of the global governance system is crucial to allow it to institutionally support the feasibility and sustainability of measures agreed among—or at least, advocated among—countries.

A better multilateral framework will lay the foundation for undertaking mutually beneficial global actions, such as establishing an information sharing centre or network, to address non-traditional threats and emerging global issues. In the mid-term, G20 countries will need to construct a common blue print for the future of cooperative organization that will assure the sustainable role of the G20, for example, establishing a permanent secretariat. Even if this kind of framework is established, it is unrealistic to expect that it could resolve or mediate various contending issues such as territorial disputes. Rather, this kind of mechanism would serve a better role in providing the "opportunity for deliberation or loose agreement on current and latent issues." More opportunities for deliberation and cooperative assessment would be significant in enhancing transparency among countries. Perhaps limited reconfiguration may be also considered on issues of mutual concern within the developmental stage of such a multilateral framework.

# G20 Summit 2013: Future Prospects in Economic and Financial Fields

*Liliana Alvarado*

The 2013 G20 Summit, scheduled to take place September 5–6, 2013 in Saint Petersburg, will be the eighth meeting of the G20 heads of governments. The G20 is the leading international cooperation forum, focusing on the most important international economic and financial issues. The core objectives of this year's summit, as defined by the host country Russia, are the development and implementation of a set of measures aimed at boosting sustainable, inclusive and balanced growth and job creation around the world. The overall agenda for the G20 in 2013 includes both the legacy from previous Presidencies and several Russian proposals. Even though G20 summits cover a wide range of issues, this essay will focus on the economic and financial aspects of this year's summit. The first section provides an outline of the main economic and financial aspects of the prior G20 Agendas. Part two describes the priorities of the Russian presidency and the third section describes the financial and economic issues which have been discussed in the meetings prior to the Leaders' summit, as well as key challenges and risks forth G20. The conclusion provides some criticism and includes personal thoughts about the priorities set by this year's G20 host.

## I. Traditional G20 Agenda—Economic and Financial Aspects

Although the G20 was created in 1999, the leaders first met in 2008. The main aim of this inaugural meeting waste prevent a future financial crisis, while securing sustainable and balanced global growth through reform of the architecture of global governance. The G20 is now considered to be a major mechanism for international economic cooperation, regulating financial markets and influencing global economic policy.

The G20 agenda traditionally addresses major challenges to the global economy, and to date, a significant number of achievements have been made. International financial institutions have been reformed, oversight over national financial institutions and regulators has been strengthened, the quality of financial regulations in economies whose regulatory problems led to the crisis have been improved and financial and organizational safety nets to prevent severe economic slumps in the future have been created (G20 website). The G20 agenda consists of eight areas, but each summit addresses them differently and includes additional issues. The purpose of the next section is to describe the priorities set by Russia, this year's host.

## II. G20 Agenda in 2013: Russian Priorities (Russia in G20)

Russia has decided to ensure continuity of the dialog on all of the traditional G20 agenda items, as well as add extra impetus to the G20 discussion by including two new topics: financing for investment and government borrowing and public debt sustainability.

For this year's summit, three overreaching priorities were defined, all aimed at starting the new cycle of economic growth: 1) growth through quality jobs and investment; 2) growth through trust and transparency; and 3) growth through effective regulation. These will receive particular attention in the 2013 G20 agenda, which is comprised of the following eight areas:

1. Framework for strong, sustainable and balanced growth
2. Jobs and employment
3. International financial architecture reform
4. Strengthening financial regulation
5. Energy sustainability
6. Development for all
7. Enhancing multilateral trade
8. Fighting corruption

To support the Russian Presidency's focus on boosting economic growth and job creation, two new topics have been proposed for discussion. These include "financing for investment," which is a component of the first agenda item, and "government borrowing and public debt sustainability," addressed under the international financial architecture reform agenda item. The following section describes the eight agenda points, focusing on the financial and economic aspects.

1) Framework for strong, sustainable and balanced growth

Since the first G20 summit, decisive actions have been undertaken to restore and strengthen global growth and to put it on a sustainable path. Despite these efforts, however, global economic recovery is still fragile and large downside risks to the outlook remain (Europe's recent debt crisis is an example of this). The Russian Presidency has decided to address this issue by taking the following steps:

a. Revision of country-specific medium- and long-term public debt targets and development strategies to achieve them;
b. Enhancement of the "Accountability Assessment Process" by extending the number of indicators to enable more comprehensive and precise macroeconomic analysis;
c. Analysis of the persistent imbalances among the G20 members in fiscal, monetary, exchange rate and structural policy domains.

Financing for investment has also been a priority in the G20 agendas following the global economic and financial crisis of recent years that led to a significant decrease of various types of investment. Russia announced that it will provide room for fruitful discussion on possible ways and practical steps to increase the amount and effectiveness of financing for investment. The G20 efforts will focus on the impact of the financial regulatory reforms on financing for investment, banking sector capabilities and barriers, multilateral and national development banks, international reserves, among others. Together with a large group of major international organizations (World Bank, IMF, OECD, FSB, UN, etc.), the G20 will exert much effort in pursuing the following results to be presented at the G20 summit in September:

a. Strengthen public policy and improve PPPs in terms of promoting financing for investment;
b. Elaborate on measures to support investments in small-and medium-size enterprises and start-up businesses;
c. Measures to meet capitalization needs of global banks;
d. Recommendations on regulatory changes that would bring about change in banking business models towards funding the real economy;
e. Analysis of the role of possible sources of financing for investment (institutional investors, equity markets, government guarantees);
f. Analysis of FDI trends, patterns and impact to maximize their growth enhancing capacity;
g. Recommendations on how to increase multilateral development bank's lending capacity.

2) Jobs and employment

Improving labor market conditions is another priority traditionally addressed in the G20 agendas. The Russian Presidency announced that it will combat unemployment and under-employment by facilitating job creation. The following topics will be addressed by the Task Force on Employment (ETF):

a. Job creation through sound monetary and fiscal policies, structural policies to foster innovation and promotion of smaller enterprises;
b. Labor activation for the vulnerable groups;
c. Monitoring of labor market development and progress on the previous G20 commitments.

3) International financial architecture reform

In order to achieve a stronger global economy and a well-balanced and efficient international financial architecture to prevent the next crisis, the Russian Presidency is committed to further increasing the efficiency and legitimacy of the IMF governance structure. Continuing the implementation of the G20 Action Plan to support development of local currency bond markets will also be an important topic. In this context the Russian Presidency will deepen work on government borrowing and public sustainability issues. Efforts to address the following topics will be undertaken:

a. Completion of the IMF's 2010 Quota and Governance reform;
b. Review of the IMF's quota formula and implementation of the 15th general review of quotas by January 2014;
c. Complete implementation of the Action Plan to support the development of local currency markets;
d. Further development of regional financial arrangements and establishment of close cooperation with the IMF;
e. Review of the "Guidelines for Public Debt Management", which were introduced by the IMF and World Bank for the first time in 2001.

4) Strengthening financial regulation

Strengthened financial regulation is considered essential to prevent a relapse of the world crisis. In order to achieve this, the following topics will be addressed:

a. Adoption of a methodology to select and apply a supervisory regime to domestic, systemically important financial institutions (D-SIFIs);
b. Promotion of shadow banking regulation;
c. Development of the global legal entity identifier (LEI) system;
d. Reduction of mechanistic reliance on Credit Rating Agency (CRA) ratings;
e. Completion of over-the-counter derivatives reform;

5) Energy sustainability

Different topics will be addressed in order to ensure energy sustainability. The following results are expected by the end of 2013:

a. Finance Ministers' progress report on the G20's contribution to enhancing transparency and functioning of international commodity and energy markets;
b. Recommendations for setting up a framework for forecasting commodity market volatility;
c. Draft principles for efficient energy markets regulation to stimulate infrastructure investments and integrate green growth and sustainable development priorities into structural policies;
d. Recommendations on the voluntary peer review process for fossil-fuel subsidies;
e. A progress report on JODI-oil, and an initial overview of the launch of JODI-gas;

f.  A draft plan for a best practice database of green energy and energy efficiency policies and management approaches used by members of the G20;
g.  A fully operational global marine environment protection website as a tool to implement the global marine environment protection initiative.

6) Development for all

To ensure economic growth, infrastructure construction and inclusive access to basic amenities have been traditional issues on the G20 agenda. This year a number of initiatives will be undertaken:

a.  Food security with a focus on increasing agricultural production and addressing undernutrition;
b.  Human resource development with a focus on developing a global skills database;
c.  Financial inclusion with a focus on financial literacy and access to financial services by women, migrants and youth;
d.  Infrastructure with a focus on long-term financing;
e.  Active participation in creating a post-2015 development agenda;
f.  Development of an accountability mechanism to assess progress on previous G20 commitments.

7) Enhancing multilateral trade

The G20 nations are committed to pushing forward strong demand for developing trade and investment as a growth driver, and developing a strong multilateral trading system as a necessary underlying prerequisite by addressing the following issues:

a.  Curbing protectionism;
b.  Strengthening and developing the multilateral trade system;
c.  Global value chains

8) Fighting corruption

Another main priority of the Russian Presidency is to fight corruption in an efficient and intransigent manner. The Anti-Corruption Working Group (ACWG) will continue its work on this issue, structured around the following topics:

a.  Start implementation of the G20 Anti-Corruption Action Plan 2013–2014. Guidance will be sought and a number of focus areas will be pursued, including the promotion of UNCAC, further independence of anti-corruption agencies, banning foreign bribery, combating money laundering and proceeds of corruption, denial of entry for corrupted officials, and other areas of the Action Plan;
b.  Anti-corruption training to build a corruption-free society;
c.  Deepening the engagement of the business community;

d.  Financial transparency and disclosure for public officials;
e.  Eradicating corruption in major international events.

## III. Meetings prior to the G20 Leaders Summit

The G20 Leaders Summit in September 2013 is preceded by a series of outreach events organized into five stakeholder categories: think tanks; business; labor; civil society and youth. This section analyses the economic and financial aspects that have been discussed to date, mainly during the Finance Ministers and Central Bank Governors' meeting.

During the first G20 Finance Ministers and Central Bank Governors' meeting within Russia's G20 Presidency, delegates agreed that tail risks to the global economy have receded and financial market conditions have improved. One of the most pressing subjects addressed were protectionist actions such as competitive devaluations. The G20 nations reiterated their adherence to exchange rate flexibility, to refrain from competitive devaluations, and to direct monetary policy at price stability and growth.

However, Japan's expansive policies, which have driven down the yen, escaped criticism. The nations decided that there would be no currency war and deferred plans to set new debt-cutting targets, emphasizing broad concern over the fragile state of the world economy. Although the G20 nations committed to a credible medium-term fiscal strategy, no specific goals were set as most delegations felt any economic recovery was too fragile. The debt-cutting pact to which delegates agreed at the 2010 Summit in Toronto will expire this year if leaders fail to agree to extend it at this year's G20 summit. At the end of the meeting the group had failed to reach agreement on medium-term budget deficit levels and concerns about ultra-loose policies were expressed (Reuters 2013).

The second G20 Finance Ministers and Central Bank Governors' meeting was held in June. Participants reviewed progress and difficulties in the implementation of countries 'commitments adopted under the G20 Framework for Strong, Sustainable and Balanced Growth. This review included perspectives and elaboration of credible medium-term debt strategies by the G20 economies, assessment of spillover effects from accommodative monetary policies of advanced economies, and G20 efforts to modernize international financial monetary relations. Further steps to promote long-term financing for investment were outlined. In addition, preliminary results of financial regulation reforms and the outcomes of the seminar on the financial benchmarks and credit-rating agencies were summarized (G20 News).

During the International Financial Architecture Working Group Meeting, delegates discussed how to further improve the efficiency and legitimacy of the IMF governance structure. Delegates also discussed the work on strengthening IMF surveillance, public debt management, Regional Financial Arrangement development and co-operation with the IMF and other entities. The implementation of the IMF's 2010

Quota and Governance reform received particular attention, with the goal of doubling the IMF quota resources initiated in 2010 and implementation of the 15th general review of quotas (G20 Events).

In July, another International Financial Architecture Working Group Meeting was held during which delegates continued working towards the IMF's 2010 Quota and Governance reform, public debt management, sustainable lending practices, and developing global liquidity indicators together with IMF and BIS. Delegates also discussed progress on implementing activity towards initiatives related to the local currency bond market.

An important innovation of the Russian Presidency will be the first Joint G20 Finance and Labor Ministers Meeting held on July 19, 2013. Delegates will primarily discuss two interrelated topics, namely, governments' role in creating incentives and eliminating barriers to investment in job creation, and cost effective social policies to facilitate job creation and inclusive societies.

## Challenges and Risks

In essence, the described objectives and policy proposals of the G20 Summit are critical in shaping the performance of the global economy and the welfare of nations given the uncertainties of the times. However, even if the main objectives and topics are very important to achieving immediate economic outcomes, the mechanisms, incentives and procedures behind supranational agreements like this one cast doubt on their implementation, efficiency and scope. For instance, the diversity of interests and economic realities of G20 members can be as contrasting as day and night. The dynamics of the group require alignment with or consideration of a variety of economic realities including the fiscal and debt problems of the United States; the monetary fragility of the Euro Zone; the stagnation in Japan's economy; the unknown risks of the Argentinean economy; the political pressures in Turkey; and the slowdown of emerging markets like Brazil, Mexico and Indonesia.

National agreements like Doha 2001, Gleneagles 2005 or the Kyoto protocol, just to mention a few, are not very forward-leaning. This is because the common denominator in the multipolar arena has typically been null cooperation, international impasse and the imposition of individual agendas. Hence, the big challenge is not only the design of effective economic policies and fiscal objectives, but the consolidation of a cooperative strategy between the contrasting interests and needs of G20 members. Moreover, the new projections of global growth published last week by the IMF are increasing the urgency of success in this Summit. The world is economy is projected to grow a mere 3%, the same amount as the last year. This meagre growth is essentially driven by emerging markets, which are predicted to grow an average of 5.4%, versus the projected 2.1% growth of advanced economies. However, the sustainability of this growth is constrained by three main risky scenarios, as identified by the IMF: 1) the deceleration of major emerging market economies due to infrastructure bottlenecks, slower external demand growth, lower commodity prices, financial instability, and social unrest; 2) a deeper recession in the Euro zone as consequence of low demand, depressed confidence, and austerity policies; and 3) weaker US economic growth due to stronger fiscal shrinkage weighing on improved private demand.

## Conclusion

Notwithstanding some considerable achievements, G20 Summits have been the subject of much debate. Criticisms of the G20 include its non-representativeness due to the fact that it only includes 20 countries and the lack of domestic legitimacy. Missing genuine ex ante engagement to build trust and support with diverse domestic constituencies has limited leaders' ability to implement the commitments of the G20 agendas. In addition, critics have highlighted the fact that the agenda topics vary substantially depending on the host country.

In a globalized world, the need for collective action seems to be obvious. G20 summits provide a platform to discuss the issues affecting the global economy at a collective level. The tasks and objectives to reduce global and regional imbalances and stimulate global growth require this kind of platform. Previous achievements have been promising, but plenty remains to be done. Consequently, the outcomes of the 2013 G20 Summit in Saint Petersburg, if successful, may not only guarantee the stability and sustainability of the global economy in the short run, but also dictate a new precedent for cooperation at supranational level in this new multipolar order.

Supervisory reform has been one of the most important topics of the summits. Important steps, such as the creation of a stress test for European banks, have been accomplished. In spite of this, results have been limited and critics have pointed out that the Spanish savings bank Bankia would have collapsed if it had not been rescued by the state, despite passing the stress test.

With respect to the priorities of this year's G20 Presidency, it is important to note that Russia decided to include two new topics into the G20 Agenda. Financing for investment has been considered an essential focus and some concrete measures and steps have been proposed. Since the G20 is only an informal platform, the most likely results will be limited to recommendations and analyses. Even though increasing investment is certainly an important goal, it is uncertain whether it will actually be achieved. The other topic added by Russia, government borrowing and public debt sustainability, will be addressed under international financial architecture reform. As with the other topic, it remains to be seen whether dialog on this topic will lead to the implementation of actual measures by the G20 nations.

## Bibliography

[1]  ANGELONI, Ignazio, What Is Wrong with the G20? Public Debt, Global Governance and Economic Dynamism, Milan, pp 159-164, 2013.
[2]  G20 Events website, http://www.g20.org/events_financial_track/20130213/7 81041922. html
[3]  G20 News, http://www. g20. org/news/20130607/781399440. html
[4]  IMF, "World Economic Outlook Update", July 2013, http://www.imf.org/exte rnal/pubs/ft/weo/2013/update/02/
[5]  KLEIN, Lawrence; SALVATORE, Dominick. Shift in the world economic centre of gravity from G7 to G20. *Journal of Policy Modeling*, 2013.
[6]  MORGAN, Matthew, Consensus Formation in the global Economy: The Success of the G7 and the Failure of the G20, *Studies in Political Economy*, 90, Autumn 2012.
[7]  RANA, Pradumna, From a Centralized to a Decentralized Global Economic Architecture: An Overview, ADBI Working Paper 401, January 2013.
[8]  Reuters "UPDATE 3-G20 steps back from currency brink, heat off Japan", February 2013 (http://www.reuters.com/article/2013/02/16/g-idUSL6N0BG0PP 20130216)
[9]  Russia in G20, http://www.g20.org/docs/g20_russia/priorities.html
[10] THAKUR, Ramesh, The G20 versus the UN: Rival Development Forums? Future United Nations Development System, April 2013.

# What is the Point of the G20?

*Gabriel Stein*

International summits have a long history. Once upon a time, the idea of a ruler leaving his country—except as the head of an army—would have seemed preposterous. Yet as early as the Middle Ages, it was not uncommon for European rulers to meet their foreign colleagues under peaceful circumstances. Two developments have spurred this change: One was the fragmentation of single empires into numerous independent states-the norm in Europe. China and much of the rest of Asia were exceptions. This fragmentation meant that rulers had to accept other rulers as equals who were likely to be around permanently. The second development was the establishment of Church Councils, which brought together clerics from numerous countries to discuss issues of concern to all.

The large numbers of independent states also meant that wars were rarely total; countries simply lacked the capacity to obliterate other countries. Wars between large numbers of participants also meant peace conferences with large numbers of participants. A key example of such a conference was the Congress of Westphalia, which ended the 30 Years War and codified many of the diplomatic rules currently taken for granted. Another crucial summit was the Congress of Vienna after the Napoleonic Wars, which reshaped the map of Europe and ushered in an era of regular conferences between the Great Powers. The Congress of Berlin in 1887 successfully defused a Balkan Crisis that had threatened to spark a wider war. In contrast, the Congress of Versailles after World War I must overall be deemed a failure.

More recently, such summits tend to concentrate on economics and finance. The European Union holds regular summits twice a year. On a global scale, we have had the G5, later revised to the G7 (to avoid the ignominy of the United Kingdom dropping out of the group) and eventually the G8 (to give Russia a way of saving face and pretend it is still important). There was the G10 (which had 12 members) and now we have the G20. In addition, whenever a new leader is inaugurated, be it in the United States, China, Germany, France or elsewhere, the first foreign trip is invested with crucial importance and believed to indicate foreign priorities. Where will the President of the United States go first, China, the UK or Mexico? Where will a new Chinese President go first, Japan, Russia or the US? And so on. Summits are part of our daily lives. However, there is a very strong argument that they should not be. This argument claims that summits, at least between leaders, do little, if any good, and are capable of doing much harm. More to the point, they are frequently meaningless. Looking at history, the Congress of Vienna was useful in that it enabled the assembled powers to quickly determine a response to the news that the Emperor Napoleon had returned from Elba. But the following congresses eventually became paralyzed as the differences between the countries became too big to be papered over. Perhaps the worst example is the Congress of Versailles.

If President Wilson had stayed in Washington, he could have dictated peace from afar; but by going to Versailles, he diminished his stature to become merely one of a number of squabbling politicians. The resulting Peace Treaty carried within it the roots of World War II. The G5 started as five heads of state and/or government meeting in private. G8 meetings became massive media circus with hundreds of attendees and staff. For the G20—which in addition to the 20 members will also have representatives of the International Monetary Fund, the World Bank, the International Monetary and Financial Committee and Development Assistance Committee—merely going through brief opening statements by the attendees will consume a couple of hours.

But there is a further issue. Namely, should heads of state/government actually meet each other at all? Philippe de Commynes, advisor first to Duke Charles the Rash of Burgundy and then to his opponent King Louis XI of France (second half of the 15th Century) addresses this issue at length in his Memoirs. His conclusion is that Princes who want to remain friends should not meet. It is far better to remain friends from afar and conduct negotiations through intermediaries (who, if necessary, can be disavowed).

There is a great deal of truth in this. Political summits are necessarily brief. The idea that one can get to know his or her opponents/colleagues during the short meeting time must be one of the more dangerous in politicians' armory of swollen egos. Occasionally it may be true. But for every Margaret Thatcher who realizes that she could "do business" with Mikhail, there is a George W. Bush who says of President Putin "I looked the man in the eye. I found him to be very straightforward and trustworthy." Not to mention a Neville Chamberlain bringing back "peace for our time" from Munich. Few would dispute the view that Winston Churchill, who never met Hitler, had a far better knowledge of him than did Neville Chamberlain—in spite of meeting him. Churchill and Stalin both clearly had a better understanding of each other and of Franklin D Roosevelt, than Roosevelt had of either of them (certainly not of Stalin).

Moreover, whenever there is a summit, there is substantial expectation built up that it will achieve something. A failure to agree is deemed a major political failure. So there has to be a unanimous communiqué, which therefore usually ends up being bland and meaningless. Moreover, the need for unanimity means that the most intransigent participants will be rewarded for their intransigence.

This does not mean that international cooperation is meaningless, far from it. Economic, environmental and other issues show little regard for borders, making international cooperation not only useful but necessary. Having means of rapid and secure communication between potential adversaries can reduce tensions and dampen the risk for conflicts. However, little if any of this work necessitates the summits. In fact, even with the summits, most of the work is done prior to the actual meetings. That work can and should continue. There is nothing wrong with having ambassadors or other representatives meet and agree on details. But the regular, top-level summits are generally meaningless—and that is even before you consider the costs in terms of time, money and (not infrequently) disturbances to and in the city where they are held.

## Economic and financial outlook for the G20

All this said, there may be an argument for a G20 summit when the largest economies all face a broadly similar and unprecedented situation; this was arguably the case in 2008. But what is the current outlook for the G20? In fact, there isn't one. That is to say, there is an outlook for each country; and some countries have a similar outlook. But the outlooks for the different G20 members vary substantially. The following provides a brief overview for the most important countries:

1) The United States

The United States recovery—as unexciting and plodding as it may be by the standard of past cycles—remains on track. Over the course of the next 18 months, the American economy should emerge from a brief and shallow soft patch in Q2 2013 toward normal trend and eventually above trend growth. The Federal Reserve has set a threshold of 6½ percent unemployment (plus minor side conditions relating to inflation) above which it will decide on further action. When it was initially announced in late 2012, this threshold was expected to be reached in 2015, and it was assumed that the Fed would leave interest rates unchanged until then. However, that was always a very pessimistic view of developments. It now looks far more likely that the unemployment threshold will be reached in the first half of next year. At that stage, the Fed should also bring its quantitative easing to an end. By rights, it should raise interest rates in the second half of 2014—not by much, possibly just one quarter-point—to make the case that the economy is capable of continued growth and that interest rates will at some stage be normalized.[1] All this also means a continued strengthening of the dollar.

2) Japan

Japan has embarked on a major experiment, guided by the mystical number "2". The monetary base is supposed to be doubled over two years, leading to 2% inflation. This policy is likely to both succeed and fail. It is likely to succeed in that Japan almost certainly will achieve 2% inflation, and probably will do so before 2015. However, this will mainly be due to a weaker yen. Internally generated inflation-brought about by an overheating economy and stimulated by monetary injection-will not materialize. This

---

[1] In the unfortunate event that Janet Yellen succeeds Ben Bernanke as Chairman of the Board of Governors of the Federal Reserve, an interest rate increase in 2014 becomes much less likely.

is because the Japanese authorities persist in targeting the monetary base, rather than broad money. While there is a relationship between broad money and activity, and eventual inflation, there is at best only a tenuous relationship between the monetary base and the real economy. This also means that the weak yen becomes increasingly important as an instrument of Japanese policy.

3) China

China is in a very different position. Its economy combines an overheating property market and excessive credit growth with the (inevitable) end of the investment and export-driven growth model that previously served it extremely well, but can no longer do so. This was always going to happen eventually, since export-led growth ultimately depends on demand somewhere else, something a nation has no control over. In 2013 this failing approach was exacerbated by the fact that everyone else was trying to achieve export-led growth as well. The crisis in the Euro area and its periphery certainly needed it; Japan needed it to achieve its economic targets; and the United States is at least keen to ensure that its current account deficit does not widen any further. Add to this a combination of China's wage inflation over the past few years, an overvalued yuan, and re-shoring of US and Japanese industrial production and the outlook for export-led growth becomes even more distant. Chinese authorities now need to reform their economy in a way that will mean lower output growth and most likely greater volatility in the short term, but will be beneficial overall in the long-term.

4) European Union

For the Eurozone, the situation is again different. Periphery countries have made great progress in terms of improving their budgets and current account balances. However, this has come at the cost of destroying domestic demand, leading to rising unemployment (with the resulting risk of social tension) and prolonged recessions. Part of the reason for the extended weakness is that policy is very much determined by Germany; and the German attitude is that austerity and discipline eventually will have the same beneficial effects on periphery countries as similar reforms had in Germany. But this disregards the fact that Germany was able to reform precisely because the periphery was moving in the opposite direction, and so was able to off-set German excess saving by its own excess spending. In contrast, German policymakers now resolutely refuse to acknowledge that increased savings in the Euro area periphery needs to be off-set by increased spending in Germany, ensuring that any periphery reform and recovery will take longer and cause more pain.

The G20, and hence the world as a whole, are thus at different stages in their economic cycle. This means they have different economic policy needs. The United States and to a lesser extent China are more likely to tighten monetary policy than to ease it. In contrast, Japan, the Euro area and the UK are still in easing mode. Hence, there is little need for policy coordination and even less likelihood of it being achieved.

Moreover, as the debate on financial regulation and banking supervision has shown, once the immediate crisis is over, even such a closely knit group as the Euro area will have difficult in achieving unity on next steps. It is unclear why some think achieving consensus would be easier, much less more desirable, on a global stage.

One final point should perhaps be made. The G20 membership consists of the 20 largest economies in the world. But size is not necessarily the most important factor. For instance, Norway has complained that it is the seventh largest contributor to United Nations international development programmes, yet it is not represented in the G20, either directly or indirectly (since it is not a member of the EU). Neither is Switzerland, despite its importance as a financial centre. Spain is merely a "permanent guest." Africa is represented by one single country (South Africa) as is the Middle East (Saudi Arabia). How long before another African or Middle Eastern country insists on being represented by virtue of its size (i.e. Nigeria, Egypt) or wealth (i.e. UAE, Kuwait)? Already considered unwieldy, the G20 could quickly become even more so as each new member raises a clamor for others to be allowed in.

## China in the G20

What, then, is the role for China in the G20? As mentioned above, the benefits of top level summits may be dubious, but multinational cooperation and contacts are undoubtedly good. Where does China fit in this world, and what are the challenges facing it? Obviously, as the second largest economy in the world, China's actions are of major importance to the global economy. Yet, in some ways, China's behavior is reminiscent of that of the United States in the 1920s and 1930s. By that time, global economic power had crossed the Atlantic to the United States; yet the United States was reluctant to act on this economic power, especially after the untimely death of Benjamin Strong, President of the Federal Reserve Bank of New York. Today's situation is not identical: economic power has begun to cross to the Pacific, but it has not left the United States behind. As the world's largest economy and most important financial sector power, the US is still more important than China and likely to remain so for many years to come.

Nevertheless, there are some signs of change. In mid-June 2013, Shibor, the Shanghai inter-bank offered rate, spiked. There were a number of reasons why this happened. Theories abound as to whether this was deliberately staged by the People's Bank of China to curb the shadow banking system and lending by commercial banks; or whether the PBoC was taken by surprise. This issue has been covered extensively in the media and by commentators and will not be discussed here. However, what stands out is that, whereas five years ago Chinese monetary policy was only of concern to China analysts, this time developments had a substantial impact on financial markets elsewhere. Moreover, it is clear that Chinese authorities were surprised by both this effect and the reactions from other countries.

What this issue highlights is that with size and power come responsibility. China cannot on the one hand claim to be a great power (as it is) and insist on due respect (which it should get), while at the same time claiming that it needs dispensations as an emerging economy, (i.e. on the environment) or to be allowed to maintain an undervalued currency (admittedly for the moment not the case) and suppress domestic demand in order to capture ever greater shares of the world's exports. There are signs that this is understood by the new Chinese leadership. Informed observers say that China is an increasingly responsible global stakeholder and an important and constructive partner for the rest of the world, something that is not necessarily the case for other major emerging markets. But, at the same time, there are still divergences between what China gives and what it expects.

The OECD notes that China has the most restrictive regime for foreign investment in the entire G20. Similarly, whereas at least EU public procurement markets are very open to Chinese companies, the Chinese public procurement market is basically blocked to foreign companies. Even on the micro level, restrictions abound. For example, foreign banks are welcome to set up branches in China. Yet it takes over a year for a foreign bank branch to be allowed in China, whereas a Chinese bank can set up a local branch in an EU country in just one week.

China is not the only country which needs to adjust its behavior, but of all countries in the G20, it does seem to be the one most determined to embark on a reform path that is both costly and difficult in the short-term, although it will bring substantial long term benefits. If—as seems likely—China persists on its path, it will also make adjustments necessary to establish itself as one of the world's economic leaders-whether through the G20 or not.

# G20: Quo Vadis?

*Zsolt Darvas*
**Paper prepared for the "The First G20 Think Tank Forum" organized by the Chongyang Institute for Financial Studies (RDCY) at Renmin University of China (RUC), August 21–22, 2013 Beijing**

## Introduction

The births of several major multinational initiatives were brought forth by major crises or disruption to economic activities. Prime examples are the creation of the IMF, the World Bank and the OECD in the aftermath of World War II, the Basel Capital Accord in1998 after the Latin American debt crisis and the savings and loan crisis in US, and the creation of the Financial Stability Forum (FSF) after the Asian crises in 1999[1]. Also in 1999, the "initial" G20[2] was also inaugurated, with the mission of promoting high-level consultations on financial stability issues. The "new" G20—consisting of the heads of states and governments of the 19 countries and the EU, accompanied by the top leaders of some invited countries and multinational organizations[3]—was prompted by the intensification of the global financial and economic crisis in late 2008, with the more ambitious self-designated goal of being "the premier forum for our international economic cooperation."[4]

As the fifth anniversary of the first G20 summit approaches, it is time to reflect on the achievements of the G20 and its future prospects. While there seems to be a consensus among analysts that the first phase of the G20, i.e. the first three summits in 2008–2009, delivered major achievements, the G20 has been criticized for being less successful in recent years. Some observers even foresee the demise of the G20 process. The G20 has been criticized for its lack of effectiveness in achieving its goals (which are assessed to be less ambitious since the Toronto summit in 2010), for its insufficient legitimacy, lack of leadership and even for irrelevance. Are these criticisms justified? Where is the G20 going from here? This paper tries to answer these questions by drawing extensively on, and providing an update to, earlier Bruegel research.

---

[1] See further examples in Table 1 of Rottier and Véron (2010a).
[2] The initial G20 meeting consisted of the group of finance ministers and central bank governors from 19 countries and the European Union (EU).
[3] At the most recent Los Cabos summit in June 2012, beyond the representatives of the 19 countries and the European Union, the presidents or prime ministers of Benin, Cambodia, Chile, Colombia, Ethiopia and Spain, and the top-leaders of the International Monetary Fund, Financial Stability Board, Food and Agriculture Organization, International Labour Organization, Organisation for Economic Co-operation and Development, World Trade Organization, United Nations and World Bank Group were also present.
[4] Paragraph 19 of the Preamble of the Leaders' Statement at the Pittsburgh summit.

## Effectiveness of the G20

Assessing the effectiveness of the G20 is a complex task, for several reasons. First, there is no counterfactual and thus it is impossible to tell which initiatives ascribed to the G20 would have been pursued anyway, for example through proposals by the IMF or the Basel Committee to avoid a repeat of the 1930s Great Depression, in the absence of the G20. Second, while there are some quantitative indicators of compliance with the summit commitments (we will report such indicators from two sources below), a high indicator score may just reflect the implementation of commitments that leaders wanted to implement anyway. There are no scoreboards for the quality of commitments and the importance of the missing commitments. Third, the latter factors could be assessed in an informal way, but this assessment would be entirely subjective.

With these caveats in mind, instead of assessing the *effectiveness* of the G20, let's look at the *compliance* with G20 commitments, based on the comprehensive dataset developed at the G20 Information Centre of the University of Toronto (Table 1). Data for the Los Cabos summit is unfortunately not available at the time of writing this paper.

The methodology behind this data is briefly described in the note to the table; here we only note that a positive value means that there was at least partial compliance on average with the commitment made, while a value close to 0 or negative signals limited or no compliance.

Panel A of Table 1 below indicates that compliance with commitments was rather high after the first Washington summit, but it declined significantly for the London summit, after which it more or less steadily increased. The scores for advanced countries are much higher than the scores for emerging countries, which may suggest unequal determination of the two country groups, fueled perhaps by the different impacts of the crisis, which was much worse for emerging countries than advanced countries. Indeed, emerging countries have negative, or close to zero scores for the London, Pittsburgh and Toronto summits. Therefore, the more recent increase in the aggregate G20 scores is largely the consequence of better compliance by emerging countries.

## Table 1 Compliance with G20 summit commitments
### Panel A: Scores by country group

| | | Washington | London | Pittsburgh | Toronto | Seoul | Cannes | Average |
|---|---|---|---|---|---|---|---|---|
| All G20 | Unweighted | 0.63 | 0.23 | 0.24 | 0.28 | 0.50 | 0.54 | 0.40 |
| | Weighted | 0.77 | 0.36 | 0.37 | 0.43 | 0.58 | 0.64 | 0.52 |
| Advanced G20 | Unweighted | 0.72 | 0.49 | 0.58 | 0.58 | 0.65 | 0.66 | 0.61 |
| | Weighted | 0.83 | 0.46 | 0.55 | 0.48 | 0.55 | 0.59 | 0.58 |
| Emerging G20 | Unweighted | 0.50 | -0.04 | -0.08 | -0.02 | 0.34 | 0.40 | 0.18 |
| | Weighted | 0.36 | -0.14 | -0.06 | 0.14 | 0.41 | 0.51 | 0.20 |

### Panel B: Scores by topic

| | | Washington | London | Pittsburgh | Toronto | Seoul | Cannes | Average |
|---|---|---|---|---|---|---|---|---|
| Macroeconomic Policy | Unweighted | 0.75 | 0.35 | 0.70 | 0.68 | 0.38 | 0.48 | 0.55 |
| | Weighted | 0.83 | 0.16 | 0.43 | 0.36 | 0.44 | 0.56 | 0.46 |
| Financial Reform | Unweighted | 0.47 | 0.50 | 0.15 | 0.10 | 0.59 | 0.60 | 0.40 |
| | Weighted | 0.68 | 0.50 | 0.43 | 0.58 | 0.73 | 0.81 | 0.62 |
| IFI Reform | Unweighted | n/a | 0.00 | 0.05 | 0.90 | 0.75 | 0.50 | 0.44 |
| | Weighted | n/a | 0.15 | 0.29 | 0.99 | 0.91 | 0.44 | 0.56 |

| | | Washington | London | Pittsburgh | Toronto | Seoul | Cannes | Average |
|---|---|---|---|---|---|---|---|---|
| Others | Unweighted | n/a | 0.15 | 0.21 | 0.14 | 0.45 | 0.51 | 0.29 |
| | Weighted | n/a | 0.50 | 0.36 | 0.28 | 0.51 | 0.60 | 0.45 |
| All | Unweighted | 0.63 | 0.23 | 0.24 | 0.28 | 0.50 | 0.54 | 0.40 |
| | Weighted | 0.77 | 0.36 | 0.37 | 0.43 | 0.58 | 0.64 | 0.52 |

**Source**: Bruegel calculations using data from the University of Toronto G20 Information Centre (scores) and the IMF (GDP used for calculating weights).
**Notes**: Unweighted: simple average of all countries; weighted: weighted averages based on GDP weights.
**Methodology**: The G20 research teams at the University of Toronto catalogue the commitments expressed in the final statement of each G20 summit, and then monitor compliance with these commitments in the period up to the next summit. For each commitment and for each meeting, each country is judgmentally assigned value of 1 if the commitment was fulfilled in full or in part, a value of 0 if the

commitment could not be fulfilled or was fulfilled only to a limited extent, and a value of -1 if the country did not act. The next step is to calculate average measures of the degree of compliance, separately for each meeting or each topic. A positive value means that there was at least partial compliance on average with the commitment made, while a value close to 0 or negative signals limited or no compliance. See more details at the G20 Research Group at the University of Toronto.

Similarly to Angeloni and Pisani-Ferry (2012), we selected three key topics among the list of G20 topics: macroeconomic policy, financial reform and the reform of International Financial Institutions (IFI). All other topics are grouped into one, which then becomes a heterogeneous group including trade, development, climate change, terrorist financing and money laundering, etc. Panel B of Table 1 reports the scores for all G20 countries for each summit for which data is available.

There seems to be a trade-off between macroeconomic policy and financial reform: for macro policies, the compliance with commitments of the first, third and fourth summits were relatively high, while for financial reforms the second, fifth and sixth summit commitments were more respected, especially in unweighted terms. There are no apparent reasons for such a trade-off, yet it may indicate that when the commitments are widespread, not all of them are pursued with equal force.

The IFI reform has very high compliance scores after Toronto and Seoul, a reasonably good score after Cannes, but a very low score after the first three summits. The heterogeneous "others" group tends to have lower scores than the three highlighted topics, especially on the unweighted basis.

The results of these quantitative assessments are not always in line with the qualitative judgements of Angeloni and Pisani-Ferry (2012), who also looked at the summit conclusions in detail (up to the Seoul summit) and assessed their relevance. For example, while these researchers had a rather positive evaluation of the London summit based on the commitments expressed in the summit's final statement, London received the lowest scores among all of the summits in the University of Toronto's scoreboard on compliance. The London statement was shorthand to the point and included major policy initiatives, including: transforming the Financial Stability Forum into the Financial Stability Board (FSB) with a broader representation and enhanced mandate; establishing the broad principles of the post-crisis bank capital standards and several other elements of financial reform (e. g. hedge funds, credit rating agencies, managerial compensation, bank risk control responsibilities); promoting bold actions in fiscal and monetary policies and banking sector repair; and significantly increasing the resources of the IMF and multinational development banks.

However, compliance with those commitments appears to have been less positive, at least during the time-frame of the Toronto G20 Information Centre assessment. Implementation of the commitment on "resisting protectionism and promoting global trade and investment" was high, but it was low in "ensuring a fair and sustainable recovery for all" (official development assistance, particularly for the poorest countries) and "the scope of regulation" (financial regulation). Also, as Angeloni and Pisani-Ferry

(2012) highlight, the increase of IMF resources, a major achievement of the London summit, is not among the priority commitments chosen by the Toronto G20 Information Centre to measure ex-post compliance with the summit, which lowers the average score.

Rottier and Véron (2010a, b) have conducted a more detailed examination of the 39 financial regulation action points of the November 2008 Washington summit, which was clearly the key focus at that time. They grade the effectiveness of implementation, cross-border consistency and follow-up initiatives taken up to the time of their writing. They score different institutions separately, but they do not score countries separately. Their analysis shows that the more the implementation of the action point depends upon action by an international body with significant autonomy in administration and resources, the more effective the implementation (Figure 1). Implementation by national authorities scores the lowest across all three criteria.

**Figure 1: Scoring of implementation of financial regulation action points in the November 2008 G20 Declaration, by type of main decision-making institution**

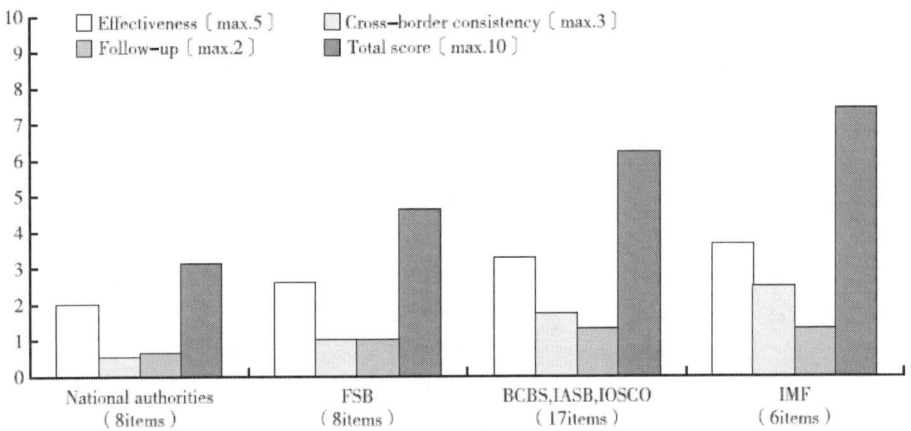

Source: Figure 2 of Rottier and Véron (2010a)
Note: See details in Rottier and Véron (2010b)

Has the G20 escaped diminishing returns? Kirton (2012) argues "yes", while Pisani-Ferry (2012) concludes "no." Kirton's main arguments for his assessment are as follows:

1. Leaders remained committed, as reflected by their attendance of G20 summits;
2. Leaders spent considerable time together and their teams produced a large number of documents;

3. The G20 is converging on the principles of democracy and human rights, even with the presence of China and Saudi Arabia in the group;
4. Leaders made a large number of commitments at G20 summits and the compliance was reasonably high[5];
5. There were steady institutional improvements of the G20; and
6. The core missions of the G20, notably ensuring financial stability and making globalization work for the benefit of all, were met.

However, some of these points are less important in terms of assessing the success of or the non-diminishing returns to the G20, while others can be seen from a different angle. For example, as discussed in the previous section, the number of commitments and compliance with the commitments is not the best measure of effectiveness. With regard to ensuring financial stability, one could also conclude that effective policies made by US authorities played the decisive role; the crisis originated in the financial sector of the US and US authorities were able to implement strong policies in shoring-up the financial system and restoring economic growth and job creation. These in turn significantly eased the financial stress felt in the US. Furthermore, a number of other G20 countries like Australia, Canada, China, and Saudi Arabia never even experienced any major financial market troubles at the height of the global financial and economic crisis. The role of the G20 in shaping US policies is unclear, but in my view, US authorities would have implemented similar policies in the absence of the G20 as well. The more medium- and longer-term financial reforms initiated by the G20 would have had a later effect, and thus may not have contributed much to the normalization of US financial markets after Lehman's demise in September 2008[6]. Moreover, financial stability was not restored in the Euro area, at least until the improvements induced the European Central Bank's Outright Monetary Transactions (OMTs) from mid-2012, in which the G20 probably did not play any role.[7]

We therefore subscribe more to the view of Pisani-Ferry (2012), discussed in more detail in Angeloni and Pisani-Ferry (2012), that in terms of macroeconomic coordination there has been decreasing returns to G20 efforts. Pisani-Ferry (2012) describes three main phases of G20 macroeconomic coordination:

1. Between the Washington and Pittsburgh Summits, a focus on stimulating the global economy;
2. Between the Toronto and Cannes Summits, a shift towards more complex objectives, with the aim of avoiding the resurgence of global imbalances; and

---

[5] See our previous section on this.
[6] See Darvas (2012a) for a discussion of the ECB's OMT.
[7] Yet we do agree that even the existence of the first and then later meetings by G20 heads of states and governments, and the fact that they act together, likely had a stabilizing impact on financial markets.

3.  From the Cannes Summit onwards, when the agenda was contaminated by the euro-crisis.

There seems to be a general agreement that the first phase was rather successful. Prompted by the urgency of the global financial crisis and the uncertain economic outlook, the G20 agenda was dominated by the management of the crisis, provision of financial resources to countries in crisis, and rebuilding of financial regulation. Such a coordinated response likely played a role in the post-2009 outcome in which advanced economies did not follow Great Depression-style policies and trade protectionism was largely avoided. In fact, as observed by Bénassy-Quéré, Kumar and Pisani-Ferry (2009), the initial G20 agenda did not explicitly address global imbalances.

This has changed in the second phase, as Table 2 indicates. While the role of global imbalances in triggering the global crisis is a controversial issue (Darvas and Pisani-Ferry, 2011), the Pittsburgh Summit in September 2009 launched the Framework for Strong, Sustainable, and Balanced Growth, to ensure a lasting recovery and strong and sustainable growth over the medium term. The main instrument of this framework is the so-called Mutual Assessment Process (MAP), which is a multilateral process through which G20 countries identify objectives for the global economy, the policies needed to reach them, and the progress toward meeting these shared objectives.

For the MAP, seven systematically important G20 countries were signaled out (China, France, Germany, India, Japan, United Kingdom, and United States) and detailed reports and country specific recommendations were made. As summarized by Angeloni and Pisani-Ferry (2012), the MAP turned out to be a cumbersome exercise and the jury is still out concerning its effectiveness. Yet after 2008, China's current account surplus reduced quite significantly[8] (Figure 2), in parallel with a gradual real effective appreciation of the Chinese Renminbi. This certainly eased the tension arising primarily from the US accusation that China was manipulating its currency.

Also, following the initiative of the French G20 presidency, reform of the international monetary system was put on the agenda. As we described in Angeloni et al (2011), this is an inherently complex issue and indeed no major achievements were reached, beyond an intensive debate which helped lead to a better understanding of the underlying issues.

---

[8] In 2011 and 2012, Germany even surpassed China as the country with the largest current account surplus in the world.

## Table 2: From Washington to Los Cabos: An Evolving Agenda

| Summit | Date | Headline priorities |
|---|---|---|
| Washington | November 2008 | Financial reform |
| London | April 2009 | Global stimulus |
| | | Financial reform |
| | | International financial institutions |
| Pittsburgh | September 2009 | G20 governance |
| | | Rebalancing of world economy |
| | | Financial reform |

| Summit | Date | Headline priorities |
|---|---|---|
| Toronto | June 2010 | Rebalancing of world economy |
| | | Financial reform |
| Seoul | November 2010 | Rebalancing of world economy |
| | | International financial institutions |
| Cannes | November 2011 | International monetary system |
| | | Commodity prices |
| | | Euro crisis |
| Los Cabos | June 2012 | International financial institutions |
| | | Commodity prices |
| | | Euro crisis |

**Source:** Updated form Angeloni and Pisani-Ferry (2012)

### Figure 2 Global imbalances (percent of world GDP), 1990–2013

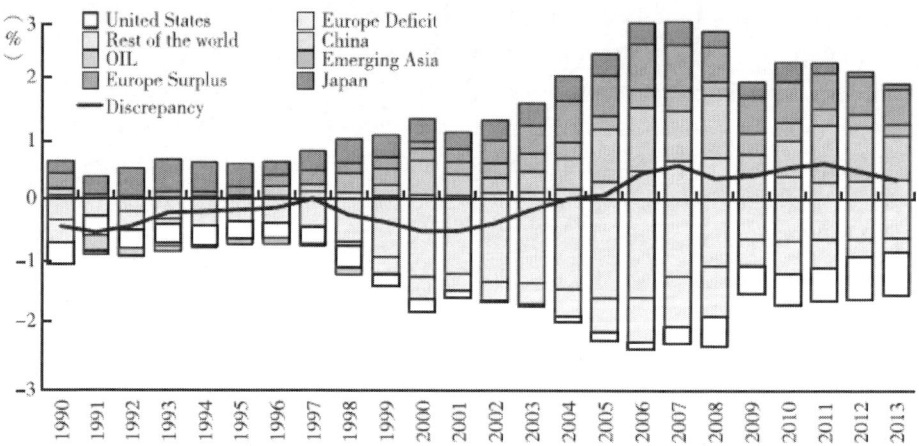

**Source:** Adopted from Figure 1 of Blanchard and Milesi-Ferretti (2010) using data from IMF World Economic Outlook April 2013.
**Note:** The composition of country groups is as follows:

1) EUR surplus: Austria, Belgium, Denmark, Finland, Germany, Luxembourg, Netherlands, Sweden, Switzerland
2) EUR deficit: Greece, Ireland, Italy, Portugal, Spain, United Kingdom, Bulgaria, Czech Republic, Estonia, Hungary, Latvia, Lithuania, Poland, Romania, Slovak Republic, Turkey, Ukraine
3) Emerging Asia: Hong Kong S. A. R. of China, Indonesia, Korea, Malaysia, Philippines, Singapore, Taiwan province of China, Thailand
4) Oil exporters: Algeria, Angola, Azerbaijan, Bahrain, Republic of Congo, Ecuador, Equatorial Guinea, Gabon, Iran, Kazakhstan, Kuwait, Libya, Nigeria, Norway, Oman, Qatar, Russia, Saudi Arabia, Sudan, Syria, Trinidad and Tobago, United Arab Emirates, Venezuela, Yemen
5) Rest of the world: remaining countries.

The third phase of the macroeconomic coordination process of the G20 was the most disappointing. It was dominated by discussions of the Euro crisis, which is in itself an inherently complex problem due to various economic, institutional and political factors (Darvas, 2012b). Also, as Darvas and Pisani-Ferry (2011) and Pisani-Ferry (2012) noted, the dual-level coordination (i.e. within the European Union and between the EuropeanG20 and other G20 partners) adds a complexity which may generate major tensions. The EU has a rules-based governance framework, relying on international treaties, whileG20 coordination is unlikely to be rules-based. Instead, the latter will likely start from a diagnosis of the major problems and responses considered in the light of this diagnosis.

Therefore, the effectiveness of the G20 in terms of macroeconomic coordination has clearly diminished. Perhaps this is the result of the nature of the problems. In 2008–2009 the whole world was shocked and the self-interest was to act together. Additionally, emerging countries realized little, if any, output loss and some non-European advanced economies left crisis mode quickly. In contrast, the complexity of the Euro crisis is such that no global policy coordination would have been able to find a quick fix.

## Conclusions

How effective has the G20 been so far? No one really knows, because measuring the effectiveness of the G20 does not equate to measuring compliance with the commitments, as there is no counterfactual to check which actions would have been pursued anyway in the absence of the G20. Also, there are no scoreboards for the quality of G20 commitments and the importance of unfulfilled commitments. Qualitative assessments of these factors are bound to be subjective. Yet quantitative indicators on compliance with G20 commitments suggest that the G20 has perhaps achieved more than is generally thought. But compliance has been uneven: advanced countries had higher compliance rates than that of emerging countries, and supranational institutions complied more than national authorities. These findings are not surprising, because advanced countries were hit harder by the crisis than emerging countries, and the G20 commitments are purely voluntary (i.e. non-binding) by national authorities, while supranational institutions are mandated to follow the will of their members, which are dominated by G20 countries.

These findings suggest that in the future, G20 initiatives can be more successful whenever they coincide with the domestic policy agenda of most members, or when the G20 gives a strong political mandate for multilateral institutions, such as the FSB or the IMF, to develop the details of an initiative for which they have their own independence and authority to implement. This also suggests that in other cases, the G20 could have a more limited impact.

While this conclusion may sound negative, I also note that G20 summits have likely helped to focus the attention of policy-makers, including the heads of states and governments, on policy priorities. It has also informed them about the policy intentions of other countries. This should have helped to design certain domestic policies and facilitated the fulfilment of the global agenda. These more informal benefits may carry over to the future.

In my view, the G20 should endeavor to discuss and coordinate major policy issues at the top-level to stimulate the thinking of policy-makers at various levels, including at the heads of states and governments. This cost will not be too high if the G20 process does not become overly bureaucratic. This also implies that while the organization of the G20 process could be marginally improved, there may not be a need for a major overhaul.

We should not expect much from the G20 in normal times, but holding a yearly gathering of heads of states (and several other meetings to prepare for these top-level meetings) should contribute to a better understanding of each other's positions, and hence provide impetus in the pursuit of a global agenda. Although the G20 may lack sufficient legitimacy, leadership and effectiveness in normal times, keeping the G20 process alive would provide the world a functioning and reliable forum should a new crisis erupt either globally, or in a major country with significant spillover implications.

## References

[1] Angeloni, Ignazio (2013) "What is wrong with the G20?" in: L. Paganetto (ed.), Public debt, Global Governance and Economic Dynamism, Springer-Verlag Italia 2013, p. 159-164.

[2] Angeloni, Ignazio and Jean Pisani-Ferry (2012) "The G20—characters in search of an author," Working Paper 2012/04, Bruegel.

[3] Angeloni, Ignazio, Agnès Bénassy-Quéré, Benjamin Carton, Christophe Destais, Zsolt Darvas, Jean Pisani-Ferry, André Sapir, and ShahinVallée, "Global currencies for tomorrow: a European perspective", July 2011, Bruegel Blueprint Volume XIII.

[4] Bénassy-Quéré, Agnès, Rajiv Kumar and Jean Pisani-Ferry (2009) "The G20 is not just a G7 with extra chairs", Policy Contribution 2009/10, Bruegel.

[5] Blanchard, Olivier and Gian Maria Milesi-Ferretti (2010), "Global Imbalances: In Midstream?", IMF Staff Position Note, 09/29.

[6] Darvas, Zsolt (2012a) "The ECB's magic wand," Intereconomics: Review of European Economic Policy, Springer, 47(5), 266-267, September, http://www.bruegel.org/nc/blog/detail/article/904-the-ecbs-magic-wand/

[7] Darvas, Zsolt (2012b), "The euro crisis: ten roots, but fewer solutions," Policy Contribution 2012/17, Bruegel.

[8] Darvas, Zsolt and Jean Pisani-Ferry (2010a), "Future developments of global imbalances," Briefing paper, IP/A/ECON/FWC/2000_040_C1, Committee on Economic and Monetary Affairs, European Parliament.

[9] Darvas, Zsolt and Jean Pisani-Ferry (2010b), "The threat of 'currency wars': A European perspective," Bruegel Policy Contribution 2010/12.

[10] G20 Research Group at the University of Toronto, "G20 Information Centre"—a website regularly updated, http://www.g20.utoronto.ca/

[11] Kirton, John (2012) "How the G20 Has Escaped Diminishing Returns," Paper prepared for a panel on "Can the G20 Escape Diminishing Returns?" at a conference on "International Cooperation in Times of Global Crisis: Views from G20 Countries" Higher School of Economics, Moscow, Russia, October 18-19, 2012, organized by Bruegel, CEPII and Higher School of Economics.

[12] Pisani-Ferry, Jean (2012) "G20: Decreasing return," in Darvas, Zsolt (ed.) EU-Korea Economic Exchange, Issue 2, Bruegel and Korea Institute of Finance, pp. 4-6.

[13] Rottier, Stéphane and Nicolas Véron (2010a) "Not all financial regulation is global," PolicyBrief 2010/07, Bruegel.

[14] Rottier, Stéphane and Nicolas Véron (2010b) "An assessment of the G20's initial action Items," Policy Contribution 2010/08, Bruegel.

[15] Véron, Nicolas (2012) "Financial reform after the crisis—An early assessment," Working Paper 2012/01, Bruegel.

# G20 from the Perspective of Green Growth and Sustainable Development[1]*

*Sung Jin Kang*
Professor, Department of Economics, Korea University, Korea

## Introduction

The eventual exhaustion of fossil fuels due to reckless overuse and global resource constraints will put a halt to the current pattern of economic growth and development models, and will lead to climate change. As demonstrated by the high dependence of economies on fossil fuels and the recent global financial crisis, we must consider adopting a new economic growth strategy based on green growth or green economy (Kang, 2012a) in order to sustain and/or improve our current quality of life.

Green growth policies for sustainable development do not just contribute to environmentally friendly economic development, but they also promote economic efficiency. However, green growth policies may cause social conflicts. This is because green growth policies do not consider social development issues in balance with the other two aspects of sustainable development: economic efficiency and environmental impact. Considering this conflict, the World Bank recently released a report entitled "Inclusive Green Growth" (World Bank, 2011).

Major developed countries have formulated strategies to take action against climate change. For instance, the European Union unveiled the Energy and Climate Change package in 2007 and the Climate Action and Renewable Energy Package in 2008. The United States ratified the American Clean Energy and Security Act in 2009 while Japan passed the Green Economy and Social Change in 2009 and Basic Act on Global Warming Countermeasures in 2010. The South Korean government also presented "Low Carbon, Green Growth" policies in 2008, garnering attention from international society.

Even China, whose rapid economic growth thus makes it a large emitter of greenhouse gases, has been establishing policies to tackle climate change. The Five-Year Plan for the National Economy and Society of the People's Republic of China (2006, 2010) includes several policies. One of the targets in the 11th Five Year Plan (2006–2010) aims to construct more resource efficient and environmentally friendly society.

---

\* This paper is a revised and abbreviated version of Kang (2012b), "Green Growth and Sustainable Development in the G20: Performance and Prospects", presented at the international conference "International Monetary System, Energy, and Sustainable Development", which is in line with the joint research project for the 2012 G20 Mexico Summit and the 2013 G20 Russia Summit (supported by Korea Development Institute).

The 12th Five Year Plan (2011–2015) aims to promote inclusive growth through fair distribution of the benefits resulting from economic growth (Hilton, 2011).

However, the priority of economic policies in developing countries is to improve absolute poverty through economic growth. Therefore, they may have difficulty balancing between environmental aspects and social development aspects. This is strikingly different compared to developed countries, which are able to consider all three aspects of sustainable development in balance. In order to successfully implement sustainable development in developing countries, international cooperation and idea sharing between developed and developing countries is therefore necessary.

The Group of Twenty (G20) was inaugurated at the 1999 IMF Annual General Meeting. The G20 summit was initiated for the purpose of resolving global financial and foreign exchange crises. Various issues such as international financial reform, development, and energy and climate change—including green growth as the strategy to achieve sustainable development—have been discussed in depth at the G20 summits.

With respect to energy and climate change issues, G20 leaders have discussed ways to improve unstable energy markets, strengthen energy security, enhance energy-related data, gradually eliminate ineffective fossil fuel subsidies, increase access to renewable energy, increase energy efficiency, protect the marine environment, and preserve biodiversity. Other topics discussed include clean energy technologies, the Green Climate Fund, the GGKP (Green Growth Knowledge Platform), and the need to establish an efficient mechanism to manage public and private funds.

At the most recent G20 Summit in 2012, two major proposals for green growth and sustainable development were made. First, leaders argued that there is a need to devise specific plan for promoting green growth in member countries currently undergoing reform. Second, leaders explained that developing and destitute nations need assistance with green growth, as well as in reducing poverty and enhancing development. Despite numerous active debates, leaders did not come to a consensus on many issues since the views on green growth held by developed nations differed from that of emerging economies.

At the upcoming 8th G20 Summit in Russia, countries should seek to narrow the gap and adopt climate change and green growth policies to achieve sustainable development. As a G2 member as well as a G20 member, China is expected to play a key role in establishing and implementing the policies to tackle the current global financial crisis as well as development aspects of other developing countries.

## G20 Future Prospects in Green Growth and Sustainable Development

One of the G20's major issues is implementation of green growth strategies for sustainable development. This encompasses a variety of sub-issues, including establishing a system to deal with energy and climate change issues, exploring ways to provide developing nations with technological and financial assistance, and addressing how to deal with volatile energy prices and their spillover effects.

Despite numerous and active debates, countries have not come to agreement on these issues. At the 8th G20 Summit in Russia, leaders must exchange ideas to achieve sustainable development. In particular, leaders must identify challenges and directions for addressing climate change and promoting green growth.[2]

1) Social Development

It has been noted that social development, one of the critical pillars of sustainable development, has not been sufficiently incorporated into green growth strategies. To achieve sustainable development, the ultimate goal, countries need to further develop their societies. Relieving poverty first comes to mind when one thinks about sustainable development. However, there is more to it than that. Countries must reduce both absolute and relative poverty, mitigate social anxieties, and increase their citizens' satisfaction in the economy.

There are many dividing lines upon which social conflicts arise, including gender, regional, generational, and social class conflicts. To resolve conflicts and achieve social integration, policies need to embrace different groups. Moreover, countries must establish a firm social safety net and inclusive social policies.

However, a mere push toward equality is not the answer. That is, fairness should not undermine social dynamics. It is disappointing that current economic and green growth policies do not take into account the complexity of social development. Even though it is possible to evaluate economic and environmental achievements objectively, not much effort has been put into the development of objective indicators for assessing social development. This is why countries need to create appropriate indicators to measure and assess social development and green growth, and also examine where they stand on the path to sustainable development. There are many different elements that affect social development. Instead of simply pursuing an equal society, countries must create an environment where different branches of government cooperate to resolve differences, resulting in the creation of policies that not only address poverty, but also economic growth. If necessary, countries must take immediate measures to reform systems on a broad scale.

2) International Cooperation

Diverse issues related to climate change are frequently debated. Global warming caused by greenhouse gas emissions affects not just heavy polluters themselves, but neighboring countries as well. Therefore, nations need to work together in addressing

---

[2] See Kang (2012a) for more detail.

climate change issues. However, due to externalities arising from environmental problems, countries are divided over which nations should bear more responsibility and costs to deal with global warming.

Developing countries, typically the largest greenhouse gas emitters, will be hit the hardest if their greenhouse gas reduction targets are set as high as those of developed nations. As a result, developing countries have not readily agreed with global action against climate change proposed by advanced countries. In addition, developing nations are less able to undertake specific measures to fight climate change even if they felt the need to. This is largely due to a lack of appropriate technologies. In order to help developing countries actively participate in international climate change actions, developed nations need to equip them with enough financial support and technology. Developed countries need to assure developing economies that green technologies will help them nurture green industries that also develop their economies, create more jobs, and improve income inequality.

Developed nations also need to make investments in developing nations and provide technological assistance, as developing countries do not have enough financial resources to promote their own green technologies and green industry. Without such assistance, a G20 declaration on its face will not achieve anything significant.

Official Development Assistance (ODA) is the most well-known, international cooperative mechanism that developed countries can take to provide direct assistance to developing nations. However, it is difficult to boost international cooperation in green growth through ODA. This is largely because definitions of green ODA are not consolidated, both at home and abroad.

Kang (2011) offers a broad definition of green growth ODA, including environment ODA, which covers environment and climate change, and a broader type of green growth ODA that is associated with the creation of new growth engines and promoting quality of life and national image. The categorization in use is based on a Credit Reporting System (CRS) code which is more detailed than that of Rio Marker, an existing environmental marker.

In this regard, Kang's definition of green growth ODA goes well beyond providing developing nations with technological and financial assistance. Kang explains that green growth ODA should not only help developing countries, but also the entire globe in achieving green growth. In the years ahead, global leaders should come up with a clear definition of green growth ODA, which can be accepted in the world and used to promote global cooperation for green growth.

The Green Climate Fund (GCF) is also an effective tool for green growth. The GCF will enable developing countries to nurture clean energy technologies and to adapt to climate changes. At the 2010 United Nations Framework Convention on Climate Change (UNFCCC) COP16, the heads of state agreed to establish the GCF, and the United Nations committed to raising $100 billion every year until 2020. At the

2011 UNFCCC COP17, the GCF Design Committee report was adopted, allowing the Fund to be launched as soon as possible.

It is a hard fact that direct technological and financial assistance is needed to spread global growth. More importantly, this assistance should be based on effective policies and public recognition that green growth is absolutely necessary. A good deal of knowledge and wisdom associated with green growth is being shared within international organizations. However, the most significant discussions are led mainly by OECD countries. At the G20 Mexico Summit, the leaders emphasized the need to establish an international mechanism through which countries can share their knowledge and enhance cooperation, similar to how the Global Growth Knowledge Platform (GGKP) performs. The GGKP should be built in a way that even developing countries can readily be involved, going well beyond a global knowledge network of developed countries. By encouraging countries to share directions for policies and action plans, the GGKP should ensure that every nation can boost their capacities and take great leaps forward in sustainable development.

3) Green Governance

In order to guarantee consistency in implementing green growth policies, each nation needs a main organization that can act as a control tower. Green growth is not just about environmental regulation and protection, but also encompasses many other issues. Green growth policies need to be properly executed whilst government departments maintain close collaboration to minimize conflicts among shareholders.

Countries like Greece, France, Australia, and Britain have a department in charge of responding to climate change and green growth. In South Korea, the "Presidential Committee on Green Growth" plays a key role in implementing green growth policies. The "Ministry of Environment and Climate Change, "and the "Ministry of Ecology, Sustainable Development, Transport and Housing," successor to "the Ministry of Ecology and Sustainable Development," are in charge of green growth for Greece and France, respectively.

Among departments such as these, Korea's Presidential Committee on Green Growth is an exemplary case where government departments work with social groups. The Committee is co-chaired by the prime minister and a private expert. There are 13 commissioners (consisting of green growth-related ministers) designated by law and 36 commissioners (consisting of professors, scholars, entrepreneurs, and other social activists) nominated by the President. The commissioners are assigned to review policies, gather extensive opinions, and make policy suggestions. They are divided into "Green Institution and Finance," "Green Growth and Industry," "Climate Change and Energy," and "Green Life and Sustainable Development" sub-committees.

Green growth is essential to the global economy, environment, and society. That is why government departments, industries, and civil society should take part in the establishment of green governance. Government departments should assume the leading role so that different opinions will be heard and that policies will be formulated. As is done in Korea's Presidential Committee, the government should make sure that diverse groups actively participate in achieving green growth. Additionally, the government needs to provide a clear legal foundation and authority for the main organization to carry out its mission. Concrete green growth policies built on progress made in theoretical and conceptual discussions will guarantee the desired outcome.

4) Energy Price Volatility

Energy price volatility is an external factor that creates difficulties for developing nations to implement green growth policies. High volatility triggers fierce competition over energy and leads vulnerable companies and countries to the brink of collapse. Increased price volatility prevents developing nations heavily dependent on imported energy from acquiring energy. Increases in price volatility still hinder short and long-term economic growth for developing countries because they usually do not have sufficient access to alternative energy. In the end, price volatility causes both economic and social anxiety, thereby discouraging developing nations from pursuing green growth. It also can have a devastating effect on the poor. Indeed, there will be a rise in the number of "energy poor" people who do not have access to a minimum amount of energy.

Since the 2009 Pittsburgh Summit, G20 leaders have had active discussions related to energy price volatility. They offered a broad range of ideas to relieve price volatility through enhancing transparency in energy markets, promoting exchanges between energy producers and consumers, and making improvements on regulations in futures markets. At the 2010 Seoul Summit, further discussions on price volatility of energy, including fossil fuels, took place and leaders agreed to support green economic policies which will ensure energy access for the poor while simultaneously promoting eco-friendly and sustainable growth. Moreover, G20 leaders committed to creating an environment where energy efficient technologies will be developed and distributed, and the establishment and implementation of clean energy policies will be promoted in both member and non-member countries. Eventually, countries must reduce the consumption of fossil fuels and other forms of energy that emits significant greenhouse gases and instead use more eco-friendly energy.

However, energy price volatility forces countries to focus on dealing with energy supply and demand issues, rather than developing environment friendly technologies and renewable energy. In the end, price volatility discourages countries from developing green technologies. An optimal energy mix can be achieved through green growth policies only when prices of energy, including fossil fuels, are stabilized. Therefore, the international community should openly discuss and put into effect methods to suppress price volatility.

Above all, conflicts between energy producers and consumers need to be resolved so that energy prices can remain stable. In order to resolve conflicts, energy-related organizations such as the International Energy Agency (IEA) and the Organization of Petroleum Exporting Countries (OPEC) should promote energy quality and raise confidence in the price determination processes. Also, they must ensure that energy is produced by internationally respected organizations and that energy-supply-and-demand problems in the market are reviewed and corrected.

In the long run, countries must push for the development of green energy technologies and decrease their vulnerability to extreme changes in energy prices. Also, they need to refrain from using energy which produces a lot of greenhouse gases. Instead, countries must use more environmentally-friendly energy. Energy-related issues have an adverse impact on individuals, as well as national economies and companies. In light of this, countries must work hard to establish policies to reduce energy price volatility.

## Conclusion

The G20 summit was originally initiated to resolve the urgent issue of the global financial and foreign exchange crises. Besides urgent issues such as international financial reform and exchange rate stability, recent G20 meeting agendas have expanded to address more long-term issues, including development, energy price stability, fossil fuel subsidies and climate change. In particular, green growth as a strategy to achieve sustainable development, was discussed in depth at the Seoul meeting. In order to improve current international collaboration, G20 summits need to better discuss global issues facing humanity, focusing on how to sustain and improve quality of life and bequeath natural resources to our descendants without further exhaustion and worsening of the climate situation.

## References

[1] Hilton, Isabel, 2011, "China's Green Revolution—Energy, Environment and the 12th Five-Year Plan."
[2] Kang, Sung Jin, 2011, "Green Growth ODA" in Green Growth: *Global Cooperation*, NRCS& Random House.
[3] Kang, Sung Jin, 2012a, "Further Steps to Achieve Sustainable Development through Green Economy," Report of International Association of Economic and Social Councils and Similar Institutions (AICESIS).
[4] Kang, Sung Jin, 2012b, "Green Growth and Sustainable Development in G20: Performance and Prospects," presented in the international conference "International Monetary System, Energy, and Sustainable Development," and conducted as a joint research for the 2012 G20 Mexico Summit and the 2013 G20 Russia Summit (supported by Korea Development Institute).

# The G20 and the Dilemma of Asymmetric Sovereignty: Why Multilateralism is Failing in Crisis Prevention

*Heribert Dieter*
German Institute for International and Security Affairs, Berlin, and
Visiting Professor for International Political Economy,
Zeppelin University, Lake Constance

## Abstract

The G20 is not able to move forward without reforms necessary to prevent future financial crises. Successes in crisis management cannot be transformed into joint crisis prevention. The global regulation of financial markets, agreed upon at previous G20 summits, was intended to make the international financial system more stable and more resilient against future crises. Alas, the resultant expectations were unfulfilled. Likewise, we cannot expect meaningful steps towards a reinforcement of the global regulation of financial markets from this year's G20 summit in St. Petersburg. At least as serious are the failure of the Doha Round and the incapability of the G20 to prevent it, despite the frequently voiced commitment to a multilateral order. The structural crisis in global regulation of today is not least the result of an asymmetric sovereignty in financial politics:

States possess only marginal influence on international financial markets, but they are liable in times of crisis. The result is a re-nationalization of financial policies. At the same time, the increasingly critical perception of globalization, in particular in OECD societies, complicates the further evolution of the multilateral trade order.

Supranational regulation of a range of issues has been on the agenda of international politics for more than two decades. "Global Governance," particularly in economic affairs, was considered a promising concept. The development of shared norms and standards in finance should have helped to reduce risks and prevent future crisis. This concept is embodied in the foundation of the Group of 20 in 1999 as a reaction to the financial crises of the late 1990s.

Initially limited to finance ministers, the G20 first met at the level of heads of states and governments in November 2008. This was deemed a breakthrough by some observers: Finally the problems of increasingly interdependent economies would be solved at the global level.

## The crisis management of the G20 raised hopes

Initially, the G20 fulfilled expectations. The global economic and financial crisis was managed without a relapse to protectionist trade policies or harmful competitive evaluations. Between 2008 and 2011, the G20 was able to implement some significant steps, for example modernizing the International Monetary Fund. At the G20 summit in Cannes in November 2011, the development of shared rules for financial markets was still high on the agenda. But only non-binding memoranda of understanding were agreed upon.

In the following two years since the G20 summit in Cannes, some countries have chosen to go their own way and it has become evident that there will be no joint approach to the regulation of financial markets. Notably, the US has not only enacted unilateral reforms of its financial markets but has also given up one of the established pillars of financial regulation. Authorities in the United States no longer accept the so called home country principle and have shifted unilaterally to the host country principle, according to which banks operating in the US must also hold capital in the US. The US terminates the former consensus of the OECD countries by implementing the host country principle in banking supervision: Financial institutions are being supervised where they operate, not in the country where their headquarters are located. This has far-reaching consequences and will lead to a segmentation of markets. In the future, Deutsche Bank for instance will have to hold capital in New York for its American business—rather than in Frankfurt as was the case up to now.

Just like the US, ever more countries are choosing individual national paths for their financial policies. For example, right from the beginning of the crisis, Brazil raised a tax on capital inflows at rates of 2 to 6 percent and has only abandoned this measure on June 5, 2013—due to a considerable drop of the Brazilian Real's exchange rate. Switzerland has chosen special capital requirements of its two large banks UBS and Credit Suisse, thereby deviating strongly from the standards of the Basel Committee of Banking Supervision. While large banks have to hold 13 percent capital by the end of the current decade, according to the set of measures known as Basel III, the Swiss banking supervision has enforced much higher capital requirements and is demanding 19 percent of risk weighted assets from its two largest banks.

## Liability in the event of a crisis

What is the reason for this development? Why do countries seem to lose faith not only in multilateral approaches, but also in the regulation of financial markets? One important aspect is the largely dissimilar experiences of countries with the financial crisis. For the societies of countries with very large financial sectors—Switzerland, but also Great Britain—the 2008–2009 crisis was a traumatic experience that the affected societies do not want to repeat. The fiercer the crisis and the closer the abyss, the stronger is the desire of these societies to not settle for the minimum global consensus in financial regulation.

Of course, establishing a set of rules for financial markets in particular not only involves the implementation of internationally agreed upon regulations, but also liability for adverse developments. In the event of a crisis, governments are at least partly responsible for the mistakes of their banks. The crises of the last several years have shown this very clearly. Whether in Ireland or in Spain, in the US or in Belgium, governments everywhere have taken great financial risks to prevent the collapse of their financial systems. In some cases—such as Ireland and Spain—the rescue operations have impaired the state budget in such a way that, without help from abroad, not only would the banks face bankruptcy but also the states themselves.

For numerous governments, the internationalization of financial markets has led to a peculiar as well as precarious situation: While countries possess only indirect influence on the international negotiations related to financial regulation, they are individually liable in the event of a crisis. Their sovereignty is thus asymmetric. So far, the governments of sovereign states have lacked the instruments to reduce the risks that come along with their bank's business; still, they were held accountable. The resulting situation has become both politically unsatisfying and threatening to the legitimacy of governments. Some G20 States have responded with the unilaterally implemented measures sketched above.

In principle, individual states would indeed have had the ability to tighten their financial market regulation well before the recent crises that struck the US and Europe. Thereby, they would have lowered the risks for their public finances. However, before the outbreak of the crises, it was politically difficult to find support for a prudent policy. Banks successfully referred to the competitive environment in which they have to operate and pointed to the liberal banking supervision in other countries. So prior to the crises, we saw a levelling of banking supervision at the lowest common level, which however—as we know today—was highly inadequate. Even more problematic has been the fact that homogeneous banking supervision made the international financial system more and not less-crisis prone. The existence of identical rules led to everybody making the same mistakes at the same time (Haldane 2009).

A second reason for the growing interest in the re-nationalization of financial politics is based on the experience from Iceland's banking system bankruptcy. Iceland's three major banks initially grew rapidly abroad, implementing daring business models. Equally quick was their demise, and all three banks slipped into bankruptcy just as quickly. The assumption that a state will guarantee the liabilities incurred by insolvent banks in other countries was plausible until Iceland failed to honor the obligations of its banks. The events in Iceland have weakened this expectation. The faith in national government guarantees—a central element of the home country principle in banking supervision—was fundamentally shaken. The bankruptcy of Cypriot banks, although somewhat different than the Iceland situation, has further fueled doubts. That is one more reason why the US is shifting towards the host country principle.

In 2013, there is increasing evidence that some countries are departing from the goal of global regulation. The US has been changing from home-country regulation—in which banks are regulated in their home country, not in the country where they do business—to the host-country principle. Large banks operating in the US will henceforth have to hold capital in America. Deutsche Bank for instance will have to hold capital in New York—a change that is vigorously opposed by that bank. The Warwick Commission (2009) has been advocating for that change in its final report. Finance would be segmented—a proposal John Maynard Keynes made in the early 1930s (Keynes 1933).

## Why do global approaches fail?

Tightening the rules for financial market regulation is not the only field where the G20 is failing. Despite the mantra-like repetition of memoranda of understanding, G20 trade ministers have not been able to overcome their conflicts of interest and reach a settlement in the Doha Round of the World Trade Organization (WTO). What are the reasons for this failure?

Although the G20 managed to prevent a revival of protectionist measures on a broad front in the midst of the crisis, there is a large gap between the announcements of the G20 and quantifiable results in trade policy. There is not one final communiqué lacking a clear statement stressing the importance of the World Trade Organization and the necessity to conclude the Doha Round. Nonetheless, the reality of trade policy looks very different. All the states that are preventing the conclusion of the Doha Round through their veto are members of the G20.

Although little information on the reasons for the deadlock in the Doha Round is publicly available, it is known that the US, Brazil and China are blocking its conclusion. The emerging economies of Brazil and China oppose the demand by the US for the complete elimination of tariffs on industrial goods. Conversely, the US resists the request to comprehensively abandon subsidies to the agricultural sector.

Thus, the Doha Round is not concluded because three important members of the G20 no longer believe in multilateral solutions and rather engage in preferential agreements. For experts in the field of international trade, this is a paradox. There is a broad consensus that single rule book for international trade would facilitate economic growth and contribute to a worldwide increase in prosperity. This, however, cannot be said for the currently popular free trade agreements. So why are the countries in the G20 incapable of further developing common rules for international trade?

One explanation is the lack of a hegemonic power that is willing to guarantee compliance with the rules of the game while at the same time establishing a system that provides member countries with sufficient economic benefits. In any event, this is how the post-war economy emerged: The US enforced the Bretton Woods system and made sure that participation in this economic regime remained attractive. Of course, the Bretton Woods regime was never a truly global system since the member countries of the Council on Mutual Economic Assistance (COMECON) do not participate. Still, within the bipolar order of the Cold War, the US managed to keep the system open and stable.

After the collapse of the USSR and the following short-lived "unipolar moment" (Charles Krauthammer) of complete US hegemony, the multilateral order came into development starting in 1995 with the founding of the WTO. Since the turn of the millennium and the parallel emergence of a multipolar order, nearly all attempts to organize cooperation without hegemony (Bob Keohane) have failed. The present multipolar world is characterized by superficial cooperation. Global Governance, whether in policies to prevent further climate change or in economic policy, remains on hold. Even worse, the world is returning to regulation on the level of the nation state and non-cooperation. The American political scientist Ian Bremmer refers to the resulting situation as "G-Zero," an era in which groups like the G20 will no longer play a vital role.

## The negative perception of the international division of labor

Apparently there is no such thing as an identity of common interests among individual states as assumed by the advocates of global regulation and global governance. In other words, the gap between the preferences of individual states is widening rather than narrowing. Governments must, however, respect the preferences of their societies in the formulation of policies if they want to retain legitimacy. Then again, the different societal preferences are the immediate result of a severely diverging perception of the international division of labor. Even within the G20, individual societies have very different perceptions of globalization and its economic effects.

In Europe and the US many people are increasingly critical of the international division of labor, if not outright hostile to globalization. According to a number of surveys, only about one-fifth to one-third of the respondents in OECD countries feels that there are greater opportunities than risks in globalization. Even in Germany, numerous politicians and citizens have expressed a critical perception of globalization, although Germany strongly benefits from open markets and the resulting intensification of international trade.

## Without a political anchoring in the member states, the G20 has no future

The critical perception of globalization and asymmetric sovereignty as outlined above has resulted in a standstill in the G20. Instead of a further development of the multilateral order, at best the status quo will be preserved. This is why we can expect nothing substantial, at least in terms of economic policy and financial regulation, from the summit of the G20 in St. Petersburg on September 5 and 6. The structural impediments to successful financial regulation and trade policies on a supranational level cannot be overcome by the heads of governments and states of the G20. At least, there is hope in those fields, few as they may be, where the countries of the G20 have identical interests. This applies primarily to measures to close down tax loopholes. In 2008, ambitious expectations of a comprehensive reorganization of international trade relations through the G20 were raised. Unfortunately, the G20 cannot and will not deliver in crisis prevention. Today, much more modest goals will have to be set. The key impediment for a successful further development of global rules in trade and finance can be found in the G20 societies themselves. The critical perception of globalization needs to be addressed by policy makers at the national level. The widespread reservations on the international division of labor in OECD countries need to be addressed. If societies continue to show diverging preferences, the development of comprehensive global economic governance in the G20 will be all but impossible.

## References

[1] Haldane, Andrew (2009): Rethinking the Financial Network. Speech by Andrew Haldane to the Financial Student Association, Amsterdam, April 2009, available at http://www.fi nextra.com/Finextra-downloads/featuredocs/speech386.pdf

[2] Keynes, John Maynard (1933): National Self-Sufficiency, The Yale Review, Vol. 22, No. 4(June), pp. 755-769.

[3] Reinhart, Carmen; Rogoff, Kenneth (2009): This Time is Different. Eight Centuries of Financial Folly. Princeton: Princeton University Press.

[4] Warwick Commission (2009): International Financial Reform: In Praise of Unlevel Playing Fields. The Report of the Second Warwick Commission. Coventry 2009

# An Australian Perspective on the G20

*Melissa Conley Tyler*[*d]
**Australian Institute of International Affairs**

## Australia and the G20

In Australian thinking, the G20 is a high priority. It has been reported that the Secretary of the Department of Foreign Affairs and Trade lists the G20 among the top priorities for Australia's foreign policy as part of a "six + two + N" formula.[2] The G20 is important to Australia both as a way to gain a seat at the table of global councils and as an effective forum for managing global economic issues. Australia is dedicated to the continued success of the G20 and has accordingly worked hard to ensure that the G20 remains both relevant and effective.

When the global financial crisis (GFC) gained momentum in 2008, Australia campaigned hard to elevate the G20, which had previously met at finance ministers' level, to a leaders' level summit.[3] Prime Minister Kevin Rudd engaged a number of the G7 nations to advocate the need for a global response.[4] Australia considers itself fortunate to be part of the body that in subsequent meetings took on the mantle of the world's "premier economic forum." The Lowy Institute's Mark Thirlwell hailed the decision to lock in the pre-eminence of the G20 as "a win for Kevin Rudd, a win for

---

[*] National Executive Director, Australian Institute of International Affairs. The views expressed are those of the author alone. Sections of this work are based on research published as M Conley Tyler, "Australia's Views on Global Summitry: The Case of the G20", *Global Summitry Journal*, vol. 1, issue 1, 2013, available online: http://globalsummitry.org/gsj/vol1/iss1/2/. The author thanks Australian government officials and others interviewed anonymously for this research. Thanks are due to AIIA interns Madeline Goldie, Simon Speldewinde and Margherita Crippa for their research assistance.

[2] This refers to the six key bilateral relationships (China, India, Indonesia, Japan, South Korea and the United States), two key multilateral institutions (G20 and the East Asia Summit) and Australia's immediate neighbourhood, the Pacific: Daniel Flitton, "Chief diplomat spells out Australia's rules of engagement", The Age, 29 January 2013, available online: http://www.theage.com.au/opinion/politics/chief-diplomat-spells-out-australias-rules-of-engagement-20130128-2dgse.html (accessed 2 May 2013).

[3] Xu Yi-Chong, "Australian Participation in the G20" in Wilhelm Hofmeister (ed), G20 - Perceptions and Perspectives for Global Governance (Singapore: Konrad Adenauer Stiftung, 2011); available online: http://www.kas.de/wf/en/33.29099 (accessed 30 September 2012).

[4] Matthew Franklin, "PM Kevin Rudd's Role in International Crisis Summit," The Australian, 25 October 2008. Available online: http://www.theaustralian.com.au/news/pms-role-in-crisissummit/story-e6frg6no-1111117850306 (accessed 30 September 2012).

Australia, and most importantly, a win for the effectiveness of the international architecture."[5] The GFC gave the opportunity for middle powers and strategic economies alike to be promoted to a position of greater influence in the global economy.

For the states involved, the G20 is an effective grouping. It has the practicality and convenience of a relatively small group, but sufficient breadth to include the key players needed. The financial crises of the 1990s had made clear that a larger and more diverse group was necessary to address financial instability.[6] The group needed to "capture the shifting geographic distribution of economic weight in the world economy"[7] while remaining regionally balanced and small enough to facilitate open and efficient discussion.[8]

The G20 is demonstrably more representative than the G8.[9] Its economies capture 87% of global GDP and 78% of world trade[10] as well as two-thirds of the world's population.[11] While the G20's greater representativeness doesn't necessarily make it more legitimate, it does make it more likely to be effective; it is representative of the major economies of the 21st century.

The G20 represents a functional approach to coordinating national action on global economic issues through what amounts to an informal "club." As such, its legitimacy is not only conferred by numbers but also by the credibility of its agenda and efficacy in producing concrete deliverables.[12] This can include outreach to non-G20 countries, improving the democratic structure of global governance and a focus on issues of inequality.[13]

---

[5]  Mark Thirlwell, "One G to Rule Them All," *The Interpreter*, Lowy Institute for International Policy, 28 September 2009, http://www.lowyinterpreter.org/post/2009/09/28/One-G-to-rulethem-all.aspx (accessed 30 September 2012).

[6]  Group of Twenty, "Group of Twenty: A History-Executive Summary,"2007: http://www.g20.org/pubindex.aspx, p 5 (accessed 30 September 2012).

[7]  Mark Thirlwell, "Towards the London Summit: Next Steps for the G-20," 2009, Lowy Institute for International Policy, p 9. Available online: http://www.lowyinstitute.org/publications/towards-london-summit-next-steps-g-20 (accessed 30 September 2012) .

[8]  Group of Twenty, "Group of Twenty: A History-Executive Summary," 2007: http://www.g20.org/pub_index.aspx, p 19 (accessed 30 September 2012) .

[9]  Mark Thirlwell and Malcolm Cook, "Geeing up the G20," 2006, Lowy Institute for International Policy.

[10]  Department of Foreign Affairs and Trade, "Trade at a Glance 2010", 2010: http://www.dfat.gov.au/publications/trade/, p 38 (accessed 30 September 2012).

[11]  Ibid.

[12]  Elizabeth Sidiropolous, "Legitimacy and Credibility: Challenges of Broadening the G20 Agenda" in Wilhelm Hofmeister (ed), G20 - Perceptions and Perspectives for Global Governance (Singapore: Konrad Adenauer Stiftung, 2011). Available online: http://www.kas.de/wf/en/33.290999 (accessed 30 September 2012).

[13]  Maria Monica Wihardja, "The G20 and Global Democracy" in Wilhelm Hofmeister (ed), G20 - Perceptions and Perspectives for Global Governance (Singapore: Konrad Adenauer Stiftung, 2011). Available online: http://www.kas.de/wf/en/33.290999 (accessed 30 September 2012).

## I. Australia as a Middle Power

To understand Australia's attitude toward the G20, one has to understand Australia's conception of itself as a middle power. Descriptively, Australia is demonstrably a middle power: it is one of "a diverse group of states that are neither 'great' nor failing, but which occupy a conceptual territory between these extremes."[14] Australia is not a small or inconsequential state in terms of geography or material attributes.[15] For example, Australia's economy is now the 12th largest in the world,[16] its military spending is 14th largest[17] and its aid budget is the 11th largest among developed countries.[18] All of these attributes give it significance. However, Australia is far from being a dominant power anywhere except in parts of the Pacific.

Most recently, the catch-phrase for Australian foreign policy has been that of an "activist middle power," in which areas for niche diplomacy are selected to both promote Australia's interests and to improve the international system. According to Prime Minister Kevin Rudd, Australia's interest in "shaping the strategic order" rates highly enough to be seen as the third pillar of Australia's foreign policy goals alongside the pursuit of economic prosperity and national security. Australia is explicitly committed to "the building of a rules-based order which protects the interests of small and middle powers as much as it does the great powers."[19]

It follows that in order to have any effect as an activist middle power, Australia needs to have access to forums like the G20 where key issues of the times are debated. Australia clearly sees that its economic and security interests are best served by a system of global governance in which its "seat at the table" ensures that its voice is heard across as many institutions as possible. The G20, in particular, could be seen as a sort

---

[14] Mark Beeson, "Can Australia Save the World? The Limits and Possibilities of Middle Power Diplomacy," Australian Journal of International Affairs, Vol. 65, No. 5, November 2011, p 564.

[15] Carl Ungerer "The 'Middle Power' Concept in Australian Foreign Policy," Australian Journal of Politics and History, Vol. 53, No. 4, 2007, p 539.

[16] International Monetary Fund, "Report for Selected Countries and Subjects," available online: http://www.imf.org/external/pubs/ft/weo/2012/02/weodata/weorept.aspx? (accessed 18 October 2012). The World Bank has Australia ranked at 13th but forecast to overtake Spain by the end of 2012: http://databank.worldbank.org/databank/download/GDP.pdf (accessed 17 October 2012).

[17] Stockholm International Peace Research Institute, "SIPRI Military Expenditure Database." Available online: http://www.sipri.org/databases/milex (accessed 19 December 2011). See also Department of Defence, Defence Portfolio Budget Statements 2011-12. Available online: http://www.Defence.gov.au/budget/11-12/pbs/ (accessed 11 January 2012).

[18] Organisation for Economic Cooperation and Development, "Net Official Development Assistance From DAC And Other OECD Members In 2011," available online: http://www.oecd.org/dac/aidstatistics/50060310.pdf (accessed 18 October 2012).

[19] The Hon Kevin Rudd MP, Minister for Foreign Affairs, "The Australia We Can All Be Proud Of," 88th Annual Charteris Lecture, Australian Institute of International Affairs, Sydney, 24 November 2011. Available online: http://www.aiia.asn.au/resources/papers-a-transcripts (accessed 12 May 2012).

of middle power paradise: the Brooking Institution's Colin Bradford has described how the G20 forces members to behave like middle powers and use ideas and consensus-building skills rather than raw power.[20]

Australia is heavily invested in maintaining the effectiveness of the G20 so that it retains its seat at the table. If the G20 loses momentum and fails to attract the leaders of the world's major economies, they will simply find other forums for economic discussion, which will likely be smaller and involve only the major players. Australia is keenly aware that middle powers like Australia will be excluded from the conversation if it moves to more exclusive forums. It is therefore very much in Australia's interests to ensure that the G20 remains the premier global forum for economic issues.

## II. Australia's Contributions to the G20

Not content with just having a seat at the table, Australia has sought to be an active contributor to the G20. Australian officials describe Australia as fully engaged across the G20 agenda. According to former Prime Minister Julia Gillard, Australia's active approach to the G20 is only to be expected: "It's not the Australian way to stand on the side-lines when we've got something to contribute."[21] Australia's contribution to the G20 has taken a number of forms. Australia's early efforts focused on contributing to the G20's crisis response with a $42 billion contribution to the 2009 stimulus strategy to combat the global economic recession.

Another key focus for Australia was improving international economic governance, including by taking an active role in promoting IMF voting reform by co-chairing with South Africa a working group on this topic This working group achieved some initial reforms in 2008.[22] Australia's position has been that the distribution of quotas should reflect developments in the world economy, and support for the inclusion and voice of rising powers in international governance.[23]

Australia has pursued specific initiatives in various niche areas, including the "Ag Results Initiative," a $100 million USD fund designed to "offer financial incentives for organizations that are able to develop and apply new technologies at an affordable

---

[20] Colin Bradford, "Australia and the G20," East Asia Forum, 30 June 2013. Available online: www.eastasiaforum.org/2013/06/30/australia-and-the-g20/ (accessed 11 August 2013).

[21] The Hon Julia Gillard MP, Prime Minister of Australia, "Speech to the G20 Heads of Mission Dinner," Canberra, 20 March 2011. Available online: http://www.pm.gov.au/press-office/speechg 20-heads-mission-dinner (accessed 30 September 2012).

[22] International Monetary Fund, "IMF Quota and Governance Publications," http://www.imf.org/e xternal/np/fin/quotas/pubs/index.htm (accessed 30 September 2012). On implementation, see Lukas Menkhoff and Reeno Meyer, "The G20 Proposal on IMF Governance: Has Any Progress Been Made?" Intereconomics, Vol. 3, 2010, pp 171-179.

[23] The Treasury, "Quota Reform and the G-20", 26 April 2006: http://www.treasury.gov.au/conte ntitem.asp?NavId=017&ContentID=1102 (accessed 30 September 2012) .

price for farmers in developing countries."[24] Most recently, Australia has sought to present itself as a model economy with potential lessons for others, for example through an open letter to G20 leaders before the Los Cabos Summit[25] and various appearances at the Summit where the benefit of "a path of openness, investment and reform which leads to jobs and fiscally sustainable growth" was promoted.[26] Australia has also worked to ensure that the G20 remains representative. Australia has taken on responsibility for representing the interests of regional non-members and sees this as an important way to build the legitimacy of the G20.[27]

Australia has much to offer to the G20 and much to gain from its continued prominence as the premier global forum for economic governance. Australia has a record of strong contributions to the G20, and hosting the G20 Summit in Brisbane in 2014[28] will provide it with its greatest opportunity for influence and impact. It is very much in Australia's interests as a middle power both to protect its seat at the table and continue to strengthen the legitimacy of the G20.

## III. The Future of the G20

The G20 remains the best-placed forum for managing the global economy. The annual G20 leaders' summit presents a unique opportunity to tackle issues that cannot be dealt with unilaterally or bilaterally. As an effective multilateral grouping, the G20 has an ongoing and vital role to play in stabilizing and managing the global economy in a world where the effects of the 2008 GFC are still being felt. It can contribute significantly in a number of areas. The G20 is an obvious forum to deal effectively with issues of global economic growth, including trade liberalization, unemployment, food

---

[24] The Hon Julia Gillard MP, Prime Minister of Australia, "New Initiative to Combat Global Hunger," Press Release, 18 June 2012. Available online: http://www.pm.gov.au/press-office/new-initiative-combat-global-hunger (accessed 30 September 2012).

[25] "Gillard-Swan Letter to G20 Leaders," 17 June, 2012, Available online: http://australianpolitics.com/2012/06/17/gillard-swan-open-letter-to-g20-leaders.html

[26] The Hon Julia Gillard MP, Prime Minister of Australia, "Address to the B20 Plenary Session, Los Cabos," 17 June 2012. Available online: http://www.pm.gov.au/press-office/address-b20-plenary-session-los-cabos (accessed 30 September 2012); see also The Hon Julia Gillard MP, Prime Minister of Australia, "Transcript of press conference, Los Cabos,"19 June 2012. Available online http://www.pm.gov.au/press-office/transcript-press-conference-los-cabos-0 (accessed 30 September 2012).

[27] The Hon Julia Gillard MP, Prime Minister of Australia, "A relentless focus on global economic and financial prosperity" in John Kirton and Madeline Koch (eds), The G20 Mexico Summit 2012: The Quest for Growth and Stability, G20 Research Group, 2012. Available online: http://www.g8.utoronto.ca/newsdesk/loscabos/gillard.html (accessed 30 September 2012); see also The World Bank, "Ag Results: Innovation in Research and Delivery," http://web.worldbank.org/WBSITE/EXTERNAL/EXTABOUTUS/ORGANIZATION/CFPEXT/0,contentMDK:23005969~pagePK:64060249~piPK:64060294~theSitePK:299948,00.html (accessed 30 September 2012).

[28] Department of the Prime Minister and Cabinet, "G20 Australia 2014", available online: http://www.dpmc.gov.au/g20/index.cfm (accessed 11 August 2013).

security and agriculture. For example, G20 nations represent 65% of the world's farmland and 77% of the world production of cereals.[29]

Australia is well-equipped to engage in agricultural discussions given its historic and advanced involvement in the agricultural sector—"a unique set of tools" that Australia can share at the G20 agricultural ministerial meetings.[30] The G20 is also able to effectively tackle issues of fairness in the international system, including issues such as IMF voting reform and tax reform. The G20 is also well positioned on issues that benefit from cooperation between developed and emerging economies, including climate change financing, infrastructure investment and anticorruption measures.[31]

## IV. Threats to the Future of the G20

### *An Expanding Agenda*

A symptom of the G20's relative success in managing the GFC is the desire to expand and diversify the group's original mandate. Since its inception the G20 has focused on promoting "cooperation to achieve stable and sustainable world growth."[32] However there is always pressure to broaden the G20 agenda.

The responsibility of expanding the G20's agenda should not be taken lightly. Numerous international organizations have a history of over-promising and under-delivering. The G20 must do its best to deliver more than empty platitudes.[33] With the expansion of the agenda, concepts such as democracy, human rights and social justice have been pushed as suitable for G20 discussion; however these issues should be properly seen as a result or by-product of a well-functioning G20, not as core topics for the G20.

A widening agenda and a loss of focus would make effective delivery of outcomes more difficult. The G20 should focus on the areas where it can contribute and build its legitimacy rather than trying to duplicate the work of existing organizations.

### *Inflated Expectations*

A symptom of an ever-expanding agenda is unrealistic expectations about what the G20 can actually achieve. The reputation of the G20 suffers when inflated expectations are not met. The G20 leaders' summit proved itself as a "crisis response" institution during the GFC; now it is being asked to deliver as a "steering committee" for

---

[29] Ibid.
[30] Julia Gillard, "Speech to the G20 Heads of Mission Dinner," Canberra, 20 March 2011: http://www.pm.gov.au/press-office/speech-g20-heads-mission-dinner
[31] M Conley Tyler and R Pitt, "Indonesia-Australia: Act Naturally," The Interpreter, 30 July 2013, available online: http://www.lowyinterpreter.org/post/2013/07/30/Indonesia-and-Australia-Learning-to-be-natural-partners.aspx
[32] Group of 8, "Final Communiqué Cologne, Germany," 20 June 1999: http://www.g8.utoronto.ca/
[33] Mark Thirlwell, "Towards the London Summit: Next Steps for the G-20," 2009, Lowy Institute for International Policy: http://www.lowyinstitute.org/Publication. asp?pid=993, p 5.

the world's economy by bridging the gap of governance between states and markets.[34] It must focus on this targeted agenda and keep expectations realistic about what it can achieve. If high expectations are let down by more modest outcomes, then disappointment and cynicism will undermine the integrity and longevity of the forum. The G20 will not survive as the premier forum for global economic discussion if it cannot deliver and the world's major powers will simply find other forums for discussion.

## Legitimacy

The G20 is vulnerable if an expanding agenda and inflated expectations lead to disappointment and questioning of its legitimacy. As a club of countries that have agreed to coordinate some parts of their domestic policy, the G20 can be criticized for its perceived un-representativeness. The G20's legitimacy is derived to a great extent from the way its decisions affect non-members. If G20 members' decisions don't harm or, better still, actively benefit non-G20 economies, then the institution is seen as a public global good. However, if the G20 is viewed as not contributing to the collective global good it will lose its legitimacy as an effective forum. Unlike the UN, the G20's legitimacy does not come from universal membership and agreed process. Its membership is self-appointed and selective, yet its decisions have global reach. To maintain legitimacy, the G20 needs to continue to deliver effective outcomes for the global economy. In the words of former Australian Prime Minister Julia Gillard, the G20 is "a unique group that can only maintain its relevance and 'earned legitimacy' through a relentless focus on global economic and financial prosperity that improves people's living standards."[35]

The G20 is at a critical time in its development. The G20 needs to continue to prove itself as a "steering committee" for the world economy.[36] As a new grouping in a world where there are a number of other potential forums, the G20 needs to embed itself and show its legitimacy by delivering on its current agenda and demonstrating that, if it does its job well, the G20 provides a global public good.

As the host of the G20 in 2014, Australia will try to ensure that the G20 concentrate on proving itself in its core business of economic issues. In Australian parlance this would be termed "putting runs on the board" to prove the G20's ability to address international finance and economics with pragmatism and authority. Australia will "fo-

---

[34] Andrew Cooper, "The G20 as an Improvised Crisis Committee and/or a Contested Steering Committee". (2010) 86 International Affairs 741, p 750.

[35] The Hon Julia Gillard MP, Prime Minister of Australia, "A relentless focus on global economic and financial prosperity" in John Kirton and Madeline Koch (eds), The G20 Mexico Summit 2012: The Quest for Growth and Stability, G20 Research Group, 2012. Available online: http://www.g8.utoronto.ca/newsdesk/loscabos/gillard.html (accessed 30 September 2012).

[36] Andrew Cooper, "The G20 as an Improvised Crisis Committee and/or a Contested Steering Committee," (2010) 86 International Affairs 741, p. 750.

cus on measures to support global economic growth, with a strong emphasis on promoting job creation and open trade"[37] in order to achieve concrete outcomes that benefit the global economy.

## V. China and the G20

Both because of what it stands to gain and what it has to offer, it is in China's interests to support Australia's agenda of promoting the G20. The G20 is the ideal forum for China to both take part in and improve the institutional world order in a way that it responds to the needs of rising powers. China's place in the world economy means that it is indispensible to any discussion of global economic issues.

### A Forum that Includes Rising Powers

While some US commentators have expressed fear about the international system being destabilized by rising powers, this is contradicted by the evidence to date.[38] Rising powers have benefited greatly from the neoliberal economic system and have become increasingly integrated into its structure over the past twenty years.[39] Looking at the statements of the Brazil, Russia, India, China and South Africa grouping (BRICS) it is clear that rising powers recognize their stake in the international system; instead of railing at the international economic regime, their key demand is to be included and given an equitable place in global governance institutions. For example, the BRICS' Delhi Action Plan recognizes "the importance of the global financial architecture in maintaining the stability and integrity of the global monetary and financial system" and argues that strengthened representation of emerging and developing countries in the institutions of global governance will enhance their effectiveness in achieving this objective.[40]

Far from resulting in the erosion of global governance, increased participation by rising powers has resulted in them becoming more committed to the stability of the system. For example, the BRICS' joint statement at the G20 Summit in Los Cabos outlined three commitments designed to stabilize the global financial system in the midst of continuing economic uncertainty and sluggish growth throughout most of the developed world. It showed rising powers acting as part of the international system in order to contribute to financial stability.

---

[37] Department of the Prime Minister and Cabinet, "G20 Australia 2014," available online: http://www.dpmc.gov.au/g20/index.cfm (accessed 11 August 2013).

[38] Melissa Conley Tyler and Michael Thomas, "BRICS and Mortar(s): Breaking or Building the Global System?" in V I Lo and M Hiscock (editors), The Rise of the BRICS in the Global Political Economy: Changing Paradigms? (Edward Elgar, 2013).

[39] Julia Oeheler-Şincai (2011) "The Strategic Character of the Cooperation Relationship Between the EU and the BRIC Countries," Romanian Journal of European Affairs, 11(2) , pp. 31-46, p. 40

[40] BRICS (2012), "Delhi Action Plan", available at http://www.brics.utoronto.ca/docs/120329-delhi-declaration.html (accessed 17 November 2012), Articles 4 and 8.

## China and the G20

As the fastest rising power, China's rising international profile and increasingly significant stake in the global economy means that China needs to find congenial global forums to pursue its interests. The G20 is very unusual in its more equal distribution of power between established and emerging powers and better representation and treatment of developing nations.[41] Embedding discussions in a multilateral body can also help with sometimes difficult bilateral relationship with other major players like the United States.[42]

The G20, as the premier forum for economic global governance, is uniquely poised to enable China to effectively manage its engagement with the global political economy. For example, with all the key stakeholders at the table, the G20 will likely prove the best forum for addressing difficult international economic issues like multilateral trade liberalization.[43]

The larger China's share of the global economy grows, the more China has to gain from the G20's role in stabilizing the global economy and providing global public goods. For China a stable, open and globalized international economy is integral to its continued economic growth: in the words of the 2009 Chinese Defense White Paper, "China cannot develop in isolation from the rest of the world, nor can the world enjoy prosperity and stability without China."[44] As the President of the China Institute of Contemporary International Relations, Cui Liru, stated in 2012:

> "China intends to realize its national resurgence and modernization through a peaceful path born of a win-win strategy for common prosperity by integrating into or accepting and participating in the existing international system.... China's peaceful integration into the process of globalization, thus becoming an integral part of it, should be seen as a matter of creative significance in world politics.[45]

Two decades of integration in the global economy has bound China to the rules and institutions of global governance. As described by Fudan University's Ren Xiao, China is a "reformist status quo power" which accepts and benefits from the existing institutional norms of world order, but also has a realistic vision for the improvement of

---

[41] Ren Xiao, "A Reform-Minded Status Quo Power? China, the G20, and Changes in the International Monetary System", Indiana University Research Centre for Chinese Politics and Business Working Paper, Unedited Rough Draft, available from author, p. 29.

[42] Geoffrey Garrett, "G2 in G20: China, the United States and the World after the Global Financial Crisis," in Global Policy, Vol. 1, Issue 1, Jan. 2010, 29.

[43] Mike Callaghan, Peter Gallagher, John Ravenhill, Mark Thirlwell, Brett Williams, "Trade and the G20" in G20 Monitor, No 3, June 2013, Lowy Institute for International Policy G20 Studies Centre, available online: http://www.lowyinstitute.org/publications/trade-and-g20 (available 11 August 2013).

[44] Quoted in Michael Glosny (2010), "China and the BRICs: A Real (But Limited) Partnership in a Unipolar World", Polity, 42(1), pp. 100-129.

[45] Cui Liru (2012), "Peaceful Rise: China's Modernisation Trajectory," The International Spectator, 47(2), p. 15.

the system.[46] As China becomes more integrated into the global system, it will have more to gain from promoting the legitimacy of the G20 by actively participating in its forums and processes and using the G20 to turn "China's influence into institutional power".[47]

---

[46] Ren Xiao, "A Reform-Minded Status Quo Power? China, the G20, and Changes in the International Monetary System," Indiana University Research Centre for Chinese Politics and Business Working Paper, Unedited Rough Draft, available from author.

[47] Ibid.

# What about the G20?

*Stefano Silvestri*
**Senior Scientific Advisor, Istituto Affari Internazionali, Rome**

Global governance is very fragmented and relatively weak. The United Nations, conceived during World War II, reflect the power balance of the past. Today trade, finance, communications, information, environment, security, etc. are increasingly global, yet the power to act remains in the hands of national powers. Common worries, such as the environment, nuclear proliferation, protectionism, human rights, etc., are not translated into common policies. Few are willing to act; many are capable of blocking action. In that situation, the hope that the G20 will be capable of managing and significantly strengthening economic and financial global governance—as if they could be isolated from all other issues—has all the appearance of wishful thinking.

In fact, the G20 has had a very strong, hopeful, start. For little more than a year it seemed that the transition from the G8 to the G20 had been successful, significantly strengthening global economic governance. This hope, however, has been fading in subsequent years, putting into question the relevance of these Summits.

Critics argue that the G20 may be too large, while the G8 is now too narrow. Certainly a large number of interlocutors increase the difficulty of reaching consensual decisions on difficult issues. It seems however impossible, in the present situation, simply to go back to the smaller Group, when most of the members of the latter are struggling still with the economic crisis, relatively slow rates of growth and financial troubles. The question therefore seems to be if we should aim for a new intermediate Group, or if the G20 can be made more effective.

A new G-n (20) doesn't seem a very sensible answer. Present global governance is already characterized by too many Summits, at the global, regional, multilateral or bilateral levels. If any, our countries may already find themselves going a Summit too far, directly involving Heads of State and Government in too many negotiations and meetings, to the point of overcrowding their agendas possibly towards irrelevance.

It is a symptom of the weakness of global governance that no significant decisions, even of a technical or emergency nature, can be reached and implemented without a show of summitry. Moreover, in too many cases these Summits have fallen well behind expectations. A proposal has been made to increase the focus of G20 Summits by shortening their agenda to a maximum of three items. This may indeed help concentrate the discussion. Yet, the proposals made to achieve this aim have until now produced very different lists and agendas, making it practically impossible to identify a consensual reduction. Also, one of the few benefits of these "less than formal" Summit meetings is that Leaders can speak frankly among themselves, voicing the subjects that most worry them at that given moment. Such an informal exchange would not be possible with a pre-cooked, rigid and short agenda. Finally, there would be very little advantage in reducing the agenda items to a handful when there is no certainty that a significant consensus will be reached on them. On the contrary, such a policy may end up widening the divergences and making any failure to agree more visible, and thus dangerous.

Others think that the G20 should develop a more formalized structure and take up clearer governance powers. In that way, the G20 could become a kind of multilateral governing body of globalization, superseding other international organizations operating in the economic and financial sector, like the IMF and the WTO.

There is no doubt that an agreement among the G20 countries can lead to important decisions in other international organizations, particularly the IMF. Yet, these structures have their own Charters and governing bodies. It may very well be a grave mistake to attempt to submit them directly to the G20, both for reasons of legitimacy and of effectiveness. For instance, IMF interventions might be time-sensitive, and their conditionality should not be predetermined by apolitical agreement among the G20 Leaders. It is necessary to maintain degree of "technical fairness" and "political neutrality" of the international organizations so as to foster global consensus and acceptance, over and above any agreement among the richest or the more powerful nations. This is even more so when it is unlikely that all the G20 leaders will agree on a specific course of action.

Other, smaller organizational improvements may marginally increase the effectiveness of the G20 Summits, such as the institutionalization of a "troika" system of rotating presidencies over a longer, three-year period that may help consolidate the agendas favored by the Government holding the Presidency, and obliging a deeper multilateral (or at least trilateral) decision making process. This and other improvements, however, remain limited and are not bound to significantly change the present global governance system. This does not mean that the G20 should avoid the issue of reforming international organizations. This is a legitimate as well as necessary item for discussion and possibly deliberation. The aim should not be to micro-manage the existing institutions, however, but more broadly build a large consensus among the major international players on priorities and path forward. To date, we have not been able to reform the United Nations Security Council, nor to conclude the Doha Round, after twelve years of useless negotiations. It would be unwise to burden the G20 with a governance role far exceeding the existing international consensus. What should be done, however, is to start a cautious, long-term consultation process to widen the areas of common agreement and to avoid unilateral initiatives.

There are some hopeful signals. The willingness to discuss a large array of issues, from finance regulations to economic growth, green economy, sustainable development goals, regulation of foreign direct investments, trade liberalization, regional economic partnerships, and so on, indicates the existence of a large number of common worries and interests, even when policy answers are bound to differ. The general preference of limiting, and even curbing, protectionist tendencies also goes in the right direction, even when implementation may be somewhat wanting.

The G20 should build on the world as it is, not as it should be. It is a fact, for instance, that the failure of the Doha Round has been marked by the rapid multiplication of bilateral and multilateral free trade agreements, putting into question global free trade principles such as the most favored nation treatment. At the same time, new large regional free trade frameworks are being built or negotiated such as the Euro-American Trans-Atlantic Trade and Investment Partnership (TTIP), or the American-Pacific Trans-Pacific Partnership (TPP), the China-Japan-South Korea framework, etc. This development is neither global nor regional, but something in between, and could evolve either way, towards the creation of competing regional blocs or towards a new global framework and a much strengthened WTO. The G20 is the logical place to consider these issues and to build a number of crossing linkages among the major free trade areas, so as to avoid the consolidation of trade blocs and to help a process of progressive globalization.

A number of sectorial issues dealing with technology regulations, internet services, foreign direct investments, sanitary standards, etc.—around which moderate possible conflicts could arise—could very well be addressed and help strengthen such process. In the end, however, the main difference between the G8 and the G20 is that the former was built on a solid common ground of shared political interests and alliances (even if the inclusion of Russia has somewhat stressed this original basis), while the latter faces the incredibly complex and daring task of building such a political consensual most from scratch. Its auspicious initial work has demonstrated that this task is not impossible, but its progressive slowing underlines the importance of the political over the economic common ground.

No one has yet found the recipe for effectively dealing with the various political and security crises facing the world. In fact, too many conflicts are complicating the Asian stability framework, from the Middle East to the Pacific, as well as Africa and the Mediterranean. The members of the G20 have different policy responses, and are sometimes at odds among them. This is not conducive to greater consensus and the building of shared goals—economic or political.

It is not possible to fully isolate the G20 from the world at large. Certainly trade and economic development can be a powerful beneficial factor, but not strong enough to fully overcome important political divisions. Specific attention should be given to China: a growing economic, political and military world power that could play a role either way, towards further disintegration or a strengthening of international consensus. It is very likely that China's main economic developments goals will help reinforce its long established preference for a peaceful and consensual approach defuse conflicts and reinforce the UN role. Certainly this is in line with many public statements of the Chinese Government itself.

Yet, China has also to manage its new objective international weight in Asia and in the world at large, and may sometimes be tempted, or be driven, to force some limited showdowns, just to assess its new international role. The problem is how to do that without provoking excessive fear or nationalistic reactions, and without fostering misperceptions that would bring about a negative assessment of its long term goals.

The basis for successful global governance can only be established through a successful process of confidence building, first of all among the G20 members, to create a common ground of shared values and policies. Of course, China is not the only power responsible for the implementation of such a process; it has to be a multilateral effort. However, inevitably, it is the growing power of China that challenges the established consensus and that, in the end, will be the first to decide to break or to mend it.

# Part 2
# The Role of Emerging Economies

At present, emerging economies contribute the lion's share of global economic growth, and have become the main reliable source of strength for the global economic recovery. China's growth is the largest among emerging economies. Set against declining demand in developed economies, development of trade relations amongst the emerging economies is extremely important for the global economic recovery. How should the economic and trade framework between emerging economies be constructed? How should a new form of cooperation between emerging economies be constructed? All of these are important topics for the G20.

# New Kids on the Block—the Growing Power of Emerging Countries in the G20

*José Luis Chicoma and Ana Dávila*
**Ethos Foundation**

- The growing influence of emerging economies in the G20 is the result of a combination of a strong economic position in the global market, and the ingenious exploitation of soft power virtues. This is a bomb of potentialities.
- Emerging economies have a unique opportunity to reshape the G20's agenda from within, tending towards a system that can better promote global equality and fairness.

If we place ourselves in a map of Washington DC, the White House is in the centre. A look northeast reveals the World Bank and the International Monetary Fund. Quite close we find K Street, the mecca of the lobbyists of the most important enterprises and firms in the world. Just a couple of steps away from President Obama's residence is the Department of the Treasury, a close walk to the Inter-American Development Bank, from where, if we look southeast, the Capitol stands out in the horizon. In the 1980s and 1990s, these institutions embraced the task of introducing structural economic reforms to Latin America and liberalizing the world economy.

But the world has clearly changed since the 1990s. The nations that were once mentored and advised by the world's greatest economic powers through institutions and frameworks such as Bretton Woods and the Washington Consensus are now, less than 30 years later, shifting the balance of power in the world order of the 21st Century.

## Might the next big idea come from an emerging country?

Since the early 1980s, pundits have predicted that one day nations of the developing world, such as China and India, would play a major role in the dynamics of the global economy. The 2008 crisis and the major financial challenges that harass the European Union have accelerated this process and opened a wide spectrum of opportunities for emerging economies to exploit. Today we see a solid Chinese economy that grows every year, a Mexican industry that is booming, a Brazilian leadership in regional and international dialogs and a strong Indian democracy and economy that promise to shift the regional dynamics of the Asian continent. According to the Carnegie Endowment for International Peace, by 2050, 60% of the G20's economic growth will come from Brazil, China, India, Russia and Mexico.

This is not only relevant to the economy and markets in these nations, but also to how the G20 will grow in the years to come, which will be much different than how they've done so for the last 3 decades. These nations are embracing a new vision of the world and the global economy. With innovation at their core, the BRICS and other prominent actors such as South Korea, Mexico and Singapore will reshape business, economy, and development. While innovation from the developed world has focused on branding, luxury, quality and hi-technology for entertainment and status, innovation from the developing world is more motivated by the social and financial needs with which they struggle. For example, developing nations are becoming the perfect environment for social innovation to take off as a structured practice.

These emerging economies cannot afford innovation to be an option or a commodity. Innovation is a tool to survive in the globalized world of today. Though some of them have vast natural resources, they are accepting the fact that their future has more to do with knowledge and innovation than with oil, minerals and other commodities. In this sense, industrial policies and innovation support have been very important lately in their public agenda.

Mexico is one of the best examples among the community of emerging economies with regard to rising awareness about the need to build an innovation economy. In Mexico, innovation has become crucial for the survival of the small and medium enterprise (SME). A recent study on economic and innovation activities shows that in Mexico, 67% of SMEs make changes or improvements in their products or services each year, while 61% introduce new products to the market regularly.

The important thing about innovation in a country is that it is the reflection of the existence of talent and creativity in terms of human capital. Leadership is a valuable asset for world power, and in the last years, emerging economies have focused on empowering their population to become a more competitive nation. A recent study by SHL, a talent management consulting firm based in the UK, shows Mexico in the #1 position of countries with potential for leadership in the future. Brazil and India are ranked #5 and #6, while the US stands at #8. The ability to innovate and generate the leaders for tomorrow demonstrates that emerging economies are finding ways to make their economic growth sustainable and crisis-proof.

## Mexico donating money to Europe

What we saw at the G20 summit in Los Cabos in 2012 demonstrated that the spectacular economic performance of the BRICS and other emerging nations would by no means remain an isolated accomplishment. The growing power of these large economies will become a predominant factor with the potential to shift the world order in the upcoming decades. Only 20 years after the Washington Consensus, Asian and Latin American nations opened a dialog during the Cabos summit to rescue the collapsing economy of the European Union through a generous donation to the International Monetary Fund. Mexico, India, Brazil and Russia each donated $10.2 billion, while China contributed $43.8 billion.

The capacity to "chip in" important sums to the IMF and the ability to become the largest contributors to the economic growth of the G20 in the following years also gives these rising economies the power to play a major role in international forums, decision-making processes and global governance. In the 1990s, institutions dominated by western powers dictated recommendations and step-by-step recipes to Latin American nations to rescue and integrate them into the global market. Now we see countries like Brazil and Mexico taking a proactive role in making recommendations to the European Union and the United States, and demanding a greater role, proportionate to their economic size and contributions, in the governance of the IMF.

International forums such as the United Nations have witnessed growing participation from and influence of emerging nations in different aspects. The behavior of the independent vote in several topics has demonstrated that the economic power and strength of emerging nations has granted them greater independence in their decision-making and votes, and a much louder voice in these forums. The Security Council has become the backdrop of a structural debate regarding the expansion of permanent membership and the number of ordinary members. India, Brazil and South Africa have assumed notable leadership roles in demanding a better representation of the current world order.

## We like these countries: soft power as a convenient strategy

Outside the framework of international organizations and forums, rising nations have also developed an interesting and independent campaign of soft power, diplomacy and cooperation. While growing economic strength was the catapult that placed rising nations like the BRICS in the right position to bargain and be heard during any economic debate, it has been their ability to gain influence and leadership in other areas that has bolstered their positions as rising power personalities. In the last decade, Brazil has become truly committed to and genuinely involved in promoting an agenda of education, global health, governance and regional cooperation. It has also taken an active role in negotiations addressing trending key global issues such as nuclear non-proliferation, HIV/AIDS, environmental regulations, climate change and global trade. India, on the other hand, has focused its attention on becoming a major player in terms of development assistance and dedicates significant effort to maintaining its global branding as "the world's largest democracy." Taking advantage of its cultural appeal and the "mysticism" surrounding the myth of Indian culture, Bollywood has become a trademark for the emerging power and a channel to shape, promote and expose its identity in a globalized era. Its diplomatic relations with its neighbors and the neutral essence that has shaped its foreign policy since the administration of Indira Gandhi has allowed India to make friends and gain sympathy in various forums and global stages. Mexico too is exploiting its reputation as a country rich in tradition, culture, kindness, gastronomy, and other virtues in order to reaffirm its position as an influential global giant.

Pragmatism in its foreign policy is perhaps one of the most valuable tools for Mexico, because it is complemented by a peaceful paradigm and a growing independence that has conditioned its support to the US, support that once was taken for granted. Mexico has also gained more presence in international events and forums in recent years, while presenting itself as a fertile territory for foreign investment.

Yet perhaps the most interesting task for which developing and emerging economies have assumed responsibly is the task of becoming the bridge that links the developed and developing world in order to serve as the most effective channel through which developing countries outside the G20 framework can make their voices heard. Within the framework of the G20, emerging powers have taken an active role in pushing forward institutional reform of the economic system and the establishment of a more balanced and fair dynamic. This has the potential to dramatically shift the paradigm that governs international relations today. The combined strengths, aptitudes and virtues of emerging powers and other developing countries in terms of economic growth, soft power and the desire for cooperation and inclusion serve as the most important tools for these countries to change the rules of global governance, and maybe even the entire game.

The emergence of the new economic powers in the international sphere of decision-making will inevitably lead to a restructuring of global dynamics. Economic and political governance will no longer be dominated by a couple of western countries that make decisions behind closed doors, but will rather become more inclusive, diverse and complex. With the new power and influence of rising nations, the dialog, paradigms and agenda can be expected to be more inclusive in terms of vision, philosophy, perspectives and priorities. The inclusion of the BRICS in institutions such as the IMF and in global debates on the future of the economic system will push a more comprehensive view of the world, with greater priority toward integrating the needs of the developing world. The whole structure and essence of the Bretton Woods arrangement will prove it insufficient and inapplicable to the realities that the world faces today. The G20 needs to reform its agenda, recommendations and models by increasing the relevance of outside mid-level powers that are allies and/or neighbors of the BRICS. All of this will inevitably lead to decentralization of global governance in the political and economic spheres.

## The New Agenda

The structure and operations of the G20 is distinctive in its flexible agenda setting, its membership system and its essence: it is a forum to stimulate dialog between nations with different economies. The democratic component of the G20 and the legitimacy of its foundation offer its members a remarkable opportunity to shape the agenda according to the needs and desires of a majority. In the last few years, the BRICS and other countries like Mexico have made clear their intention to utilize the G20 framework to reform the Bretton Woods structure and increase the influence and presence of developing nations in the decision-making processes of the economic system. At the 2005 summit, China took advantage of its role as host to introduce to the G20 agenda reform of the internal structures of the World Bank and the IMF in order to increase the participation and influence of emerging economies and to better represent the current world order, characterized by a dynamic multi-polarity.

This year's G20 summit is particularly promising for the BRICS and the developing nations in and outside the framework of the group. As a member of this group and host of the G20 summit 2013, Russia has recognized the need to draw international attention to the issue of raising the BRICS' voting share in the IMF and the World Bank. Russia's position as host of this year's summit is a unique opportunity to shape the agenda from the standpoint and priorities of the economies that are shaping the world today, rather than that of the traditional Western powers. According to Russia's First Deputy Chairman, "The priorities for the agenda of the summit will include stabilizing the world economic system, overcoming the debt crisis in the Eurozone, addressing problems in the American economy and creating conditions in which developing economies can become locomotives of global growth."

Since 2005, the debate over reforming and restructuring Bretton Woods institutions has intensified and will continue to do so in the coming years. The influence and power of emerging economies are not restricted to the economic sphere; these nations are finding the power to dramatically shift the paradigms that rule international organisms, forums and decision-making processes towards a more inclusive, multipolar and complex structure. The G20 offers these nations a powerful framework to do so, and that will certainly evolve in the near future into a more representative forum for both members and non-members. The ability to shape and reshape each year's G20 agenda has allowed countries such as China to prioritize issues that are relevant for them, as emerging nations, and for their partners, neighbors and allies. The G20 gives voice to those without a membership through the leadership of the emerging economies, who are concerned with a greater equilibrium in the global arena in the upcoming decades.

Additionally, the position of Russia as host of the 2013 summit will allow the BRICS and other developing nations to preserve some topics in the agenda that have been proposed in recent years by emerging economies. Among the topics that developing economies are working to introduce to the global economic agenda and to the table of debate at the next G20 summits include: sustainable and renewable energies; actions against money laundering and illicit investment; exchange of financial information for greater transparency; the creation of resources to increase transparency and prevent corruption, reform the IMF's structure and membership system in order to increase the representation and activity of developing nations in the decision-making process; and creating special funds to fight poverty.

The Troika, the group that includes the past, present and future G20 chairs, has proven to be an effective channel to introduce topics and concerns to the present and following year agendas. It is important to note that Mexico is one of the three members of this year's Troika, and thus has the power to influence the agenda meaningfully. Mexico is working to include the following topics into the pillars of the G20 Action Plan: inclusive green growth, cost reductions of shipping remittances, financial inclusion, and food security. Mexico is particularly interested in including the crusade against hunger (Cruzada contra el hambre) in the upcoming St. Petersburg Action Plan as one of the main issues to address.

As Nancy Birdsall and Francis Fukuyama stated in 2011, developing countries are more concerned and committed to a sensible social policy in recent years, as demonstrated by the priorities that the developing world has for the upcoming global agenda. Countries have witnessed and experimented with complete separation between economic growth and social development, modelled by the Washington Consensus and liberal reforms exported to the world. However, economic efficiency can no longer be dictated by the developed to the developing world in vertical procedure that excludes considerations, exceptions and particularities. Rather, an inclusive process that is debated and shaped in a holistic manner at every level is needed.

Developing nations seem to agree on the fact that it is important to "humanize "the economy and global markets. At the centre of this premise lies the issue of inequality, which has become a major topic of debate worldwide, brought to the table by increasingly concerned emerging economies. Social policies, while always a touchy subject for their probability to lead to a socialist model, have been reconsidered and rethought, a lesson to the developed world taught by developing nations. In Asia, China has become more engaged in social issues, creating programmes for the elderly and expanding educational opportunities for the youth. In Latin America, Brazil and Mexico have taken a leadership role in social policy that, despite room for improvement, has already taken the decisive steps towards a change in the conception of progress and development. Global, regional, national and sub-national inequality has been one of the greatest trends in the last few decades, and now, there is an urge to reverse this process and place equality and fairness at the core of economic reform. In this way, industrial policies are also a determining factor, but these types of policies have not found proper regularization in the rapid paced dynamics that rule the economy today. This is a need arising from underdeveloped and developing nations that is now being inserted into the frameworks of the G20, the United Nations and other remarkable forums of international cooperation.

This unique effort to integrate nations from various continents in order to stimulate economic growth, development and innovation in its member countries is a clear piece of evidence that the world order is changing. Today, we see emerging economies that no longer simply follow the instructions and recommendations from the developed world, but take the proactive initiative in finding creative and authentic means to maximize their potential in the globalized economy of the 21st century. Emerging economies are taking an outstanding leadership role and are breaking the barriers between the developing and developed world to propose a more integrated and complex economy that intends to revolutionize the system of labor division as we know it today and the working methods of the institutions that have long dictated the fate and development of the global economy.

## On our way to a new geopolitical order?

The rapid emergence of nations such as Brazil, India, China, South Africa and Mexico in recent years has been a significant event for global governance. Economic growth and predominance in the financial dynamics of the globalized era are not the only main characteristic of their growing influence, but the catapult that has vaulted them to a position where they can be more influential and integral than ever before. Such relevance inevitably opens a wide spectrum of possibilities in areas of both hard and soft power for these actors. The active engagement in diplomatic relations, the energetic participation in international forums, strong leadership in the promotion of a more inclusive agenda and economic system and the focus on innovation and efficiency have become the perfect complement to best exploit the virtues of a growing economy.

Although the coming of power of these nations in such a short period of time is changing global political and economic dynamics, a long path still lies ahead of developing nations. No one can deny that the unipolar, hegemonic system that ruled the world in the last decades is tending towards a multipolar system, where complexity, inclusion, multilateralism and a more democratic representation of the world system are becoming the core of the new paradigm. However, the occurrence of a profound system change is still a hazy long-term vision.

Emerging countries still face challenges and have profound areas of opportunity. While it is likely that BRICS will represent at least 60% of the G20's economic growth by 2050, these nations will not have the largest internal GDP in the world and are at risk of becoming low income but big economy markets. There is also significant scepticism lately about the sustainability of the economic growth models of the emerging nations.

Speculation about the end of the economic miracle of countries such as China and India could affect the reliability of such economies in the future. The strength of such economies has not yet proven to be crisis-proof. Moreover, though innovation seems to be the possible vaccine against dependence and economic vulnerability, these countries still face severe issues in the formation of solid structures to create an innovation-based economy, mainly due to the reliance on their natural resources and unqualified labor force. Overall, emerging countries have accomplished plenty. It's admirable that emerging countries are becoming part of the world's most influential forums, institutions and groups and accumulating enough leverage in various aspects to have the ability to bargain and improve their BATNAs (best alternative to a negotiated agreement) in more than just economic related issues. Now the new kids on the block will have to demonstrate that their growth and strength is reliable, sustainable, independent and positive.

# Note on the Recent Progress of the G20 and China's Future Role in the Multilateral Economic Agenda

*Edison Benedito da Silva Filho*
**Researcher, Institute for Applied Economic Research (IPEA), Brazil**

## Introduction

First summoned in response to threats to global economic stability, the G20 is today a privileged space for discussion on various topics ranging from the financial agenda to regulation of trade and investment, from social policies to environmental sustainability.

The expansion of the forum's agenda denotes its growing importance as a mechanism for building consensus around common public policies to promote balanced and sustainable development. However, this diversity of issues can also lead to fragmentation of efforts and amplify latent conflicts between countries, thus constituting a major challenge to the effectiveness of cooperation.

Above all, the success of the G20 stems from the recognition that it is important for developing countries to participate in global governance. These economies are no longer limited to passively approving the decisions of the biggest economies, but today seek to effectively influence and support the implementation of global policies through their growing economic capacity. In this sense, strengthened coordination of the BRICS (Brazil, Russia, India, China and South Africa) can also contribute to increasing the G20's legitimacy by representing to that body the interests of the developing world.

Given that the problems of developed economies have dominated the agenda, most of the progress achieved so far by the G20 has been in the field of reforming the international financial system. Now, however, several countries are stressing the need to expand the forum's discussions on other sensitive issues related to international trade and investment.

This brief report draws on the recent discussions within the G20, focusing on the role played by emerging countries, especially China. The text consists of four sections, including this brief introduction. The second section resumes describing the key areas of progress in the reforms of international financial system. The third section discusses the challenges faced by the developing countries and their efforts to broaden the scope of G20 agenda. The fourth section analyses China's transition to a new growth model and its implications to global governance. Finally, we conclude by pointing out future perspectives of the G20 forum.

## Recent progress of the G20 reform agenda

Until the outbreak of the recent global economic crisis, there was a prevailing confidence in the strength of the financial system in developed economies. However, this optimistic view was challenged by the speed and depth of the impact on global financial markets following the collapse of Lehman Brothers Holdings in 2008. The subprime crisis quickly spread to other markets in the wake of the huge losses incurred by global banks. The overall decline in prices spanned from commodity markets to sovereign debt securities. The weaknesses in the European bloc subsequently amplified the effects of the crisis, and the ongoing slowdown of emerging economies seemed to decide the debate on decoupling.

The increasing complexity and imbrications of financial transactions bring new challenges for regulation and highlights the limits of its effectiveness at the national level. Instruments such as derivative contracts, structured debt obligations and credit default swaps became increasingly opaque, hindering the proper internalization of risks by economic agents. The lack of transparency of global financial corporation led to the spread of risk to other countries. These problems illustrate the need for a multilateral approach to the regulation of financial markets.

The debate on international finance reform has focused on the search for increased robustness, efficiency and transparency of financial institutions as well as the cooperation of countries and multilateral economic organizations to prevent a widespread collapse like the one seen in 2008. In this sense, progress in recent years has been significant. Basel III recommendations are in advanced implementation stages in major economies, and most banks in some emerging countries already meet the committee requirements.

In addition to these recommendations, other measures have been proposed to enhance the transparency and soundness of the financial system. These measures include separation between commercial and investment banking, prohibitions on proprietary trade and additional capital requirements and controls for institutions deemed systemically important ("too big to fail"). Certainly some policies are controversial, such as capital adequacy requirements for subsidiaries of foreign banks operating in the United States and the proposed European tax on financial transactions. In addition, emerging countries still resent the lack of stronger commitments by the developed world to adopt macroeconomic policies that favor the resumption of growth, not just the recovery of market confidence. However, the prospects for cooperation in this field are positive: countries agree on the urgency of adjusting their financial systems in order to achieve recovery of sustainable economic growth. Hence, most of the pending differences in this field relate to the time required for adjustment or possible inaccuracies and gaps in the proposed regulatory framework.

One of the major recent advances in the field of financial regulation is recognition of the need for a macro prudential approach aimed at minimizing the social costs of adjustments in the financial sector. Regulators should pay attention not only to the problem of moral hazard, but also to the effects of adverse selection during credit crunches, in order to prevent a further deterioration of the economy.

The new approach to regulation attempts to bring more effectiveness to moderating business cycles so as to avoid both the emergence of speculative bubbles as well as a financial crisis. A corollary to this is that in order to ensure economic stability, not only is it necessary to have effective banking regulations, but also monetary and credit policies that are consistent with the process of adjustment in financial markets. Although seemingly trivial, this goal has proven extremely difficult to achieve. This is not only due to the difficulty of identifying speculative bubbles in time to prevent them, but also because of the perceived high costs of adjusting national economies, especially in emerging markets.

## Challenges for developing economies and the search for a broad G20 agenda

In the last decade, developing countries have achieved remarkable improvements in terms of economic fundamentals. This is due to the adoption of sound fiscal policies, as well as the rapid accumulation of reserves in the wake of rising commodity prices. Their banks also enjoy high levels of liquidity and capitalization, which can be partially explained by the strong regulatory requirements imposed on them. Moreover, the late development of the financial sector in emerging economies also makes them less complex and facilitates regulatory activity.

However, emerging economies remain susceptible to short-term shocks, especially through the currency market channel. Disruptions in capital flows (sudden stops) produce rapid changes in the price of the local currency, with non-negligible impacts on inflation and the solvency of companies that are exposed to short-term foreign debt. Some of these countries also face the problem of shadow banking. Since non-regulated institutions provide a large ratio of credit to the private sector, it is difficult to measure the impact of a shock to the real economy in the event of a liquidity crisis. Shadow banking will almost certainly represent a major challenge for emerging economies, especially China, over the next decade. Further, some of the macroeconomic measures adopted by various countries, although justified, may result in deleterious consequences for their economic partners, which increases the risk of setbacks to global integration. Developing countries have been especially disadvantaged in this regard, partially because of the loss of competitiveness following appreciation of their currencies, but also because of the freezing of free trade negotiations in multilateral forums, coupled with the adoption of protectionist measures in the advanced economies.

Furthermore, the existence of tax havens and other important asymmetrical legal frameworks that regulate capital flows around the world also reduce the effectiveness of national policies aimed at regulating financial activity. These asymmetries hinder the establishment of homogeneous competition rules for financial institutions and enable illicit practices such as money laundering and tax evasion. These issues will become even more pronounced if free trade agreements like the US-Europe FTA and the Trans-Pacific Partnership are successfully concluded, since global companies will pursue advantages provided by asymmetries created by these new regulations.

Although there has been progress in overcoming these difficulties, important challenges remain. International macroeconomic coordination remains poor; current account imbalances in major economies will demand much more consistent effort from governments in order to promote the necessary adjustment. Emerging countries will continue to push fora greater say in the decision-making of the International Monetary Fund and the World Bank. They will also demand that these institutions recognize the legitimacy of certain policies such as the imposition of capital controls, preservation of public credit institutions and investment and limits to the exposure of private companies to foreign currency debt.

Besides reform of financial institutions, emerging countries intend to bring regulation of international trade and capital flows to the G20 agenda, discussion of which has been hindered in other multilateral forums. The main objective of developing countries is to ensure the support of growth and employment and a more equitable distribution of the "costs of development" among nations. They contend that adjustment toward more sustainable and balanced global growth should not obstruct ongoing policies aimed at eliminating poverty and reducing inequality.

In fact, many of the measures proposed by emerging economies reflect the more ambitious political agenda of these countries. Specifically, they envision reform of international economic institutions as an opportunity to endorse an alternative development model, in which the state plays a more significant and pervasive role. This development agenda is already taking shape with initiatives that will certainly dominate much of the economic debate in the next decades. One example is the transition of China towards a new growth model based on its internal market and innovation, as discussed below.

## China's transition and its role in the G20

China's participation in the G20 and other multilateral forums is widely recognized as being constructive in character, with an emphasis on the need for consensus-building and strengthening multilateral governance to solve global economic problems. In particular, China has long argued for more effective coordination of macroeconomic policies among major economies. It also supports the ability of developing countries to pursue alternative policies in order to support high levels of growth and employment.

As argued before, there is a current trend toward expansion of the G20 economic agenda. At the same time, negotiations among regional trading blocs exacerbate the risks of weakening multilateral regulation and increasing protectionism amidst competition between major economies. In this context, it is likely that China will emphasize issues such as the harmonization of infrastructure investment rules and the consolidation of global value chains in the G20 in the near future.

Recently, Chinese authorities announced a commitment to changing towards a new growth model based on domestic household consumption and technological innovation, rather than the current model of reliance on exports and investment in infrastructure. Certainly the most significant impact of these changes is the expansion and strengthening of the already large middle class in China, whose increasing purchasing power will require higher diversification and quality of both private sector goods and services and public services. The adoption of more restrictive credit policies should contribute in the medium term to a substantial reduction in the levels of inflation in China, which will also improve the purchasing power of the population and contribute to diminishing social inequality.

However, there are significant risks in the process of adjustment. Since shadow banking represents a significant portion of the volume of credit, a successful transition to a new economic model will be conditioned by the Chinese government's ability to reduce the rate of output growth without causing massive losses in the private sector, given the likely disruption to informal channels of finance. This will require Chinese companies to shift focus towards the internal market, rather than maintaining their dependence on international markets. Chinese companies are already anticipating this transformation, moving towards higher technological content in production and higher value added in global value chains, which also require higher wages. The inexorable increase in costs can be partially compensated by productivity gains, facilitated by the government's implementation of various policies to raise the skill level of the country's working population.

Today, Chinese companies manufacture some of the world's most sophisticated goods to which they own the patents and proprietary rights that assure the man increasing share of value in global value chains. Government incentives ensure that a high percentage of companies' revenues are channeled to technological innovation and modernization of industrial parks. Although there are criticisms related to the opacity of the Chinese regulatory framework and poor protection of property rights of Western companies, it is undeniable that the country has advanced in developing a dynamic business environment, which favors enterprise and innovation. Recently, the Chinese government has identified several technologically intensive sectors as strategic to the success of the country's future international integration. The main focus today is renewable energy, for which specific policies are designed to encourage exports and innovation. China seeks to be a world leader in the production of solar panels and invests heavily in other "green" technologies that will dominate future daily life in cities, such as hybrid vehicles, intelligent energy management in homes and low carbon mass transport. Technological progress will therefore play a decisive role in the economic transition envisioned for the country.

Although it is too early to predict the success of the new model of Chinese growth, there is undeniable merit in expanding the well-being of the population and moving toward a more balanced and sustainable economic environment. The most important remark is that these changes will not only alter the distribution of wealth and political power in society, but are part of a bold strategy to strengthen the economic capacity of the country and prepare it for a new global reality. Therefore, these initiatives constitute more than an inevitable adjustment: they represent a new development proposal that deserves to be diligently observed by the rest of the world, and in particular, by the other members of the G20.

## Concluding remarks

This note attempts to briefly outline some trends for the G20, as well as the role played by China and other emerging countries in shaping the reform agenda of the forum. We summarize below the main points in this debate.

Given the urgency imposed by the global financial crisis and the difficulty facing multilateral institutions in advancing changes to international governance, the G20 has taken the lead in this process. The growing importance of this forum is evidenced by its widening agenda, which originally was limited to reform of the international financial system. Today, the G20 agenda covers a much larger list of themes, including trade, investment and sustainability.

Yet the broadening of the G20 agenda also poses risks to its effectiveness, due to greater dispersion of efforts and the increasing likelihood of conflict insensitive subjects. However, this expansion is inexorable. Overcoming the financial crisis will require not only greater macroeconomic coordination, but also the harmonization of trade and investment rules, so as to avoid a major setback to global economic integration. The current account imbalances of the major economies of the world, for instance, cannot be corrected only through adjustments of exchange rate regimes.

In addition, the G20 offers clear advantages for an expanded agenda of reforms. On the one hand, developed countries need a more agile multilateral institution that allows for direct cooperation between government agencies, UN agencies, OECD systems and organizations representing the private sector without the requirement of prior formal commitments. On the other hand, emerging economies see the G20 as an ideal arena to coordinate efforts to defend their growth models, since they face much greater resistance in other multilateral forums.

As emerging economies look for more influence in the G20, one can expect some conflicts stemming from the concentration of power in advanced economies and the lack of political representation of developing countries. The current decision-making process in the G20 still favors the agendas of US and Europe. European countries in particular are overrepresented in the forum, and their economic problems differ significantly from those of the developing world. This political representation problem is related to the very foundation of the G20 forum, which from the beginning was based on ad hoc criteria for selecting its members. Even the rise of the BRICS and their self-appointment as representatives of the interests of developing countries is unlikely to settle the question. There is no doubt that in the near future some fast-growing Asian and African economies will seek direct representation in the forum.

Finally, we address China's ongoing process of structural change. Despite its huge economic size, China still depends on the resumption of growth in developed countries to ensure the success of its transition towards a consumption-based economy. Because of this, it is expected that China will play an increasingly important role in future G20 discussions. Also, the Chinese experience of economic transformation will be a good "laboratory" for evaluating several strategies that emerging countries might seek as alternative development models.

# G20: Governing Development?

*Mohammed Saqib*
Secretary General, India China Economic and Cultural Council, India

## Introduction

Since its inception as a group of finance ministers and central bank governors formed in the wake of the 1997–1998 Asian financial crisis, the G20 has come a long way. It started as a forum with rather a limited agenda of encouraging the adoption of the "Washington Consensus" by Asian and other emerging economies to prevent another financial meltdown. This objective has been well achieved. The elevation of the G20 to a summit level was imperative in achieving global solidarity and collective action to tackle the financial crisis and subsequent global recession. This collective action by the G20 leaders helped ease global financial markets, which prevented the recession from turning into a depression. It also gave credence to the G20 as the principal global forum for financial and economic governance.

## Governance

The policy announcements and commitments that G20 leaders make at the summits are non-binding, and the implementation record of these commitments is wide ranging. Examples of major G20 initiatives that have been completed include coordination of fiscal policies during the global financial crisis, tripling of IMF resources, and strengthening the Financial Stability Board (FSB) to coordinate and monitor international progress on regulatory reforms. However, progress on other G20 commitments has been much slower, such as correcting global imbalances, concluding the multilateral WTO Doha Round trade negotiations, increasing the voting share of emerging economies at the IMF, and eliminating fossil fuel subsidies. Yet the issues keep adding to the G20 agenda with each new presidency.

It seems that the G20, like the G8, is unable to bridge the differences in approaches to handling the recovery. Members seek to go their own way in deciding to continue or exit from fiscal stimulus depending on national circumstances. Collective action, it seems, is limited to crisis management. There is continued disagreement on financial sector issues like imposing a tax on banks for funding future bail outs. The UK and the US have both gone ahead with their own measures for improving financial sector regulation without waiting for final recommendations from the expanded Financial Stability Board. There is precious little agreement on trade and protection, aside from repetition of the desirability of completing the Doha Round but with no suggestions on how to achieve this. It is safe to say that convincing G20 leaders of the forum's continued usefulness will be increasingly difficult. The forum, it seems, is suddenly in need of a major boost to achieve greater coherence and relevance.

If the G20 is unable to improve its implementation record, both its legitimacy and credibility will be fatally affected. This will result in the forum quickly losing its relevance. At this stage, it is critical that leaders focus on these existential issues. They should be paying far more attention to establishing mechanisms for follow-up and implementation, which includes the issue of whether or not to establish a secretariat. It would do well to consider creating an appropriate incentive structure that will produce greater compliance with the collective decisions by member countries. Adding development issues to the G20 agenda will be useful only if the group remains relevant and is perceived to be effective in implementing its avowed objectives.

## Development Agenda

"The G20 development agenda is central to the issues facing the G20. Development issues and global economic issues can no longer be treated in isolation.... At a time when economic uncertainties regarding world growth are on the rise, and global imbalances must be eliminated, economic growth can contribute to global economic recovery by creating new focal points of growth and helping to reduce disparities" (G20 DWG, 2011).

Development was added to the G20 agenda at the Seoul Summit in November 2011. This apparently marked a new stage in the evolution of the G20. Yet the question remains whether development should be on the G20 agenda. While global development and poverty is of concern to all G20 members, and the existing body of international institutions could be criticized for ineffective results, it is uncertain whether the G20 would be able to do better. Is there a set of potentially successful G20 initiatives that would add to its credibility? "The G20 development agenda has had so far limited value addition to ongoing global development processes. It lacks both institutional strength and a convincing narrative. Moreover, short-lived celebrity initiatives, such as the financing report submitted by Bill Gates, cannot distract from the weak performance of the G20 as a development driver" (Schulz, 2011).

Based on this criterion, it appears that development should not be on the G20 agenda. Why, then, did Korea add this to the G20 agenda? Why did following G20 presidencies keep it on their agendas? Why is Russia keeping it on the agenda? The rationale for its inclusion was to try and achieve a more balanced outcome from globalization and improve equity across countries and within each economy, with the goal of giving greater legitimacy to the G20 and ensuring greater attention to global equity concerns. Secondly, the inclusion of development on the agenda makes the G20 more relevant and acceptable to developing economies, which are not included in the grouping. Thirdly, promoting the development agenda will help accelerate growth in developing economies and reverse the three decades long trend of worsening equity across countries. Without a development agenda, the G20 will be perceived as an extension of the rich nation cartel that seeks to maximize the benefits from globalization to the detriment of the poorer countries. This is a compelling rationale for the G20 to give greater attention to development issues.

It has been suggested that the G20 should oversee practically the entire range of development activities in developing economies. In other words, it should address the whole gambit of developmental issues. However, there is a danger that the development agenda being suggested for adoption by the G20 will become too large that it precludes effective follow-up or implementation. This is far too ambitious and impractical an agenda for a summit-level forum and is duplicative of the mandates of existing multilateral organizations like the World Bank, Regional Development Banks and UN agencies and organizations.

While it is important to include development issues on the G20 agenda, this could be done with greater advantage once the future existence and efficacy of the Group is assured. Furthermore, the G20 should focus on a select minimum number of development issues that are seen as critical constraints on achieving rapid, equitable and sustainable growth in developing economies. By spreading itself too thinly, the G20 risks becoming yet another layer in the hierarchy of agencies overseeing global efforts for promoting development.

There are certain concerns that must be addressed to improve the G20's existence, efficacy and legitimacy and to make its development agenda effective. The G20 could take up the issue of global aid architecture and the adoption of globally accepted norms for channeling aid flows by old and new donors. Presently, these issues are overseen by the Development Assistance Committee (DAC) of the OECD. However, large emerging economies like Brazil, China, India and Turkey have emerged as major donors, but are not party to the DAC initiatives as they are not OECD members. This prevents effective coordination and in some cases works against the implementation of desirable sanctions against truant governments. On the other hand, nearly all existing DAC members (save perhaps Sweden and Japan) are in violation of their own pledge to allocate 1% of their GDP for development aid. There is apparently insufficient peer pressure within the DAC to hold them to their commitment. Issues like this where the global community would benefit from greater coordination between emerging and advanced economies and which require a degree of accountability would be ideally suited for adoption by the G20.

A coordinated G20 effort to improve the volume, design and delivery of development aid for the world's poorest countries will surely produce a win-win outcome. It could lead to higher allocations by advanced economies, greater compliance of governance norms by new donors and more effective coordination and delivery of the programmes (Rajiv Kumar 2010). The issue of access to necessary technologies and now green technologies has long divided the global community into "Us and Them" or between "Owners and Users". These divisions are especially harmful for technologies needed to overcome the deleterious consequences of extreme poverty (for example malnutrition, illiteracy and morbidity etc.) and addressing climate change issues. By agreeing to a collective approach and action on these issues, the G20 could help reinforce the awareness that all of us are in it together to tackle global public "ills" (poverty and climate change), and that divisions across income or other lines are disastrous.

The issue of the movement of labour is also very important and needs to be addressed. Complete freedom of movement of capital and highly restricted movement of people are no longer possible in the globalized world. This is a highly controversial issue, but it must be addressed at some stage. The G20, acting at the highest Summit level, is the appropriate forum for taking on such apparently difficult issues, the resolution of which requires the maximum generation of collective political will that only the G20 can achieve.

## In Conclusion

The G20's successes at the height of the financial crisis are laudable. During this time, the G20 played a unique, strong, and central role in steering the recovery efforts. Even if members are not able to reach agreement on policies, the G20 serves as a critical forum for discussing major policy initiatives across key countries and encouraging greater cooperation. The G20 was the source of major decisions regarding fiscal stimulus, regulatory reform, tripling the IMF's lending capacity, and other response efforts. The G20 also tasked other international organizations, such as the Bank for International Settlements (BIS), the IMF, the World Bank, and the Financial Stability Board (FSB), with facilitating, monitoring, or implementing various aspects of the response to the crisis. The G20 will be an effective forum for international economic cooperation moving forward, as it includes all the major economic players at the table, representing two-thirds of the world's population, 90% of world GDP, and 80% of world trade, but at the same time is small enough to facilitate concrete negotiations. Also, the involvement of national heads of state in the negotiations could serve to facilitate commitments in major policy areas. Moreover, as the issues discussed by the G20 leaders expand, the G20 may be able to facilitate cooperation by enabling trade-offs among major concerns, such as climate change and trade, which are not possible in issue-specific forums and institutions.

Emerging market economies, especially BRICS countries, have a very important role to play in the success of G20. Developing countries have lots of expectations from the G20, as they see it as their own institution. As the most powerful developing country, China has to somehow steer the cause of developing countries. Developing nations have placed lots of hope on China to take up their causes in the G20, and hope is the most dangerous thing to betray.

# The Future of the G20 Countries*

*Jakkie Cilliers*
**Speaking notes prepared for the international think tank conference "Great Finance, Great Cooperation, Great Governance" hosted in Beijing China, August 21–22, 2013**

Created in 1999, the G20's visibility and influence in world affairs has rapidly increased since 2008. The need for greater representation of emerging economies following the global financial crisis was the main catalyst for this increase, and with its current membership the G20 economies together account for roughly 80% of world's GDP and two-thirds of the world's population. According to the G20 website, its major accomplishments include: "…strengthening the role of emerging economies, such as BRICS, reforming international financial institutions, improving discipline and tightening oversight over national financial institutions and regulators, improving the quality of financial regulations in economies whose regulatory problems led to the crisis, and creating financial and organizational safety nets to prevent severe economic slumps in the future."[1]

The G20 is also a focus of much opposition from officials and public action groups, although less so than the G8 group of countries. Norway's foreign minister in 2010 criticized the G20 as having no mandate and no clear functions, as well as for including the EU as a member.[2] As a major forum of global economic power, the G20 is also a significant target of anti-globalization criticism and protest. Other sources of criticism come from countries that are not members of the G20 but believe that they should be regional contenders to current members.

Understanding how G20 member nations are likely to grow and change internally incoming decades can therefore yield insight into which issues are likely to dominate global political and economic debates. The sections below present, in graphical form, some of the key changes expected for G20 members in two dimensions only. The first section looks at the expected changes in population and labor force. The second looks at the expected shifts in economic size and impact between the various G20 members. The conclusion touches on the impact of climate change.

---

\*   Members of the G20 consist of: Argentina, Australia, Brazil, Canada, China, France, Germany, India, Indonesia, Italy, Japan, the Republic of Korea, Mexico, Russia, Saudi Arabia, South Africa, Turkey, the United Kingdom, the United States of America plus the European Union, which is represented by the President of the European Council and by Head of the European Central Bank.
1   http://www. g20.org/docs/about/part_G20.html, accessed on 5 August 2013.
2   http://www.spiegel.de/international/europe/norway-takes-aim-at-g-20-one-of-the-greatestsetbacks-since-world-war-ii-a-702104. html, accessed on 5 August 2013.

The forecasts rely upon the International Futures system, developed and hosted by the Frederick S. Pardee Centre for International Futures at the University of Denver.[3] The Institute for Security Studies and the Pardee Centre have been collaborating for several years within the framework of the African Futures project.[4] It is important to note that only the individual members of the G20 who are not part of the EU27 group are included in the associated forecasts that follow.

Forecasts are not predictions and the interpretation and representation that follows is only one in many that could be made in looking ahead. As such it is a useful aid to our understanding of how events may unfold, but no more.

## Population

Partly due to the fact that Africa, the youngest continent, is not well represented in the G20, the G20 population as a percentage of global population is slowly declining. This decline is modest however, from around 61% in 2013 to a little over 50% in 2040 (also see figure 1).

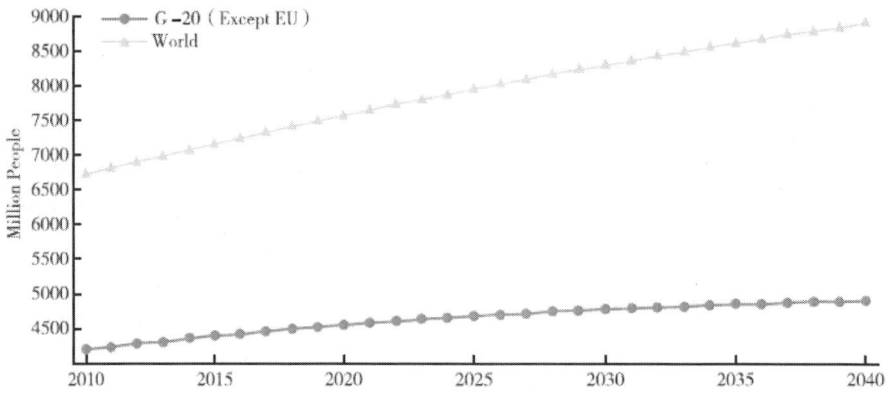

Figure 1: G20 population as a percentage of the world's population

Underlying this shift is the trend towards fewer children per family in many of the G20 nations, with impacts on aggregate population that are offset partially by a corresponding increase in life expectancy. This shift away from high historical birth and death

---

[3] See www.ifs.du.edu. IFs is an integrated assessment model for 183 countries in the world. It has sub-models on: demographics; economics; health; education; infrastructure; agriculture; energy; environment; governance; and international politics. These sub-systems are all endogenous to the model, so the outputs of each system provide important inputs for other systems. This creates the interactivity necessary to create dynamic integrated forecasts and scenarios. The forecasts are all drawn from IFs version 6.7 and represent results from the Base Case. The Base Case is a central tendency scenario that reflects patterns of world development observed over the past 20 years. For our analysis, only individual European countries that are members of the G20, and not the EU as a whole, are included.

[4] See http://www.issafrica.org/futures/.

rates is the much talked-about demographic transition. Looking more closely at population structure and age, we can group the G20 countries into three broad categories:

- Those with old and rapidly aging populations: currently Japan, Italy and Germany. Eventually South Korea and China will join this group as both are aging much more rapidly.
- Those with younger populations: Argentina, Brazil, Turkey, Indonesia, and Mexico, but particularly India and South Africa.
- The rest (the middle group) includes the US, which, if historical patterns of migration continue, will age slower than most of the rest in this group in part due to migration patterns.

In the four G20 countries with the largest populations—China, India, the US and Indonesia—contrasting profiles both of demographics and of education are evident. The pyramid-like structure of India's profile reflects its relatively youthful population and high fertility rates, while in China, the impact of the one-child policy is evident in the constriction of its middle-aged cohort that also reflects an imbalance between more men and less women. In Indonesia, the slow levelling off of its pyramid base reflects fertility rates that have declined to just around the replacement rate of 2.1, a trend seen at a later stage in the population structure of the US. India and China continue to face huge education challenges since large sections of the population continue to have only primary education or less while Indonesia is expected to make much faster progress in educating its population.

Equally striking are the shifts in education profiles. Incompletion of primary school is increasingly disappearing, and advancement in completion of secondary schooling is seen across the board. Figure 2 contains a forecast for the four most populated countries to 2040, which includes a summary view of expected education levels. These four countries do not, of course, have the same population size with the result that the graph presents a slightly skewed picture indicating largely equal numbers of people. By 2040, India should have 1.61 billion people, China 1.37 billion people, and the US 380 million people and Indonesia 289 million people.

**Figure 2: Population and education structure for China, India, USA and Indonesia in 2040**

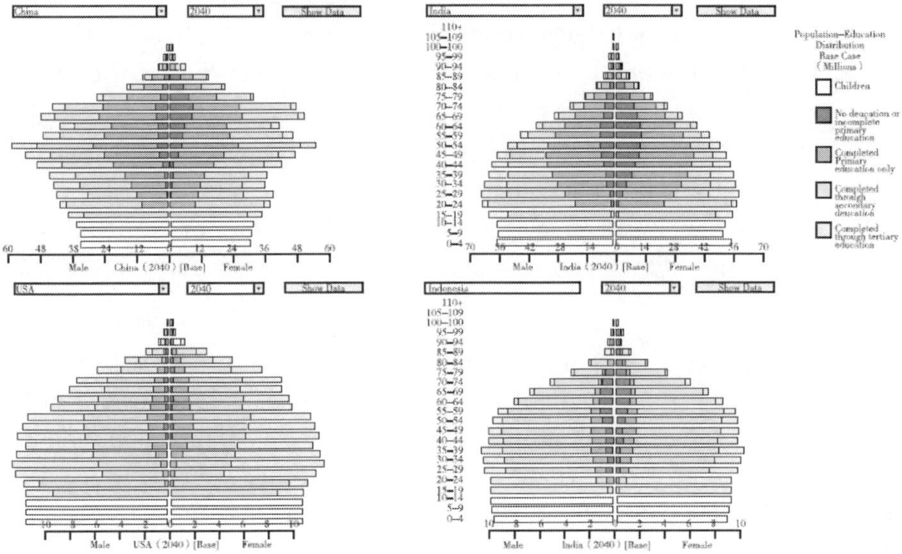

The imbalance between men and women in China, one of the more striking features when looking ahead, is more visible in looking at an age graph of its population separately. The graph (Figure 3) is a forecast for 2020.

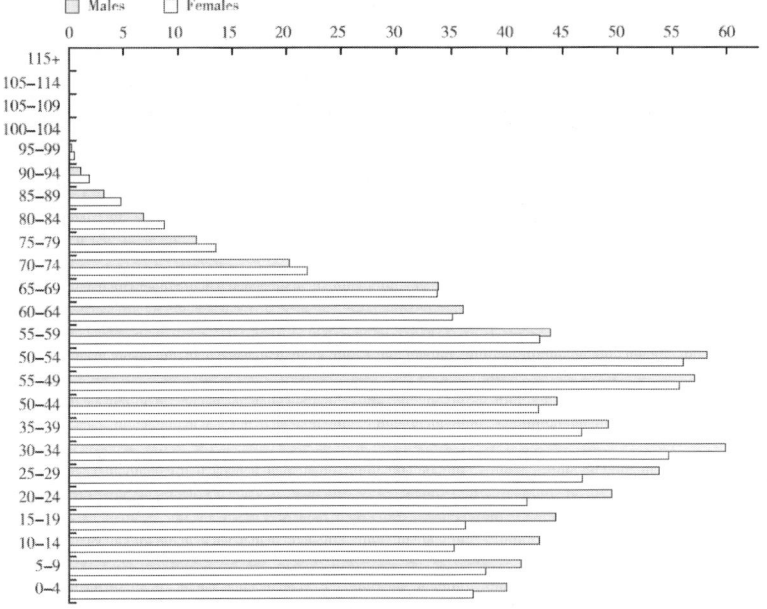

**Figure 3: Population Distribution for China in 2020**

The size of working populations is always interesting and shows how relationships will change over time, particularly dependency ratios. In Figure 4 one can see the extent to which the size of the potential labor force (people aged 15 to 65) of China and India dominate all other G20 members. Figure 4 also shows the closing of the gap between these two countries both as a result of youthful population growth in India and aging of the Chinese population. The US, Indonesia and Brazil constitute a second group of countries with large working age populations, which are consistently larger than the remainder of the G20 members, all of which have comparatively small working age populations if seen as a percentage of the global working age population.

If we are to look at completed years of education at age 25+, the picture changes radically. In Figure 5 we see how the education levels of the US, Germany, Australia, South Korea, Canada, Japan and France outstrip that of the rest, while the countries with the lowest level of education are India, Indonesia, Turkey and Brazil. Again one must be careful in comparing since the absolute numbers of students at different levels are quite different.

**Figure 4: Size of working age (15-65 years) population**

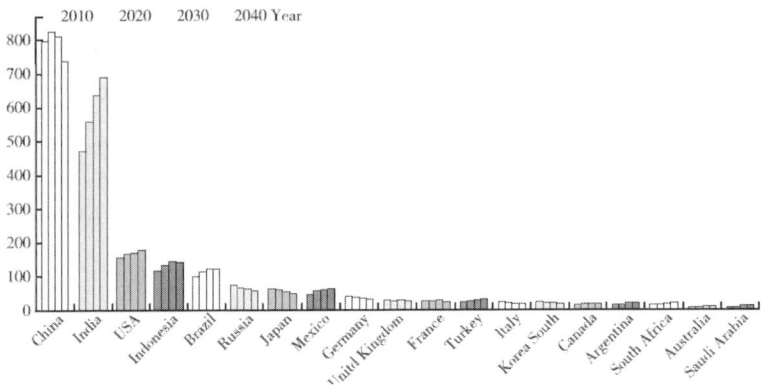

**Figure 5: Education Years, average at age 25+**

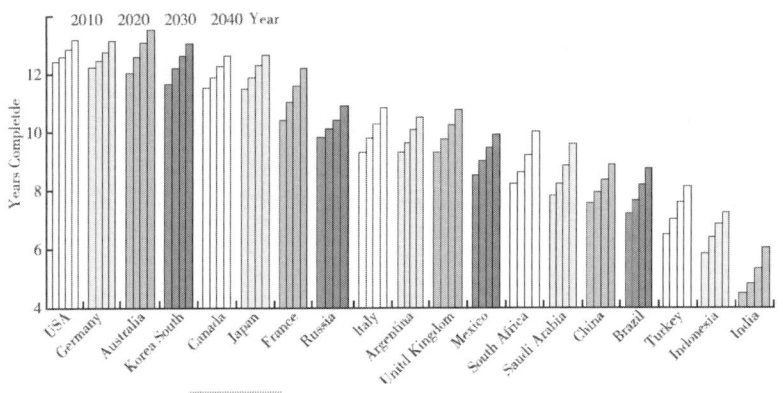

## Economics

We now turn to expected economic developments and patterns. Globally we continue to live in times of amazing advances of wealth and prosperity—a path that should generally continue although, as indicated below, the impact of climate change will increasingly impact upon all aspects of social co-existence. The G20 countries constitute the largest component of the global economy and will continue to do so for the foreseeable future, reflected in Figure 6 below.

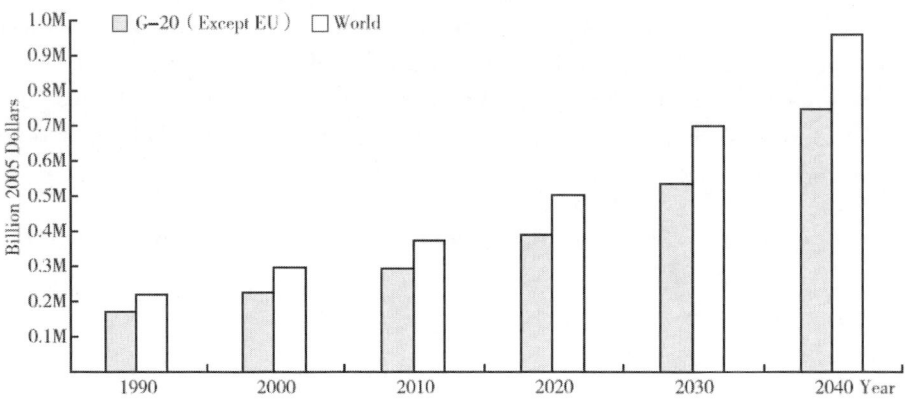

**Figure 6: Size of the global economy and G20 economies**

If we were to divide the G20 into countries with a GDP per capita above $20,000 by 2020 (G20 developed) and those with a GDP per capita below $20,000 by 2020 (G20 developing), the subsequent results are interesting:

- G20 developed countries would consist of Australia, Canada, France, Germany, Italy, Japan, South Korea, Saudi Arabia, the UK and the US.
- G20 developing countries would consist of Argentina, China, Brazil, India, Indonesia, Mexico, Russia, South Africa and Turkey.

The total economic contribution of G20 developing countries (of which China is the largest) as a share of total contribution by G20 members will steadily increase over time. As indicated by Figure 7 below, the G20 developing group is expected to contribute almost all future growth. The economies of China, India and the US will increasingly dominate within the G20 (and indeed the world). Of course, any number of events can shift the future away from base case forecasts. If Prime Minister Shinzo Abe succeeds in turning around the slow growth of the Japanese economy, we might see a slightly different picture from that represented here. However, it is highly unlikely that Japan (or the EU27 for that matter) can turn around their falling share of the global economy in such a way.

The table below provides a summary of the forecasted growth rates for the top five best performing G20 countries for 2020, 2030 and 2040. These forecasts show India and China as growing the fastest, but this is only possible if India is able to overcome many of the hurdles that it faces. Generally, there will no longer be double-digit growth rates for G20 countries. The table below indicates more modest growth rates even for those G20 members that are the best achievers.

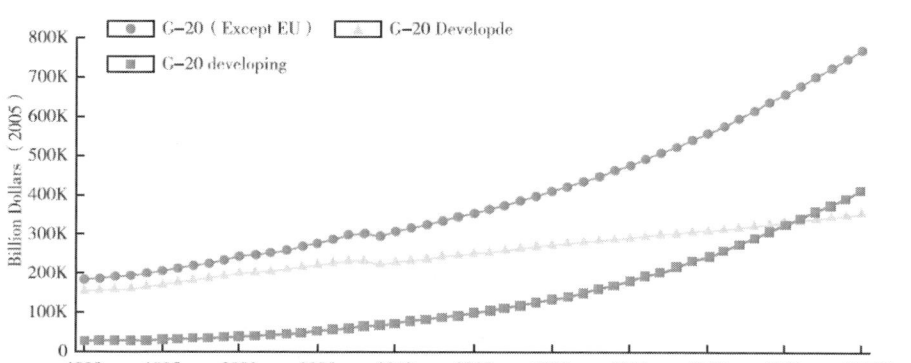

**Figure 7: Size of the G20 economy and relative contribution from G-20 developed and developing countries**

Going forward, the fastest growing countries will almost all be found in Africa, although growth will occur from a very low base. In fact, by our forecast India will only be the 20th fastest growing economy by 2040. 15 of the countries with the potentiality to grow faster than India are in Africa. Despite this rapid growth, Africa will constitute an ever decreasing part of the global economy in the decades ahead.

| In G20 | 2020 | 2030 | 2040 |
|---|---|---|---|
| 1st | India (at 8. 2%) | India (at 8. 4%) | India (at 6. 7%) |
| 2nd | China | China | China |
| 3nd | Indonesia | South Africa | South Africa |
| 4th | Saudi Arabia | Indonesia | Indonesia |
| 5th | Argentina (at 4. 2%) | Saudi Arabia (at 4. 5%) | Turkey (at 3. 3%) |

The various G20 members are, of course, at very different levels of wealth if measured in per capita terms. Here the G20 can be divided into a first and a second class. First class is led by the US and includes Australia, Canada, South Korea, UK, Germany, Japan, France and Saudi Arabia. Looking long-term, Italy slowly falls out of this group and becomes a member of the second class, a poorer group that includes most of the remaining countries within the G20.China continues to make the most impressive performance, graduating from almost bottom of the second class to knocking at the door of the first. India and Indonesia are consistently placed at the bottom of second class due to their large, young populations, despite doing quite well in terms of GDP growth rates. Even Brazil and South Africa don't show dramatic increases in per capita income for the same reason, despite the sterling growth levels that IFs scenario analysis suggests could be possible in South Africa. Both countries seem to be caught up in a middle-income trap.

We can expect the composition of these G20 economies to also undergo important changes. Taken as a whole, the size of the services sector will grow fast and outstrip the contributions from other sectors such as manufacturing (which also continues to grow) although not in relative (proportional) terms. While there is much talk of global convergence or greater global inequality, the gap between the G20 developing and developed groups will probably remain unchanged in the years that lie ahead, reflected in Figure 8 below.

**Figure 8: GDP comparison between G20 developed and developing groups**

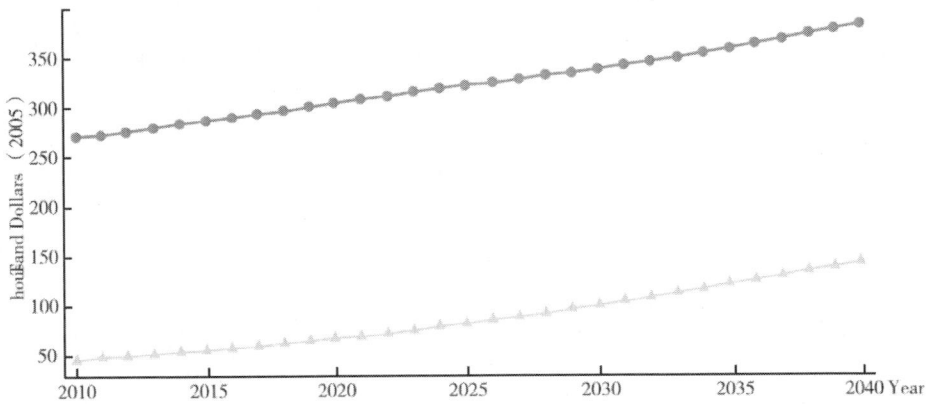

For all practical purposes, extreme poverty has been eliminated in the grouping of developed G20 countries. The number of persons living in absolute poverty, i.e. less than $2 per day, also falls dramatically in the G20 developing group, largely on the back of the continued trends in China, but also due to growth and greater prosperity in other countries. These advances, however, may not be enough to address global problems of inequality, either within or between nations. In terms of equality of income, we can expect that the situation may become worse for both groups in coming decades, while any reductions in the gap in HDI between the two groups of developed and developing countries will only occur very slowly, if at all.

**Figure 9: G20 developing countries: millions of people living on less than $2 per day vs population size**

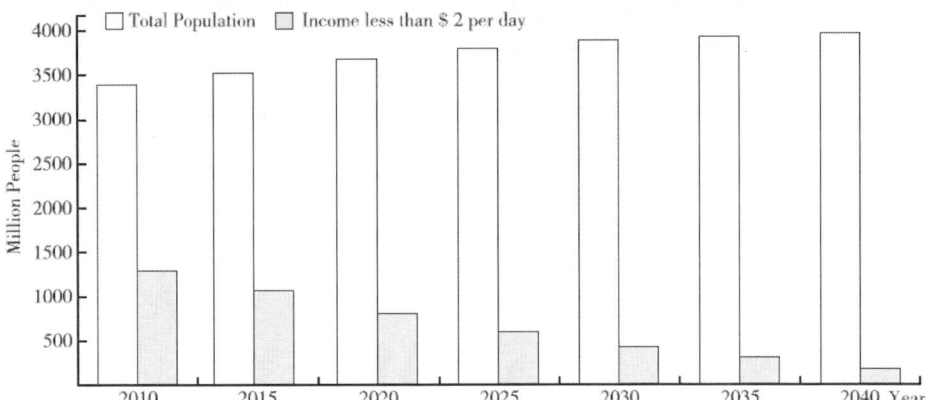

## Conclusion

The pace of global development is rapidly becoming unsustainable. G20 countries currently emit around 78% of carbon emissions from fossil fuels—a percentage set-to decline very moderately by 8% by 2040. As a result, action on climate change is overwhelmingly dependent on action by G20 members, of which the developed world members are the historical culprits, but today the emerging countries are the major emitters. The gap between the two is expected to grow as developed economies become more energy efficient on the back of their lower population growth and the developing group has to look after the needs of their much larger young populations.

**Figure 10: Carbon emissions- World, G20, G20 developed and G20 developing**

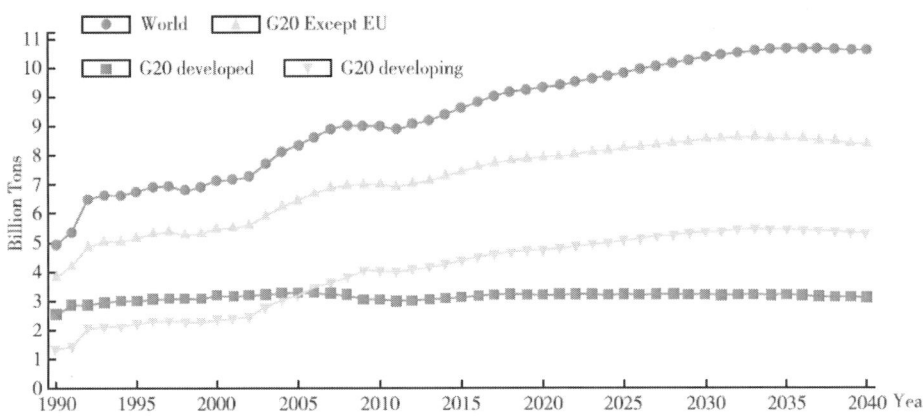

It's well known that amongst the G20 members the US, China and, in the future, India, are the largest polluters. The analysis presented here highlights a few of the major challenges of the coming world, including demographic transition, rising consumption, and environmental degradation. All G20 countries can expect to play a role in meeting these challenges, yet as we have seen, each has unique circumstances with which they will have to cope. We can expect, then, that their incentives and motivations will change over time as their circumstances change. Understanding the likely directions and pace of these changes is therefore crucial for planning our collective future.

# "Great Finance, Great Cooperation, Great Governance" Statement to the International Think Tank Conference

*Taher Hamdi Kanaan*
**Member of the Board of Directors**
**Arab Centre for Research and Policy Studies-Doha Institute, Qatar**

## About the G20

The G20 is an important component of the continued efforts of nations to establish an effective system of "global governance." In order to prevent a repeat of the two major economic recessions of the past and present centuries, such a system has to be based on democratic participation of all nations and should endeavor to establish international law and order towards a peaceful and prosperous world.

Political globalization must catch up with economic globalization in the form of international institutions that enable countries to work together and prevent countries from taking actions that adversely affect others. Originally, the seven richest nations (G7) came together in 1973 to undertake collective action to deal with the first economic crisis of global dimensions, namely the oil price shock. The crisis was blamed on Arab oil-exporting countries, so much so that the President of the US at the time described it as "The Moral Equivalent of War". The initial G6, enhanced to G7 to include Canada in 1976, was established with wealth as the sole membership qualification. In 1997, with the demise of the Soviet bloc, Russia officially became the 8th member. The G8 membership represented about 80 percent of world output, but less than 20 percent of the world population.

However, the issues underpinning the formation of the G8 were at least of equal concerto the welfare of the other 80 percent of the world population. Democratic principles dictate that those who are deeply affected by a policy should have a say in their formulation, and those who are responsible for massive failures and injury should be held accountable. Our present system of global economic governance does not meet either of these fundamental tests of democratic governance.[1]

The platform for equitable representation of the majority of mankind is the United Nations (UN). Yet, considerations of "real politic" have prevented this platform from effectively addressing issues involving the vital interests of the big powers. This task was relegated to thief and the World Bank Group, where the governing

---

[1] United Nations, Chairman Joseph Stiglitz, Report of the Commission of Experts of the President of the United Nations General Assembly on Reforms of the International Monetary and Financial System, September 2009, Foreword.

boards provided platforms for the voice of all nations, but subjected decisions to the biased voting power of the richer nations.

The very large number of board members of the IMF and the World Bank made deliberation of issues complex and prone to lobbying by politicians back home. Hence, a smaller membership platform was needed, but with larger representation than provided in the G8.

Under the shadow of the world economic crisis of October 2008, the G8 was enlarged to become the G20 with the additions of China, India and 9 other so-called "emerging countries, "along with the institutional member of the European Union. Despite this expansion, the membership of the G20 has remained deficient in equitable representation of developing countries and their developmental concerns. It is noted, for example, that in the course of seven G20 summits held between November 2008 and June 2012, only two announcements specifically addressed such issues, namely: 1) the pledges made at the April 2009 London Summit to increase funding for the IMF and the MDBs by $1.1 trillion, including a tripling of the IMF's lending capacity; and 2) the announcement at the November 2010 Seoul Summit of the "Seoul Development Consensus" that emphasized, inter alia, the positive role of governments in influencing development and the importance of infrastructure in development. This does not mean of course that other policy recommendations reached in the various summits were not beneficial to developing countries.

Over time, the polarization between the haves and the have-nots among IMF and World Bank member states has boiled down to two groups:

1. The G20, which is comprised of the original G7/G8 members, augmented by the addition of "emerging countries," i.e. those with high economic performance that makes their weight in the global market too significant to be ignored. The G20 mandate consists of cooperation and consultation on matters pertaining to the international financial system.
2. The G24 was established in 1971, preceding the G20 by about three decades. It goes back to the zenith of the Cold War when the US-led West (1st World), and the USSR-led East (2nd World) vied to bring the South (3rd World) to their side in their bi-polar conflict. Under the triad leadership of China (Zhou Enlai), India (Nehro), and Egypt (Nasser), the South exercised considerable influence by organizing themselves into articulate international groups, such as the G77, the Non-Aligned Nations, and the G24. These groups focused on coordinating the

positions of developing countries on international monetary and development issues in global institutions, particularly the IMF.[2]

The end of the Cold War and the implosion of the Soviet Union resulted in the marginalization of the poor countries of the South, and neglect of their concerns. This is evident in the fact that the G20 does not seem to interact with the G24, although they have similar and interrelated mandates. Recent communiqués of the G20 hardly mentioned the G24 in any context, and vice-versa. To be sure, the exclusivity of the G20 to rich and newly rich countries does not detract from its success in guiding the recovery efforts of the financial crisis, and the important decisions made regarding fiscal stimuli, regulatory reform, tripling the IMF's lending capacity, and other efforts related to vital concerns such as the environment and food security. On the debit side, note is taken of G20 failure to provide effective leadership in dealing with the Euro zone crisis, and in pursuing a positive conclusion to the Doha negotiations.

## Future Prospects of the G20

The crises which gave birth to the G20 and similar international initiatives are systemic in the deepest sense. The recurrence of such systemic crises can only be prevented through collective and cooperative deliberation and action undertaken by international institutions that equitably represent the community of nations and that combine democratic representation of nations with supranational enforcement modalities. Only by this means can the global community gradually establish an effective system of global governance.

International and national endeavors over the past decade have registered certain progress in global economic and financial reforms, but have been unsuccessful at overcoming certain shortcomings, both old as well as new. Since the 1990s, substantial economic reforms in countries like China and India have managed to sustain high rates of economic growth, with a substantial material impact on poverty. Several hundred million people have been lifted out of extreme poverty as a result of this economic growth. Yet these achievements could have been even more significant if reforms had been deeper and extended more broadly to areas of policy.

In addition to outstanding issues of economic and financial reform, the future agenda for the G20 and other relevant multilateral institutions includes issues associated with "development-centered globalization", as usefully outlined by the UNCTAD Panel of Eminent Persons in their second report. Due to space limitations, this article

---

2   Members of G-24: Region I (Africa): Algeria, Côte d'Ivoire, Egypt, Ethiopia, Gabon, Ghana, Nigeria, South Africa and the Democratic Republic of Congo. Region II (Latin America and the Caribbean): Argentina, Brazil, Colombia, Guatemala, Mexico, Peru, Trinidad and Tobago and Venezuela. Region III (Asia) : India, Iran, Lebanon, Pakistan, Philippines, Sri Lanka and Syria.

lists only the titles of the issues in the UNCTAD report along with a brief outline of recommended actions.[3]

1) Global economic and financial governance

Build a "Development Observatory of Global Economic and Financial Governance" and develop a "Virtual Consortium of Think Tanks" on globalization and new development strategies.

2) Trade

Establish a multilateral and multi-stakeholder platform for fostering dialog among regional trade blocs, identify opportunities for "open regionalism," emphasize the development angle and ultimately support multilateralism.

3) Commodities

Foster diversification in commodities dependent low-income countries by creating an aid-for-diversification facility.

4) Investment

Work towards creating a multilateral platform where international investment policies can be coordinated.

5) Enterprise and supply chains

Build local enterprises and develop domestic productive capacity to integrate into global supply chains. Develop operational strategies for strengthening the productive capacity of developing countries' enterprises.

6) Technology capabilities

Help LDCs, through disseminating "soft" technology, make use of the skills and knowledge of retired professionals and skilled emigrants.

7) International migration

Undertake research and policy analysis on the economic development impact of migration, particularly with respect to the development of finance, trade (services model) and the economic empowerment of women.

8) Green economy

Possible actions involve advocacy and knowledge dissemination at a firm level, and establishing an international technical assistance centre for green investment and technology to drive change at the national and international governance level.

---

[3] UNCTAD, *Op. Cit.*

9) Women in development

Work toward mainstream gender parity in the economic and sustainable development spheres. Identify and deploy meaningful and effective actions where differentiated approaches for women rather than a gender-neutral approach are warranted.

10) Inclusive growth

Undertake research to understand the challenges and opportunities faced by the informal sector in order to facilitate its formalization. A platform should be established for the international community to engage on these questions and provide technical assistance to facilitate the formalization of the informal sector.

## China's Role in the G20

China shares major challenges with less developed countries in terms of managing both its internal economy as well as its external relations with the global economy. We shall focus the rest of this statement on one of the most pressing of those challenges, namely the issue of global financial imbalances and their impact on international monetary system reform. The huge trade imbalance between China and the US and between China and other countries of the global North is a haunting threat to the sustainability of its miraculous economic growth, which to date has been grounded in export-oriented industrialization, low consumption and high savings.[4] This developmental model is associated with extreme economic dependence on meeting export demand at the expense of impoverishing domestic consumer demand, particularly in the countryside. This generates a continuous exodus of the rural population to urban centre's in coastal towns and cities, where export industrialization is concentrated. The competitive advantage of Chinese exports owes a great deal to cheap labor migrating from the countryside.[5]

Organized under a Japan-centric and multi-layered subcontracting production network, different Asian exporters occupy different segments of the value chain, and each of them specialize in goods exports to developed industrial countries. Japan specializes in the highest value-added items, while the economies of Hong Kong, Singapore, South Korea, and Taiwan specialize in middle-range products, and emerging economies in South East Asia specialize in low-cost labor intensive products. This so-called "flying geese formation" of Asian exporters constitutes a reliable network of suppliers for all sorts of consumer products to the world market, particularly markets in the global north. In the 1990s, when China started establishing itself as the most

---

[4] Ho-Fung Hung, China in the Global Crisis, in Bagchi, Amiya Kumar, and Anthony P. D. Costa(Ed.), *Transformation and Development, The Political Economy of Transition in India and China.* Oxford University Press, New Delhi, 2012, Chapter 5, p. 135.
[5] Ibid. p. 138.

competitive Asian exporter of products at various levels of technological sophistication, incumbent Asian exporters in East and South East Asia were put under intense pressure to adjust. China's export competitiveness induced the relocation of export manufacturing from other Asian economies to China. A new China-centric export-oriented industrial order emerged, under which most Asian economies increased the weight of their exports of high value added components and parts (esp. Korea and Taiwan) and capital goods (esp. Japan) to China.

In China, these parts and capital goods are assembled into finished products to be exported to the global North. This China-centric production network has resulted in increased dependence of East Asian economies on China's growth performance. Accordingly, the vulnerability of these Asian economies is tied to the limits and vulnerability of Chinese development, which is in turn overly dependent on consumption demand in the US and other countries of the North. The rebalancing of China's development model is important for both the sustainability of Chinese economic growth as well as for the collective future of East Asia as an integrated regional economic block.[6]

Over the last two decades, China has emerged as the leader of the regional East Asian network of production described above, and has attained the status as the largest creditor to the United States and the largest holder of foreign reserves. The downside of this status is that it depends on sustained high levels of domestic consumption in the US. This dependency is volatile and in the long run unsustainable. Eventually, domestic US consumption could take a fall caused by a decline in thevalue of the US dollar, a collapse in the US Treasury bonds market or a sharp rise in interest rates in the US economy. This will be a deadly blow to China's export engine and will cut down China's global financial power through a drastic devaluation of its investments in Treasury bonds. China can rescue itself from this nightmare scenario by fighting and winning battles on three fronts:

a.  Stimulate the domestic economy: By utilizing the potential of China's economic, geographic, and demographic size, stimulate domestic consumer demand so that the country becomes the market of the world on top of being the "workshop of the world."[7]
b.  Reform the international financial system: Advocate for international collective action through the G20 and other multilateral institutions to reform the international financial system in two respects:
    a.  Create a new reserve currency to replace the dollar

---

[6]  Ibid. pp. 140-143.
[7]  Ibid. p. 147

b. Strengthen multilateralism by democratizing, reforming, and funding the IMF and the World Bank so that developing countries find less need to turn to bilateral support in times of need.
c. Pursue and upgrade the Chinese time-honored tradition of South-South cooperation: China should resist the temptation to join the club of rich nations and acknowledge the benefits to China of assisting developing countries in raising their economic performance.

In the following paragraphs we shall highlight specific aspects of these three approaches.

## Domestic Economic Policy

China's government is well aware that further accumulation of global financial power is counterproductive because it would increase the risk to assets that China holds. Reducing China's export dependence requires prioritizing the growth of domestic demand by increasing the disposable income of the lower classes. This involves the shift of resources away from the coastal urban areas to rural inland areas where the room for consumption growth is abundant. It might be useful here to point to the experience of India, whose rapid development in the past decade has been grounded more on the expansion of domestic private consumption than on exports. India's robust growth in private consumption relative to its overall economic growth has partially contributed to relatively lower rural-urban inequality, which in turn is related to improved terms of trade for the agricultural sector compared with manufacturing since the 1980s. In contrast, China's agricultural sector has declined compared with manufacturing in China. The Economist's "the World in 2010" referred to the strength of rural demand in India as one reason why India escaped from the global financial crisis of 2008 so lightly.[8]

## Reform of the International Monetary System

There is something terribly wrong with a system that allows poor countries, desperately in need of investable capital resources, to lend hundreds of billions of dollars to the world's richest country. The money that China and other developing countries, particularly the Arab oil-exporting countries, put in dollar reserves are essentially loans to the US at negligible interest rates. They instead could be used to stimulate the global economy, contribute to global aggregate demand for consumption and investment, and help to maintain the world economy at full employment. China and other trade surplus countries do not need to export goods to the US in return for pieces of paper of diminishing value that finance American deficits. Rather than lending money to the US to increase consumption there, these countries could use this money to investing

---

[8] Bagchi and Costa, Op. Cit. p. 148

their own countries and advance their own people. Given the right level of decisiveness by the international community, freeing the global economy from the overwhelming hegemony of the dollar as the world reserve currency is simple. As proposed by Keynes in the 1940s, the international community can provide a new form of reserve if countries agree to exchange this money for their own currency when needed, e.g. in a time of crisis. This form of provision of international liquidity has already been adopted, albeit in a feeble and lame manner, in the form of Special Drawing Rights (SDRs). The SDR is a kind of international money that the IMF can create. However, the problem with the SDR system as currently practiced is that SDRs are created only on occasion and are given largely to the wealthiest countries. An effective substitute to the dollar as a global reserve currency should not only provide the liquidity needed for the efficient functioning of the international financial system, but also for tackling some of the deeper problems facing the world today, such as global poverty and environmental degradation.[9]

Indeed, at the time of the East Asian crisis of 1997 an important initiative in that direction was taken by Japan in the form of a proposal to establish an Asian Monetary Fund (AMF) with seed money amounting to $100 billion contributed from Japan. This Fund was to provide Asian countries with financial resources needed to help their economies recover from the crisis. The IMF managed to terminate this early initiative. Pursuing the earlier Japanese initiative, members of Association of South-East Asian Nations (ASEAN), plus China, Japan, and South Korea, signed the Chiang Mai Initiative at a meeting in Thailand in 2000. This initiative sowed the seed for a new regional cooperative arrangement that would enhance the ASEAN's ability to deal with financial crises. Instead of putting their sizable reserves in Western countries, each country agreed to hold currencies of the others, thus keeping the reserves within their region. Under this arrangement, they would lend money to support consumption and investment in countries of their region instead of lending resources to rich Western countries to finance their deficit spending. Holding one another's currencies in reserves has the same effect as a line of credit, commitment on the part of other countries to allow a fellow country in a time of need to have access to the resources in reserve. Nobel Laureate Joseph Stiglitz illustrates how this initiative might work as follows:

> Each year each member of the New Reserve Currency Agreement—the countries that signed up to the new global reserve system—would contribute a specified amount to a global reserve fund and, at the same time, the Monetary Authority of this system would issue units of the new currency of equivalent value to the currency which they would holding their reserves.

In 2010 the Chiang Mai initiative, dubbed the Chiang Mai Initiative Multilateralism agreement (CMIM), was turned into a formal arrangement binding the ASEAN+3 countries. However, because the committed money remains in individual central banks,

---

[9] Stiglitz, Joseph E., Making Globalization Work, New York, 2006, Chapter 9, pp. 260-265.

the CMIM is a set of promises that is not close enough to the original concept of an Asian Monetary Fund (AMF). This shortcoming was characterized by The Economist as progress "albeit at the snail's pace." This appears grossly unfair. Establishing an AMF that results in a successful new reserve system is no small undertaking in institution building. To do this, the AMF has to act as a supra-national central bank which has all the critical attributes of such an institution, including highly competent, dedicated, and visionary management, endowed with all the necessary material and human resources while diligently protecting the institution's independence and devotion to its objectives. Such a demanding institution building effort can only proceed gradually with every step consolidated and secured before taking the next step, particularly in light of the ferocious political opposition it will inevitably encounter from global vested interests. In effect, this is a case of "better late than never." In fact, by virtue of fidelity to the region I come from, I believe there is a unique opportunity here for what might develop into a historic process of interregional cooperation between the Middle East North Africa Region (Arab Countries + Iran) and the ASEAN+3 Region. Both sides have strong potential to become founding partners in initiatives that, among other potential achievements, may prove successful in the daunting task of re-directing the enormous trade surpluses they continue to accumulate into upgrading the economic performance of less fortunate populations in their respective regions.

From the Chinese policy standpoint, this is in keeping with China's longstanding tradition even before China emerged into the era of high performance development. Least developed Arab countries, Yemen and Sudan, were early recipients of Chinese development assistance to upgrade their infrastructure. China's involvement in financial assistance for development was institutionalized both within the Asian region through China's membership in the Asian Development Bank, and reached as far as the Latin American region through membership in the Latin American Development Bank. In the Middle East North Africa Region, a regional development bank is still an unfulfilled need. As the maiden venture for institutionalizing interregional cooperation between China and the Gulf oil-exporting countries, both sides could agree to establish a regional development bank designated as the Middle East North Africa Development Bank (MENA Bank).[10] The financial resources and trade base that would strongly underwrite such venture is clearly indicated by the figures shown in the following two pages, and with a supporting Excel file attached separately.

---

[10] To distance this venture from World Bank nomenclature, it might be more appropriately named as WEST ASIA NORTH AFRICA Development Bank (WANA).

## Statistical Annex

*Middle East, North Africa (MENA) Trade with rest of the World*

|      | Exports<br>US$ billions | Imports<br>US$ billions | Trade Balance<br>US$ billions |
|------|-------|-------|-------|
| 2005 | 554.8 | 319.5 | 235.3 |
| 2006 | 705.1 | 447.7 | 257.4 |
| 2007 | 799.9 | 556.2 | 243.7 |
| 2008 | 1127.8 | 748.2 | 379.6 |
| 2009 | 712.1 | 624.3 | 87.8 |
| 2010 | 960.7 | 709.4 | 251.3 |
| 2011 | 1252.6 | 841.4 | 411.2 |
|      | Exports to China<br>US$ billions | Imports from China<br>US $ billions | Trade Balance<br>US $ billions |
| 2005 | 32.01 | 26.96 | 5.05 |
| 2006 | 42.31 | 35.38 | 6.93 |
| 2007 | 52.83 | 51.42 | 1.41 |
| 2008 | 73.3 | 70.93 | 2.37 |
| 2009 | 55.17 | 63.48 | -8.31 |
| 2010 | 83.19 | 73.08 | 10.11 |
| 2011 | 125.6 | 95.52 | 30.08 |

**Charts**

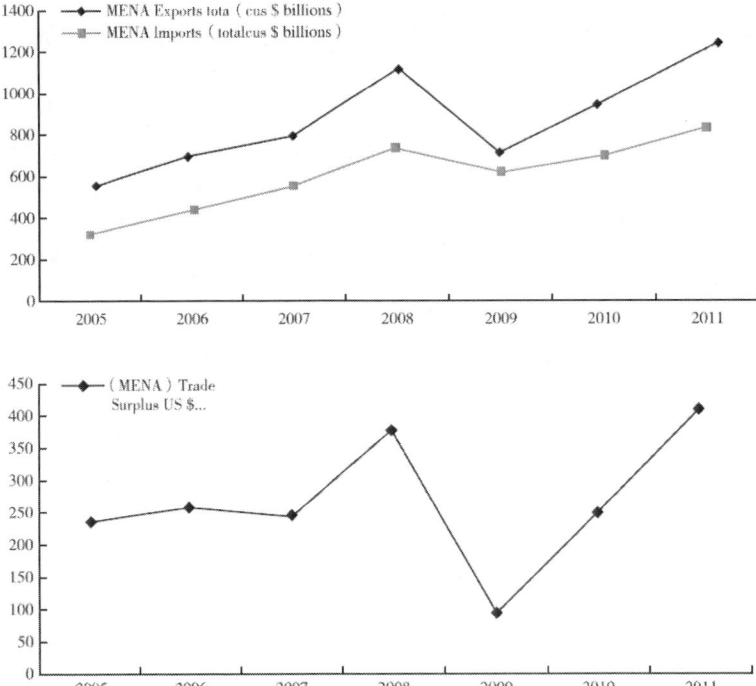

## MENA Trade with the World

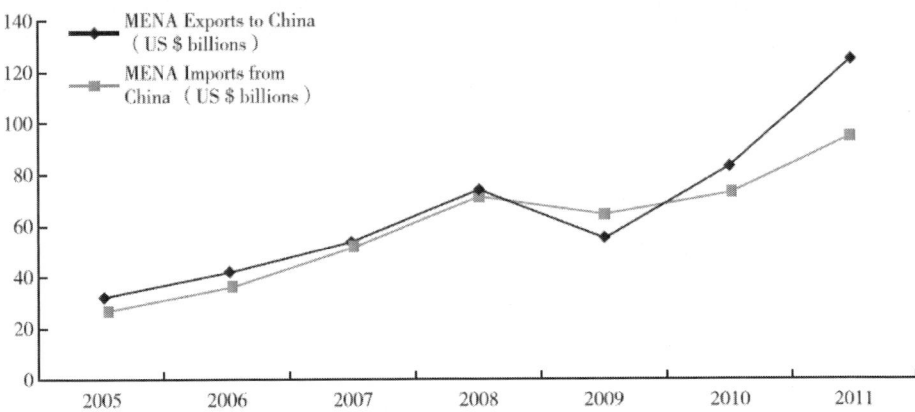

## MENA Trade with China

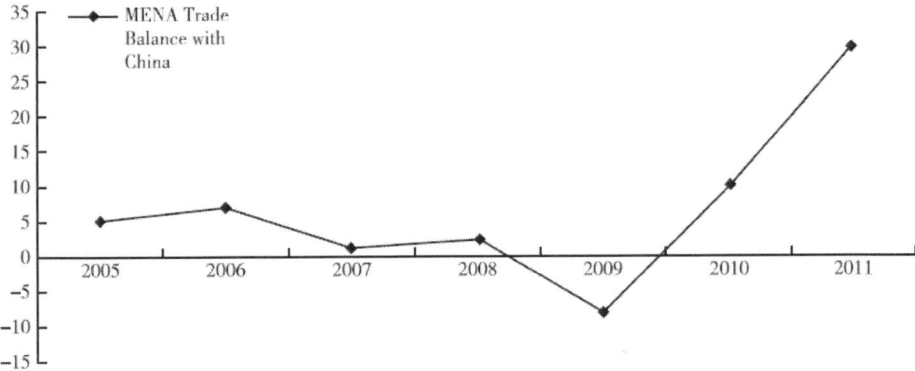

# G20 and Turkey

*Cafer Sait Okray*
**Member of the Executive Board
of the Marmara Group Foundation, Turkey**

## Introduction

The G20 is a platform that was established with the goal of ensuring increased representation of developed countries and countries whose importance and weight is growing within the international system and in the global economic decision-making process. Established in 1999 following the 1997 Asia and 1998 Russia crises, the members of the G20 are as follows:

> EUROPE: Turkey, England, Germany, France, Italy, Russian Federation and EU Commission[1]
> AMERICAS: US, Canada, Mexico, Argentina, Brazil
> ASIA-PACIFIC: China, India, Japan, South Korea, Indonesia, Australia
> AFRICA: South Africa
> MIDDLE EAST: Saudi Arabia

The G20 stands out as an organization that brings 90% of the world's economy, 80% of the world's trade and 2/3 of the world's population together. It also stands out for its inclusive structure, bringing together both developed countries and emerging economies from different continents. Its profile in the international economic community has been consistently rising. The G20 has gathered at the Leaders level since 2008, with the goal of working to overcome the challenges of the global economic and financial crisis. At the time of this writing, a total of seven G20 Leaders Summits have been organized: 1) Washington, November 14–15, 2008 2) London, April 2, 2009 3) Pittsburgh, September 24–25, 2009 4) Toronto, June 26–27, 2010 5) Seoul, November 11–12, 2010 6) Cannes, November 3–4, 2011 and 7) Los Cabos, June 18–19, 2012. Today, the G20 is considered the premier platform for international economic cooperation.

The G20 agenda was initially formulated towards solving the economic crisis, but today has expanded to encompass development issues related to the global economy, trade, energy security, climate change, poverty, employment and re-structuring of the economic and financial system in accordance with today's realities and needs. Turkey considers the G20 to be the most suitable platform for global economic cooperation due to its high rated representation capacity and quality. Turkey is actively involved in the global efforts of the G20, and Turkey's Prime Minister has attended the Washington, London, Pittsburgh, Toronto, Seoul, Cannes and Los Cabos G20 Summits.

---

[1] Although Spain is not a member of the G20, it has been attending the G20 Summits and other meetings under the status of " permanent guest country"

The rise of the G20's profile after the global crisis and participation by Government/State heads of the biggest economic, political and military powers of the world also carries great importance for Turkey as a member state of the G20. We think that Turkey's position in the G20 presents opportunities for Turkey to increase its influence in international economic organizations that collaborate with the G20, such as the OECD, WTO, IMF and World Bank. Turkey views the G20's efforts to increase the influence of developing countries in the IMF and World Bank, the decision to transfer 5% of IMF quotas from the share of developed countries to developing economies and Turkey's membership in the Financial Stability Board (FSB)—the most important institution next to the IMF—as positive developments for Turkey.

The activities of the G20 can essentially be divided into two work streams: the Sherpa work stream and Finance work stream. Development, energy, trade, employment, climate change, fighting corruption and other similar subjects constitute the Sherpa course of the G20 efforts and activities. This work stream is diplomatic in nature and G20 countries are to assign representatives as Sherpas to the meetings of the G20. The finance course consists of international financial and economic issues, which are usually coordinated by relevant ministries, under secretariats and Central Bank administrations.

## Russia's Term Presidency

The Russian Federation has taken on the Presidency of the G20 from Mexico as of December 1, 2012. The priority issues under Russia's presidency are as follows:

1. "Growth through Efficient Regulation": Strengthening financial regulation; encouraging multilateral trade (easing trade, fighting protectionism, free trade agreements), energy sustainability (infrastructure and regulations, energy markets, green growth, GMEP initiative);
2. "Growth through Qualitative Employment and Investment": strong, sustainable and balanced growth; financing for investment; employment (fighting structural unemployment, employment of delicate groups); development for everyone (nutrition security, infrastructure, human capital, spreading the financial base);
3. "Growth through Trust and Transparency": reforming the international monetary system (IMF quota and governance reform, public debt and sustainability of public debt); fighting corruption.

The G20 Leaders Summit under the Russian Federation's Term Presidency will gather on September 5–6, 2013 in St. Petersburg.

## Turkey's Position

As decided at the 2011 Cannes Leaders' Summit, Turkey will assume the Presidency of the G20 in 2015. As of December 2013, Turkey will join the Russian Federation and Australia as part of the G20 Troika, the group of the previous, present and future G20 Presidencies.

Within this framework, the Republic of Turkey has established the "G20 Term Presidency Direction Committee" in order to manage the relevant preparations for Turkey's upcoming presidential term and to maintain cooperation and coordination among relevant government institutions. The Committee will be chaired by the Deputy Prime Minister responsible for general coordination on economic matters and will consist of the Undersecretary of the Prime Ministry, Undersecretary of the Ministry of Interior, Undersecretary of the Ministry of Foreign Affairs, Undersecretary of Treasury and the Chairman of the Central Bank. If seen necessary by the Committee Chairman, other ministries, relevant government institutions, universities, NGOs and private sector representatives will be invited to the Committee meetings.

## Concluding Remarks

In the existing complex and global economic and political atmosphere, the job of the G20 is rather a difficult one, especially when one considers the questions and problems detailed in this report. Yet the fact remains that G20 countries can take some steps towards solving or at least making progress on some of the important and urgent issues that concern the activities of other international organizations and platforms.

Turkey places significant political emphasis on the G20 group. For this reason, Turkey may be considered one of the more active participants in the G20 compared to many other member countries. As a result of its political interest and willingness, Turkey will be the host country of the preparatory meetings of the G20 in 2015 and, ultimately, will host the leaders' summit. As it prepares for its presidential term, Turkey, like Russia and Australia, should bear in mind all the points that have been called to attention in this paper. In this way, Turkey may be able to learn some lessons from the mistakes and failure to create a successful agenda with respect to continuity, urgency, importance and selectiveness between terms, as well as the inability of some countries/leaders in fulfilling their tasks. It is important for Turkey to start preparations for the 2015 summit early, and to be careful, realistic and selective when determining the summit's agenda in order to bring about a successful summit.

During this term, Turkey should give a primary importance to the issue of "green growth for sustainable development from an environmental perspective "with a long-term approach on national and global levels. If G20 countries, who make up a large share of production and trade of international goods and services, decide to work together, this will have a huge and positive impact on the inevitable transformation of the global energy system and the fight against global warming, poverty and hunger. However, it is important to make one thing clear: if the issues of "a new financial structure" and "reform of financial organizations" (which seem to be more quickly resolvable compared to other topics) are not brought to a concrete resolution during the Presidencies of Mexico, Russia and Australia, they may infiltrate the agenda of the G20 in 2015. In this respect, it is clear that big steps on financial issues need to be taken in Mexico.

# Part 3
# China's Development and the G20's Future

With China's increasing economic strength, China's economy and the global economy are becoming more closely intertwined. At the same time, the international community is intensifying its call for China to become a responsible international power commensurate with its economic strength. Through the platform of the G20, China can acquire more opportunities to participate in global affairs, and more opportunities to cooperate with other nations in areas of mutual gain. Set against the backdrop of globalization, how can China further strengthen its competitiveness and influence? In the future, how can the G20's development trend satisfy calls for greater diversity, and achieve an optimum state of equilibrium?

# Interest Camps in the Framework of the G20 and Strategic Space of Emerging Countries

*Wang Wen and Wang Ruijing*
Translated from Chinese by Sam Overholt and Wang Ruijing

*Wang Wen*
Executive Dean
Renmin University of China Executive Director
Chongyang Institute for Financial Studies

*Wang Ruijing*
Deputy Director of the Macro-economic Project
Renmin University of China
Chongyang Institute for Financial Studies

## The G20 and a New World Order

As an organization, the G20 is the result of two financial crises that shook the world. The first was the 1997 Asian Financial Crisis, during which "The Wealthy Nations Club" of the G7 discovered it was impossible to manage the financial crisis alone. The G20 Finance Ministers and Central Bank Governors' Meeting emerged as a new co-ordinated response. Second was the 2007 United States sub-prime mortgage crisis. In this case, the G7 itself was "ground zero" for the crisis. Hoping to bring about a fast recovery, developed countries were forced to rely on help from emerging countries and other world economies. The G20 Leaders' Summit gradually replaced the G8's function as a primary means to influence international financial affairs and policy.[1]

The European Commission President Jose Manuel Barroso sees the current financial crisis as the first major crisis of the globalization era.[2] Globalization is the basic development trend of the 20th century international political economy. Global financial crises influence the international political economy mainly by changing the course of globalization. Currently, globalization is understood as a process of "Americanization", or pursuit of global implementation of Western style governance models oriented according to the interests of the United States.

The G20 is the product of a transitional era. New international powers are replacing the old, creating a new model for international governance. Leaders of the old

---

[1] Hajnal, Peter I. (2007), *The G8 system and the G20: Evolution, Role and Documentation.* Aldershot, Hampshire: Ashgate Publishing.
[2] 21st Century Business Herald (2009). European Commission President Jose Manuel Barroso: G20 summit should Reconstruct Globalization. Retrieved April 1, 2009, from http://money.163.com/09/0401/02/55PHUTCM002538OL.html

order still want to maintain their status as global rule makers. Because of their increased economic strength, proponents of the new order hope that they can become core partners in making new rules, and have more of a say in international affairs after the coming structural shift. G20 members are destined to have vastly different interests and standings on many issues. Reaching a consensus will be extremely difficult.

## Three Major G20 Camps

The G20 includes 19 countries and one regional organization, the European Union. The struggle of competing interests among the 20 members is divided along three main camps.[3]

The first camp consists of developed countries who maintain the old order. The core member of this camp is the United States. The United States can trap vast global wealth at very low cost in the dollar-based international monetary system. The United States has great national interest and rule-making power in the present international economic order. It is improbable that the US will relinquish these vested interests easily. Other nations that have been bound by this system are forced to save large amounts of national wealth as dollars, and in the process have their own vital interests controlled by the United States. In the short term, they are unable to simply do away with this system. The United States hopes to limit the role of the G20 to crisis management and harness the strength of the G20 emerging economies to aid its own recovery while giving up the least in terms of its current vested interests.

A Brookings Institution working paper on the G20 noted that in order to protect its vested interests, the United States from the very beginning has chosen to pursue solutions that would least change the current framework, thus excluding the establishment of a new type of international system. However, the G20 has instead chosen to expand the range of dialog on the basis of the existing framework. Because the G20 is consensus-based, and not voting-based, the inclusion of more developing nations cannot by numbers alone exert any influence on the course of international affairs.[4] While the G20 has helped to improve the status of developing countries, they have not been able to use the G20 to increase real influence. The United States has taken a resistant attitude toward any reform measures that may limit its overall power and vested interests, such as supranational financial regulation and limits on economic stimulus plans.

The second camp consists of developed countries that actively promote financial reform.

This camp is primarily comprised of European Union member states, with Germany and France as the core nations. In the second half of the last century, Europe's

---

[3] Yang, Jiechi (2011). The Transformation Choice and Development Prospects of G20 Members. *International studies*, Vol. 6, 50-60.

[4] Martinez-Diaz, L. 2011.*The G20 after Eight Years: How Effective a Vehicle for Developing Country Influence?* The Brookings Institution Global Economy and Development Working Paper no. 12.

support of the United States was the result of its political and military dependence on United States military strength to balance the threat of the Soviet Union. After the dissolution of the Soviet Union, European Union nations created the euro to compete with the dollar for the status of the world's reserve currency.

After the European debt crisis, France and Germany led the Euro area to call for the creation of a supranational financial regulatory system to limit excessive and speculative investments and capital flows from Wall Street and elsewhere. At the 2009 London summit, German Prime Minister Merkel once expressed that international financial crises are the result of un-moderated free market behavior. "…The world is currently situated at a watershed, we must learn lessons from this disaster, we cannot repeat a disaster like this, and we need to create a constitution for financial markets."[5] At the same time, most European Union member states took a position of cautious opposition to American economic stimulus plans. This was meant to prevent any more European Union member states from falling prey to speculation. Confronted by the rise of emerging economies, the European Union pushed forward the climate change issue and the establishment of trade carbon emission exchange systems in an attempt to restrict their industrial competitiveness. But it also attempted to bundle the euro and carbon exchange markets together to support the euro with enough capital to compete with the dollar as the world reserve currency. If Europe wants to raise the international status of the euro it can join with developing countries to limit dollar hegemony.

The third camp of developing countries and emerging economies has China, Russia, India and Brazil at its core. While the first two camps were mired in financial crisis, the status and role of large developing countries and emerging economies increased significantly as the overall power of developed countries dwindled within the international order. This third camp of countries became the backbone of strength promoting multilateral international structures. The industrial and natural resources of emerging economies are the external forces that the first two camps must rely on to fully recover from the financial crisis. It is also the political capital that developing countries must use to influence a new round of international rule-making. Under the leadership of the BRIC nations, the total share of quotas within the IMF belonging to developing nations has risen. They now also hold more voting rights in the World Bank. The larger goal of emerging economies is to cast off dollar hegemony. Many of the leading emerging G20 economies, including the four BRIC nations, have all expressed an appeal to promote reform in the international financial system.

---

[5] Xinhua Net (2009). German Chancellor Angela Merkel Reasserts Fostering Supervision of Financial Markets. Retrieved March 23, 2009, from http://news.163.com/09/0329/15/55J604VS000120GU.html

# Emerging countries' development space in the framework of the G20

The G20 is a platform for emerging economies to participate in international affairs at a standing commensurate to their abilities. Following the rise of emerging economies like China, India and Russia, the ability of the G7, the precursor to the G20, to influence international affairs became unstable. From the expansion of the G7 to G8 to the G8+5, from beginning to end emerging countries were not able to achieve equality in international affairs. The G7 and G8 are seen as the West's "Wealthy Nations Club." To join this elite group not only confers the ability "to play a role" in global governance, but also means a status change in the world. China has long expressed such a worry that joining the G8+5 will undo its status as a developing nation and force it to take on obligations not suitable to its current stage of development. Besides this, G8+5 type groups will not grant emerging countries equal status in any dialogs. In comparison, the G20 is a better platform for emerging economies to promote their national interests in international discourse.

As a leading representative of emerging economies, China has made three proposals to reform the international economic system. The first proposal centers on reforming the international monetary system. On the eve of the 2009 G20 London Summit, PBOC Governor Zhou Xiaochuan issued a cable promoting the creation of a reserve system that guarantees stable valuation, orderly supply and adjustable aggregates. This avoids the common defects experienced when a sovereign credit currency also serves as the international reserve currency.[6] This proposal directly addresses dollar hegemony and an international monetary system dependent on one sovereign currency as the international reserve. China's proposals were enthusiastically received by emerging economies that have suffered the burden of dollar hegemony. However, the response from the European Union has not been equally as warm.

The second proposal is to strengthen international regulation of finance. The root of the current global financial crisis is a severe lack of regulation. Capital movements lack necessary restrictions. The United States has consistently resisted any form of outside financial regulation because of the great benefit it stands to gain from an unregulated system. The European Union and emerging countries both strongly support strengthening international financial regulation as part of an effort to limit the harm caused by dollar hegemony and excessive capitalization.

The third proposal is reform of the international financial institutions. International financial institutions mainly refer to the IMF and the World Bank, which both have governance and discourse power skewed severely toward developed countries.

---

6  Zhou Xiaochuan (2009).Thoughts on Reforming International Monetary System. Retrieved March 23, 2009, from http://www.pbc.gov.cn/publish/hanglingdao/36/2010/20100914193900497315 048/20100914193900497315048_.html

Countries of the third camp support this proposal and believe the architecture of international governance should be reformed to align with changes in the real distribution of world power.

Since the 2008 financial crisis, each G20 member has taken part in financial reforms in some way to impose greater regulation on financial markets. However, the effects of global financial and monetary reforms are quite limited on the whole. The United States Dodd-Frank Act passed in 2010 does not amount to a substantive reform. This Act has only made banks bigger and seemingly much safer, but achieves no significant improvement to the regulation of derivatives and money market funds. The European Union is comparatively more active in financial reforms than the United States. Recently, the proposal of a single supervisory mechanism has already been approved. Yet there is still a long way to go before it is possible to realize G20 joint statement goals internationally because more than just regional efforts for reform are needed.

The current financial system is not in a periodic crisis, but a fundamental crisis dealing with profound problems in the economic and financial systems of the United States and Europe. It mainly reveals two problems. One is that the consumption driven economies of the United States and Western Europe supported by strong financial industries and weak real economies are difficult to sustain much longer. The other is that their financial systems are riddled with interlinked problems due to excessive financial innovation and loose financial supervision over the past few decades. These issues can't be solved with a single stroke. The economy and financial markets of the United States and Europe seem to have resumed functionality, but in fact their financial systems are no more different from that before the crisis. The risk of financial crisis remains.

Right now China and other emerging countries need a robust and stable international economic system oriented toward development and stability. The persistence of the international financial crisis underscores the inadequacy of traditional international coordination. It also exposed the defects within the international monetary and financial system. As a result, emerging countries' national interests are very hard to guarantee in the current environment, especially for those countries without a robust financial protection system against risk in international financial markets.

Emerging countries in the third camp should utilize the G20 as a sound platform to engage in global governance. They should stand side by side with each other and European Union second camp countries that share common views on specific issues and strategic developments. Within the G20 they can work to correct aspects of the world economy that endanger their interests in international financial markets and reform the world economic order toward a sound and healthy direction of development.

# G20's Future and China's Role in the G20

*Carlos Magariños*
**Chairman of Global Alliance of SMEs,**
**Former UNIDO Director General, Argentina**

## Abstract

As requested by the organizers of the forum the present report outlines some ideas on three topics: a) opinion on the G20; b) its future prospects, especially in the financial field; and c) the role of China in the group. The content of the paper will be presented at the International Think Tank Conference in Renmin University of China in late August, this year.

It will argue that the G20 represents a significant innovation as a mechanism of Global Governance for the 21st century, an opinion based on the relative success of the group's actions to coordinate economic measures to stabilize global macroeconomic imbalances, reform the international financial architecture and improve supervision of financial entities and activities. These actions have steered the world economy out of the worst financial crisis experienced in the last 8 decades.

The second section of the paper will consider the growing agenda of the G20 and its potential consequences for the G20's present activities and working mechanisms. Section III concludes with some considerations on the role of China in the G20 as a bridge between different countries' interests based on its recent experience of vibrant self-development over the last three decades.

## Section I: G20 Opinion

The emergence of the G20 at the dawn of the new century was a clever move towards crafting a new equilibrium in the balance of power at a global level. Its very existence is a sort of recognition that the limited boundaries of the G7 and G8 did not provide enough room at the end of the 20th century for the relevant actors whose opinions, actions and political will were then—and are ever more now—necessary to properly address the world's economic and social problems. Some analysts, especially at the moment of the G20's birth, consider it a mere enlargement of the G7 to secure broader consensus for initiatives in a changing world. These analysts even talk about the "G7ization" of the world through the bringing of the eleven new actors "within the framework of the Bretton Woods Institutions". In their view, the non-G7 members would remain just passive spectators destined to influence decisions only on the margin.

Others, later on, compared the G20 to a sort of "Board of Directors" of the world economy due to the powerful position of G20 countries within it, which together represent around 90% of the world's GDP, 80% of its trade, and two-thirds of the world's population.

During the heated discussions in the context of the ongoing United Nations reform process, some observers have connected the emergence of the G20 to the world stage with the proposed re-organization of the UN Economic and Social Security Council. Many analysts consider the G20 to be a mechanism to democratize top economic decisions on world affairs and to increase the importance of economic and social issues in world negotiations mirroring, in a way, the UN Security Council on matters related to peace and security. Whether those observers are right or not, the G20 represents a much needed breath of fresh air to the multilateral system and the way countries interact on international affairs.

Unlike the typical UN organizations, the G20 embodies a very interesting concept quite popular among players of the multilateral system at the end of the 20th century. While reforming the United Nations Industrial Development Organization (UNIDO) from 1998 onwards, I had the opportunity to explore the idea that nations can work together on important world issues beyond traditional multilateral country groupings (developed and developing, rich and poor, north and south) around sorts of "coalitions of the willing" that assume responsibilities to cooperate and lead the process of change.

The issues chosen by the G7 members in 1999 to launch "cooperation to lead the process for change" were quite ambitious, defining the G20 in its own words "as a new mechanism… to broaden the dialog on key economic and financial policy issues among systemically significant economies and to promote cooperation to achieve stable and sustainable world growth that benefits all."

The informal character of its deliberation was meant to facilitate dialog and stimulate open exchange of experiences among its members and to avoid "hard statements" on political positions. Two clear phases can be identified over the life cycle of the G20 divided by the financial crisis started in 2007and the decision in 2008 to upgrade the political might of the grouping by moving from a gathering of finance ministers to full-fledged meetings at the level of Heads of State and Government.

The central focus of the first G20 meetings was to coordinate policy responses to the crisis, ensuring financial stability through the coordination and adoption of proactive economic measures to enable the world economy to return to the path of growth and employment generation. In twenty four months between November 2008 and November 2010 (running from the first meeting of G20 Leaders in Washington to its fifth meeting in Toronto), the Heads of State and Government of the G20 met five times, an average of around one meeting every four months and three weeks. This series of meetings marked the transformation of the G20 from a deliberative body into a decision-making forum, which was central to designing the way out from the worst financial crisis to hit the world in almost a century.

More recently, the G20 Leader's Summits have included a number of innovations that have brought business and civil society to the fore. Beginning in June 2010 in Toronto, the G20 summits have included Business Summits called "B20" where the representatives of the major industrial and trade unions of the G20 countries gather to consider global economic challenges and propose ideas and measures at the Heads of State and Government formal gatherings. Business is celebrating its fifth formal meeting at the Russian Summit.

Last year in Los Cabos, México academia gathered at a Think Tank Forum that continued its activities in Russia last December. Civil society summits of G20 countries (C20, first held in Russia last month) also started to work towards preparing and forwarding recommendations to the Leaders meetings.

These processes involving business, academia and civil society organizations (including Youth and Non G20 Member States called Extended Dialog under the Mexican Presidency) are providing a source of much needed legitimacy and transparency to the G20 decision-making process. Gathering together, rather than lobbying individual governments in isolation, also provides an opportunity for trade union leaders, NGOs and active members of civil society to rise to the challenge of addressing global problems in a participatory fashion.

Although it is far from perfect, the whole process can be regarded as a reasonable innovation in overcoming the limitations of the architectural design of multilateral institutions that anachronistically reflect the balance of power of the 20th century world. Such power relations and economic patterns don't exist anymore and the G20 tries to fill the gap in a dynamic fashion. No doubt, for all its shortcomings, the G20 remains the most significant innovation in Global Governance for the 21st Century.

## Section II: The Future Prospects of the G20

With the increase in globalization, trade and financial flows have become more complex as a result of either financial innovations or new technological developments. In the context of global macroeconomic imbalances, the capacity of one country—or a concentrated group of countries—to influence global economic performance on their own, however great it may be, is fading away towards a broader group of leaders who are better suited to provide certainty and stability to the modern world economy.

This process was well understood by the first promoters of the G20 in the wake of the crisis in the late 1990s, which included the devaluation of the Thai and Brazilian currencies and the Russian default, among other woes. These earlier promoters were probably wondering how to improve global governance without creating a world government. The financial crisis starting in 2007–2008 proved very clearly the point already on the table at the birth of the G20: an increasingly integrated world economy requires the provision of certain global public goods.

In this particular case, the provision of global financial stability—or the lack of it—dramatically showcased the critical importance of having effective decision-making multilateral mechanisms to supply much-needed collective leadership and consensus-building across traditional multilateral divides (of the sort mentioned before, advanced vs. emerging; north vs. south, etc.). It seems that there is no other proper way available in the short term to secure those critically important global public goods for managing globalization.

There is considerable literature on the provision of global public goods and, in particular, on the way they can be provided, the characteristics of the international architecture to ensure efficiency and their contributions to development and prosperity.

At the national level, the work to provide public goods is obviously done by domestic governments. At the international level, however, the provision of public goods relies on a patchwork of institutions created more than half century ago. Under the existing multilateral financial architecture, it is necessary to secure a new power equilibrium to improve the coordination process for policy implementation and expand the mandates of institutions charged with supervision and lending to renew and reinforce their responsibilities.

Working as a Board of Directors—or a "Council of Governors" as some call it—for the global economy, G20 countries can claim some reasonable success in building consensus around a common set of actions to bring the international financial crisis under control, preventing further damage and minimizing its social costs. The G20 succeeded in getting emerging economies more engaged in and committed to redressing problems at the multilateral level, enabling them to play a constructive and important role when differences between the United States and Europe threaten to cause global gridlock. The G20 also provided a platform to stimulate consideration for a renewed process of multilateral cooperation, making room for bringing regional agreements into multilateral negotiations.

In the short term, the G20 must maintain coordination mechanisms and direct its individual and collective efforts to address a three-pronged economic situation: 1) deceleration of the emerging market economies; 2) a deeper than expected EU recession; and 3) a milder than forecasted economic recovery in the US. Within this context, advanced economies will be obliged to sustain a macroeconomic environment that supports industrial activity while devising, simultaneously, appropriate measures to ensure debt sustainability. In parallel, those countries will need to stabilize companies' balance sheets and restore credit channels. Although vulnerability risks vary across emerging markets and developing economies according to their different economic stages, these developing countries will have to balance emphasis on reinvigorating economic activity with policies to contain capital outflows, probably through the implementation of structural reforms and prudent macroeconomic policies.

Both groups of countries—advanced and emerging economies—are facing increased volatility in financial markets. If the forecasts for reduced volatility in the coming months (due to monetary stabilization in the US) do not materialize or take longer than expected, emerging economies should be ready to handle further investment portfolio shifts through macroeconomic policies-essentially further monetary easing—although weaker growth, the price effects of monetary depreciation and low real rates will, most probably, reduce the room for that. In the medium to long term the G20 will have to continue working towards redressing structural macroeconomic imbalances in the world economy and improving the multilateral financial architecture in order to improve global growth prospects and create sustainable employment. The "Los Cabos Growth and Jobs Action Plan" seems to fully reflect those intentions. Such a collection of measures reaffirms, and even deepens, the commitments already assumed by the Group at its meeting in Cannes.

The documents outlining the objectives and focus of the 2013 Russian chairmanship reaffirm those intentions, clustering the group's growth goals around three main pillars: quality jobs and investment; trust and transparency; and effective regulation. They further signal eight areas of primary focus building on (its predecessor's) G20 agenda: a) Framework for strong, sustainable and balanced growth; b) Jobs and employment; c) International financial architecture reform; d) Strengthening financial regulation; e) Energy sustainability; f) Development for all; g) Enhancing multilateral trade and h) Fighting corruption.

It is interesting to recall that the Mexican Presidency outlined just 5 areas, including Food Security. Items "a", "c", and "d" form the core of the G20's mandate and item "f" was already present as a priority in previous meetings.

The Russian proposed agenda items-in growing number-are showing Botha strong commitment to work on short-term decision-making to consolidate the positive results achieved so far to emerge from the crisis as well as degree of collective ambition (mixed with responsibility) to translate good interaction into an effective multilateral tool for strategic planning to address the world's most substantive challenges in areas like food security (present during Mexican Presidency), energy security, development for all, trade and corruption.

It's very interesting to note the role that the G20 is gradually taking, for example, at the formulation process for the Post-2015 Development Agenda. 2015 is the year that the international community will have to set up new global targets for development aid and global cooperation for social and economic development. The G20's approach seems active, articulate and committed towards concrete contributions in the agenda setting process, facilitating consensus building and promoting constructive interaction. It shows a new dynamic for multilateral interaction when compared with the formulation process of the Millennium Development Goals currently in place, at which time the G20 did not even exist.

This year in Moscow, the G20 Ministers of Labor met for the first time, adding an important new dimension for the Group's attention to job creation. The Russian presidency also gave considerable room and visibility to Energy Sustainability (as could have been expected duet its own vision on the subject) which became a central topic for its term. It seems evident that the G20 agenda is getting larger and deeper with the aim of strengthening the mandate for its members, built on the Group's earlier success in steering the course of the international financial crisis towards safer and calmer terrain.

In a way, such an attitude could well be recognition that systemic crisis needs holistic solutions looking beyond the proximate causes and acting on structural, long-term issues.

At the same time, it poses a challenge to the G20 working mechanisms. Those routines and mechanisms seemed to work reasonably well to confront concrete and immediate problems such as those faced at peak of the crisis; it remains to be seen how well they would do for strategic planning to address longer term challenges, such as those posed by food or energy security, the environment or development for all.

Given the vacuum in the multilateral framework for addressing these issues, one could find it reasonable for the G20 to fulfil this role. The real challenge, however, would be to keep the Group's focus and dynamism and avoid the temptation to address all the problems at the same time. It is important for the G20 to discern clearly where there is room and consensus for collective action that is likely to produce significant results within a reasonable period of time and where it is necessary to refrain from overlapping existing multilateral mechanisms without failing its responsibility to act boldly and decisively to ensure growth and prosperity.

It is useful to recall that the Group's effectiveness can be regarded as the result of a bottom-up approach on very specific and relatively immediate problems. The Leaders' meetings started as a means of coordinating the many individual policies adopted by different members to address the financial crisis and its main purpose was to adopt common positions on issues that were unsolvable by any single country.

It would be difficult to anticipate how well the Group's dynamics would adapt to topics that differ in nature, urgency and complexity from those that gave birth to the G20'smandate in the second phase of its life from 2008 onwards, through the Heads of State and Governments Summits, and how other non-members would react to the G20 addressing these topics.

In other words, it would be necessary to assess how and when the G20 would transition from decision-making on crisis-related issues to strategic planning on substantive long-term challenges. In such context, the key question is whether the G20 will become the central pillar of an effective multilateral system (and its design architect) to strengthen the supply of Global Public Goods or if it would attempt to replace the multilateral system altogether (with itself). Was the latter the attitude they were forced to assume during the peak of the financial crisis?

## Section III: China's role in the G20

China has chosen to be a responsible contributor to global governance and a positive economic force to pull the world economy out of its crisis. While having decided to position China as a responsible leader state that contributes to global solutions, China's leadership, however, maintains that this role should be played without losing China's status as a developing country. In a way, China's dual role on the world stage and its participation in the G20 mirrors its longhand lengthy negotiations to accede to the WTO. Such a gigantic trade partner entered the stage defending its position as a developing nation.

China's role in the G20 then seems to be two-fold: a) that of an engine of growth and a stabilizer for the world economy, and b) a model and a partner for emerging economies and developing nations to defend the policy space needed for nurturing development processes, strengthening social assets and living conditions. China thus bridges the interests and ambitions of different countries, including advanced ones.

Typically, once a country achieves a leadership position in the international arena (not to mention rising to hegemonic status), it tends to resist any movement towards strengthening multilateral institutions or mechanisms. China's singular situation of being both a leading economy and a developing nation at the same time could provide the first opportunity to build a stronger multilateral system without the privileges (like veto powers or special majorities) usually reserved for the "winners" of any international order.

For such an outcome to materialize, China's partners would also have to play a constructive role. Many analysts, still trapped in bipolar ways of thinking, predict the polarization of power between China and US in the years ahead. Conceding that the US-China relationship is already complex and the challenges will only grow over the next years, and that history has demonstrated natural rivalry between emerging and dominant powers, such scenario shouldn´t be the single way to see the relationship between these two nations.

China's peaceful rise and the determination of its leadership to stay focused on its many social challenges means that other major international players must refrain from using China alone to counterbalance US influence and political might. This is a natural temptation, but must be resisted for the sake of building a stronger multilateral system that is able to secure the provision of some essential global public goods for development and progress.

As mentioned, how well the G20 completes its transition from decision making to strategic planning, and whether it will strike the right cords to build an effective global governance system for the 21st century, all depends very much on a basic degree of harmony in the interactions between China and the US, but also on the trust and confidence of China's partners in China's exceptional condition as a leading power while remaining solidly in the realm of emerging countries.

## References

[1] The Group of Twenty: A history. Produced by G20. 2008.
[2] From Toronto to Saint Petersburg: Assessing G20-B20 Engagement Effectiveness.
[3] Draft Report. G20-B20 Dialog Efficiency Task Force. International Organizations Research Institute (IORI) Higher School of Economics. National Research Institute and Munk School of Global Affairs, University of Toronto G20 Research Group. June 2013.
[4] Achievements of the G20 Mexican Presidency. Draft Report. Mexican Ministry of Foreign Affairs. January 2013.
[5] The Russian Presidency of the G20: Outline. December 2012.
[6] G2012. Los Cabos, México. Leader's Declaration. December 2012.
[7] Global Trends 2030: Alternative Worlds. US National Intelligence Council. December 2012.
[8] The Role of Emerging Countries in the G20: Agenda Setters, Veto Player or Spectator? Katharina Gnath and Claudia Schmucker. Bruges Regional Integration and Global Governance Papers. United Nations University and College of Europe. February 2011.
[9] Saving Multilateralism. Renovating the House of Global Governance for the 21st Century. Jennifer Hillman. The German Marshal Fund of the United States. 2010.
[10] G2 in G20: China, the United States and the World after the Global Financial Crisis. Geoffrey Garret. University of Sydney. 2010.
[11] Economic Development and UN Reform. Towards a Common Agenda for Action.A Proposal in the Context of the Millennium Development Goals. Carlos Magariños. United Nations Industrial Development Organization (UNIDO) 2005.
[12] China in the WTO. The Birth of a New Catching up Strategy. Carlos Magariños, Long Yongtu and Francisco Sercovich. Palgrave Macmillian. 2003.

# G20 Governance for the Future: Performance, Prospects, Possibilities and China's Role

*John Kirton*
**Co-Director, G8 & G20 Research Group, University of Toronto, Canada**

Paper Prepared for a conference on "Great Finance, Great Co-operation, Great Governance," of the "First G20 Think Tank Forum in China," Chongyang Institute for Financial Studies (RDCY) at Renmin University of China (RUC), Shangri-La Hotel, 29 Zizhuyuan Road, Beijing, China, August 21–22, 2013.

## Introduction

On November 14–15, 2008, the leaders of the world's 19 systemically significant countries and the European Union (EU) assembled in Washington, D.C. for the first "G20 Leaders Summit on Financial Markets and the World Economy." They did so to cope with the great global financial crisis that had erupted in the US on September 15th that year. US President George W. Bush had decided to respond to the crisis through a summit of the established G20 that had been working at the ministerial level since 1999. All G20 leaders, led by China's Hu Jintao, readily accepted the invitation, and the G20 summit was born. Five years later, by the time of its seventh summit in June 2012, the G20 had provided an effective response to the global finance shocks generated by a globalized, 21st-century world. It did so by acting as a powerful leaders-level group of diverse equals from the advanced and emerging worlds and from a declining Europe and a rising Asia too. The G20 was not merely a concert of major powers based on capability but a group of systemically important countries based on connectivity as well. It rapidly expanded its role, agenda, and institutionalization, moving from a crisis response committee to a crisis prevention and steering committee for finance and economics, social and development policy and political security issues such as terrorism as well.

## G20 Performance

Since its start in 1999 and after its upgrade to the leaders' level in 2008, judgements about the course, causes and consequences of G20 governance have been the subject of a vigorous debate (Kirton 2013a). The first school sees the G20 as redundant in the long term, because it is too large and diverse in its membership, too informal in its institutionalization, or has inspired the older Bretton Woods, United Nations (UN) and Group of Seven (G7) or Group of Eight (G8) bodies to revive. The second school rejects the G20's claim to be the primary centre of global economic governance, due to the superior power or performance of the established, hard-law, multilateral bodies, the dominance of the old G7 within the new G20, or the G20's lack of legitimacy as a small, self-selected body without clear membership criteria, rules of governance, authorization from anyone else or developing country members, or benefits for G8 members. The third school sees the G20 reinforcing the G8 and similar groups, delivering its two key tasks of providing financial stability and making globalization work for all, by adding the emerging country buy-in that the G8 lacked. The fourth school sees replacement by the G20 of the G7, G8 and G7 in practice the Permanent Five members of the UN Security Council.

The fifth, currently dominant school sees a reduction in the G20 summit performance after its initial, crisis-inspired high performance in 2008–2009. Some see only selective decline, with the difficulty and delay in delivery of key G20 decisions, notably the 2010 summit promises on fiscal consolidation and banking capital. Others note a decline in macroeconomic policy performance, in contrast to the expansive success on an even more challenging agenda in financial regulation for developed countries.

However a more comprehensive, systematic examination shows that the G20 has emerged as a global governance hub whose performance has grown across a widening, more demanding, more domestically intrusive agenda and across all the governance functions that such international institutions have. Since 1999 the G20 has grown to govern a broadening agenda, including some core security subjects such as terrorist finance, corruption and good governance. Especially with the advent of G20 summitry in 2008, the G20 has moved from its initial focus on domestic political management, deliberation and direction setting into decision making, delivery and the development of global governance within and beyond the G20 (Appendix A). After its initial crisis-response success in 2008–2009, it has successfully moved to effective crisis prevention, by stopping the continuing Euro-crisis from going global, agreeing on International Monetary Fund (IMF) and banking regulatory reform, preventing trade protectionism from spiraling into a trade war of a 1930s sort, and advancing development, the environment and climate change protection, energy and food security, and corruption control. Yet with rising inequality within most G20 members, it is still struggling to make globalization work for all.

The first G20 summit set principled directions, initiated a process to apply them and took 95 concrete decisions, including holding another summit very soon. The second summit, hosted by the United Kingdom's Gordon Brown in London on April 1–2, 2009, produced major spending stimulus. The third G20 summit, hosted and chaired by the newly elected US President Barack Obama in Pittsburgh on September 24–25, 2009, proclaimed that the G20 would henceforth be the permanent premier forum for its members' international economic cooperation. The fourth G20 summit, chaired by Canadian Prime Minister Stephen Harper in Toronto on June 26–27, 2010, produced a hard-won agreement to exit from the exceptional fiscal stimulus over the medium term.

The fifth summit, hosted by Korean President Lee Myung-bak in Seoul on November 11–12, 2010, saw hosting move from the established G8 Atlantic countries to the emerging, non-G8 Asian-Pacific countries, albeit remaining among members with democratic governments. This trend toward balance was reinforced by the sixth summit, hosted by French President Nicolas Sarkozy in Cannes on November 3–4, 2011, the seventh by Mexican President Felipe Calderón in Los Cabos on June 18–19, 2012, and preparations for the eighth, to be hosted by Russian President Vladimir Putin in St. Petersburg on September 5–6, 2013. The eruption of the European financial crisis in early 2010, sparked by the spiraling sovereign debt of Greece and threatening to spread beyond Europe to become the third global financial crisis in 13 years, underscored the need for permanent G20 summit governance.

## G20 Prospects and Possibilities in Economics and Finance

Projecting the future prospects for the G20 requires a well-developed, empirically tested causal model that specifies why the G20 has performed well in the past and why it is likely to do so in the future if similar conditions prevail. This is provided by the model of systemic hub governance (Kirton 2013a), which shows that the G20's effective and expanding performance is due to proliferating shocks that exposed the equalizing new vulnerary abilities of all countries, the failure of the older international institutions to cope, the rising capabilities and increasing openness of most members, the domestic political cohesion that participants brought, and their rational attachment to a still compact G20 club at the hub of a global governance network in the world.

Summit success has been driven in the first instance by shocks, initially in the financial and economic domain from 1997 to 2001, again with the much larger shocking 2007–2010, and then in smaller but steady form from Greece in January 2010 through to Cyprus in March 2013. Success in expanding the agenda has also been spurred by shocks in other fields, notably from terrorism since 9/11 in 2001 and from energy, the environment, food and natural disasters since 2007. These shocks grew in scale, rate of spread and contagiousness, extending with destructive impact to sectors and societies of still legally sovereign states. The geographic sources of these shocks have changed, from an emerging Asia in 1997–1999, to a once hegemonic but now highly vulnerable US in 2008, to Europe in 2010. These shocks show that globalization has created, materially and socially, a complex, adaptive global system characterized by compounding interconnectedness, complexity and uncertainty.

In the face of such shocks that exposed and equalized the vulnerability of the major powers, the formal multilateral organizations that America and its Atlantic allies have constructed since the 1940s and controlled to this day could not cope on their own. Nor could the more select G7/8-centreed and often informal plurilateral institutions that had arisen since 1975. In the field of finance, the IMF failed to eliminate its new G20 competitor between 1999 and 2008. The IMF depended on the G20 to reform the "voice and vote" system at IMF meetings in China in 2005 and in Korea in 2010, to raise resources for the IMF in London in 2009 and Los Cabos in 2012, and to create a new institution for financial stability with the birth of the Financial Stability Board (FSB) in London in 2009.

Unlike its many international institutional competitors, the G20 alone includes as full, equal members countries that increasingly possess the collectively predominant and internally equal capabilities required to respond to shocks. At the G20's third ministerial meeting in Ottawa on November 16–17, 2001, America, recently attacked on September 11th, depended on Saudi Arabia, Indonesia and Turkey to explain how informal Islamic finance worked and thus how terrorist finance could be controlled. At the summits, the US was similarly dependent on others, intellectually and materially, to respond to the financial crisis that had importantly been born in the US.

G20 members since 1997 have increasingly, if unevenly, become more economically, socially and politically open polities, as a way to maintain their desired domestic stability in globalizing age. The financial and macroeconomic success of the London summit was driven by the vivid memory of what economic depression in the 1930s had bred in Europe, above all in Germany at its core. All members share a profound aversion to terrorism, as seen in 2001, and increasingly to corruption, as another assault on their domestic sovereignty and rule of law.

The G20 further benefited from the domestic political control, capital, continuity and competence of its participants. At the summit level, continuity has been led by China's Hu Jintao and India's Manmohan Singh from the BRICS, Germany's Angela Merkel, Canada's Stephen Harper and the EU's Jose Manuel Barosso from the G8, and Mexico's Felipe Calderon, Turkey's Recep Tayyip Erdogan, Indonesia's Susilo Bambang Yudhoyono, and Argentina's Cristina Kirchner from beyond. These nine leaders, balanced institutionally, geographically, and economically, and constituting almost half of the G20 membership, have been to all seven summits thus far.

Above all, the G20 has become a club with the unchanging country membership and constricted participation necessary to reduce transaction costs, foster learning and promote socialization among the established and emerging country members, and confer on them the status, identification and new conceptions of systemic interests that came with membership in a new top-tier club. This has been reinforced by the increasing intensity of interaction at the leader, minister, and official levels, after the autumn of 2008. The G20 also became the hub of a growing global network in which combinations of its established and emerging country members connect in overlapping combinations in many other relevant plurilateral institutions of global relevance that joined the G20 at the centre with the rest of the world all around. It was the non-

G20 members of the Commonwealth that helped get climate change on the G20 agenda at the London Summit, where the five Commonwealth members (UK, India, Canada, Australia, and South Africa) were members and host.

Looking ahead, all of these causes are likely to remain in force. Increasing multidimensional vulnerability and multilateral organizational failure will continue to expand the G20 agenda. Emerging country members will continue to grow more rapidly than the G8 ones, in both GDP and currency values. Openness in most G20 countries is not likely to reverse and will increase, in the medium if not the short term. A more experienced Barak Obama and returning Kevin Rudd could help smooth the arrival of several new leaders for the eighth summit, in Deauville in May 2011. Beyond Singh and Harper, however, few can claim professional competence in the field of economics or finance. G20 summits have recently regained a perfect attendance record. Finally, even with the advent of the leaders' level BRICS in 2009, and a revived G8 again governing economics and finance, no other rival plurilateral summit institution has arisen to challenge the G20 as a global governance hub. In short, to meet the growing demand for global governance, there is nowhere else to go.

To serve even more effectively as a global steering group for the bigger, broader challenges that the G20 alone can solve, the future G20 will likely evolve in several ways. These can be done more quickly and effectively, in both the issue-management and institutional development realms, through proactive reforms in the following ways.

In its issue management, three items stand out. The first concerns the G20's core mission of producing financial stability. The initial task is to complete the financial crisis prevention job in Europe and to prevent another crisis erupting in the fiscally challenged and fragile United States, in second-ranked China and in third-ranked Japan and in member countries beyond. The crisis prevention task will remain central to the G20's work, given the core characteristics of an intensely, interconnected world. The G20 will therefore need to move more quickly and ambitiously to develop and act on the analytic models that captures how the global economy and financial system in this new age, especially in the critical component of the emerging countries that has robustly arrived within the global top ten.

The second issue concerns fiscal consolidation. The task is to more effectively control soaring fiscal deficits driven by rising health care as well as pension costs. Fiscal consolidation will remain central to the G20's work, and expand as member countries public sector debts, at all levels of government, steadily rise. Pensions can be and are easily addressed by adjusting the age when payments and entitlements start. Health care costs are much more difficult. The G20 can help enhance action on health promotion, starting with preventing and controlling the major non-communicable diseases of cardiovascular and chronic respiratory diseases, diabetes and cancer. These are also the top killers of human life in most G20 countries, and raise employers' costs and workers' productivity as well.

The third task concerns financial regulation, at a time when the demand for tax revenues, tax fairness and tax transparency is on the rise. This involves completing a single, high-quality global set of accounting standards for all major firms and governments to use in a globalized economy. It also could involve pioneering a multilateral agreement on investment, to replace the kaleidoscope of bilateral arrangements and the limited multilateral ones.

The fourth task concerns the G20's second core mission of making globalization work for all. Here the task is to foster strong, sustainable and balanced growth by reducing the economic inequality that is increasing almost everywhere. There is now firm evidence from the IMF that economic equality is a new source of such growth. It can be secured by generating better employment and education especially for the young. It includes giving greater attention to gender equality and social policy as a whole.

In the realm of reforming the summit process, three items stand out. The first is increasing the supply of G20 summit governance to meet the growing demand. TheG20 leaders will and should meet more often, and for longer than the 24 hours they will come together after over a year when they again assemble on September 5–6, 2013. G20 governance works, but only when its leaders show up for work. They need to put in more time to ensure delivery of the key decisions that they have made but remain undone. They should meet as often to do crisis prevention as they did to do crises response from 2008 to 2010. Resuming to two summits a year would also enable more members to share the responsibilities and rights of hosting and reduce friction about who will host after Australia in 2014 and Turkey in 2015 (Ng 2013).

The second item is having more ministerial meetings than just those for finance and more civil society institutions to work with them and the leaders. G20 trade ministers will need to meet more often, just as they do in the BRICS, to strengthen the anti-protectionist pledge and advance an offensive liberalization agenda separate from the overdue, dead-locked Doha development agenda. There could also be good grounds for officials from the judiciary, law enforcement and other economically-relevant regulatory parts of G20 governments to meet.

The third item is improving accountability, on which both the effectiveness and legitimacy of the G20 ultimately depend. Many of the G20's major achievements—fiscal consolidation, Basel 3 financial regulation, reform of international financial institutions, and phase-out of fossil fuel subsidies—are still waiting for all members to convincingly comply with the commitments they have already made. G20 leaders now know they need more than the polite report cards on their performance issued at their request by some of the international institutions they control and fund by themselves. Many recognize the value of independent compliance assessments produced, with input from many stakeholders, by professionals with no immediate stake in the result.

The fourth step is to foster the emergence of an Academic 20 (A20) to fulfil the leaders' promise at Seoul to work more closely with the academic community. In addition to conducting independent accountability assessments, such an A20 could, in ways similar to the Intergovernmental Panel for Climate Change, come to research-based, scientific consensus on key subjects such as what level of debt burden a country can stand under different conditions before its strong sustainable and balanced growth and its income equality are harmed.

## China's Role in the G20

Such developments and advances will depend increasingly on the choices of China's new leaders. China's role in G20 governance thus far has been the subject of considerable debate. The first school sees China as a passive, self-interested status seeker, embracing its equal status in the G20 over its second class status in the G8 but using its G20 position to protect its immediate, narrow interests, taking no initiatives and free-riding on the contributions other members made in providing global public goods and shaping global governance as a whole (Kirton 2012). A second school sees China as the leader of the increasingly powerful emerging country, non-G8 caucus within the G20 or just the BRICS, aligning with them in a fixed coalition to challenge the established countries and their existing global order. A third school argues that China, along with a declining US, does or should constitute a new "G2" that would deliver better global governance than the G20 did or could (Spence 2013). A fourth school, dominant in China, sees China as an active and cooperative reformer in G20 summitry due to its elite epistemic economic consensus at home. In the narrow "reluctant cooperator" variant, Zhang Bin and Wu Ping (2011) believe that "because of its privileged position, the US cannot be expected truly to fulfil the responsibility for correcting global economic imbalances. China should, therefore, participate actively in the G20 dialog, and work with other members with common concerns to promote the reform of international governance mechanisms" (Wang 2012: 571). Similarly Z. Pan (2011) argues that although China is the second largest economy it is still only 40% of the US economy and that all G20 members should thus contribute to eliminating imbalances according to their own conditions.

Zhang Boli (2009) feels China's priority should be raising the representation and voting power of developing countries in the IMF and World Bank and enhancing early warning and surveillance in these organizations. In the expansive "cooperate first with all" variant, Yong Wang (2012: 580) argues:

> "Chinese leaders have urged joining hands to combat the global financial crisis and revive the growth of the global economy by strengthening multilateral collaboration forums such as the G20, and they believe that the momentum of economic globalization must be maintained. As Chinese leaders promised at each G20 summit, the Chinese government actively cooperates with other major economies to stimulate the recovery of the global economy and do its best to contribute to the

objectives of global economic rebalancing by carrying forward the structural adjustments of the Chinese economy."

This evidence, however, suggests more ambitiously that China has been an essential, increasingly active, expansive and effective global leader in G20 governance since the start, steadily moving to more robust leadership roles (Kirton 2013b). A fast growing China has been a constant producer rather than consumer of global financial and economic security through three financial crises, Asia in 1997, America in 2008 and Europe in 2010, along with its Asian colleagues of economically stagnant Japan, India, and Australia.

China has been a voter, defensively protecting its own specific domestic preferences, such as tax havens at the London Summit in 2009, and exchange rates, imbalances, trade protectionism and climate change throughout. It has been an accommodating adjuster, increasingly accepting the preferences of the US and other partners to have the Framework and its Mutual Assessment Process (MAP) advance in promising ways. Under its new leadership it is clearly transitioning from export-led growth to enhanced domestic demand through structural reform, just as its major G20 partners have long asked. In 2013 it has also allowed its exchange rate to rise against the US dollar, even as most other partners have seen theirs drop. It has increasingly been a reliable complier, implementing the priority commitments that successive summits have made. Over the first six summits, China's compliance performance stood at 0.35 compared to a G20 average of 0.40. Yet for the Washington Summit its score was 0.25 compared to the G20's 0.66, and for the crisis-consumed London Summit it had a score of -0.17 compared to the G20's +0.17. This score then rose for the Pittsburgh Summit to 0.36 to surpass the G20's 0.31 and did so again for the Toronto Summit with 0.50 compared to the G20's 0.37. For the Seoul Summit it was 0.30 compared to the G20's 0.37. For Cannes in November 2011 it reached a new high of 0.53, almost identical to the G20's new high of 0.54 (Appendix B). China's compliance has been high in macroeconomics (.63) and financial regulation (.50) (Appendix C). But it has also been high in climate change (.80) and energy (.56), areas where a broader and growing set of vulnerabilities rise.

China has been a G20 institution builder. China's agreement was necessary to create the group in 1999, to elevate it to the leaders' level in 2008, and to make it the primary forum for international economic cooperation among its members in 2009 and beyond. It has been a global governance institutional reformer. The ministerial meeting China hosted in 2005 led to the first agreement on IMF voice and vote reform. Its accommodation with its BRICS partners led to the agreement on the second stage of IMF reform at the Seoul Summit in 2010. It has been a systemic financial and macroeconomic supporter. It provided its share of critical public goods in fiscal and monetary stimulus since the Washington Summit, intellectually initiated the increase of Special Drawing Rights (SDR) at the London Summit, and initiated a new IMF firewall fund at Los Cabos. In the latter two cases, China did so even before the advanced countries promised or delivered China's appropriately enhanced place at the IMF.

Throughout, China has combined flexible issue-specific coalitions with both advanced and emerging countries to pursue and secure its multifaceted interests, while skillfully adjusting to the preferences of others to achieve larger global growth, stability and other goals (Schrim 2013).

In the coming years, China's evolving G20 leadership is likely to increase. On the demand and supply side respectively, its vulnerabilities and economic capabilities are likely to grow faster than those of any other ranking member of the G20. It will be increasingly called up to respond and deliver leadership within the G20. It should find it in its own interests to do so, to expand the economic, financial and institutional agenda for the future G20.

## References and Bibliography

[1] Kirton, John (2012a), *G20 Governance for a Globalizing World* (Farnham, Ashgate).
[2] Kirton, John (2013b), "Prospects for the BRICS and G20 Summits through China's Contribution," *Peoplebution*, May 2.
[3] Kirton, John (2007), "Strengthening Global Governance: The G8, China, the HeiligendammProcess and 2010, " paper prepared for delivery at SHISU, Shanghai University of Financeand Economics, Soochow University, Fudan University, Shanghai, China, December 17-20,2007. Version of December 13, 2007.
[4] Ng, Teddy (2013), "China wants to chair G20 talks, Xi tells Holland, " *South China MorningPost*, May 7.
[5] Pan, Z. (2011), "China's participation in quantifying the global economic rebalancing: a feasibility analysis, " *Guoji Maoyi (International Trade)* 5.
[6] Schrim, Stefan (2012), "Global Politics are Domestic Politics: A Societal Approach to Divergence in the G20, " *Review of International Studies* (July): 1-22.
[7] Spence, Michael (2013), "The Sino-America decade, " *Japan Times May* 29.
[8] Wang, Yong (2012) "Seeking a balanced approach on the global economic rebalancing: China's answers to international policy co-operation, " *Oxford Review of Economic Policy* 23 (3): 569-586.
[9] Yongding, Yu (2011), "China comes to Cannes with an open mind, " in John Kirton and Madeline Koch, eds. G20: The Cannes Summit: *A New Way Forward*, (Newsdesk: London), pp. 60-61.
[10] Yongding, Yu (2005), "China's Evolving Global View," in John English, Ramesh Thakurand Andrew F. Cooper, eds. *Reforming from the Top: A leaders from the To*(United NationsUniversity Press: Tokyo), pp. 187-200.
[11] Xu, Ting (2011), "A Low Carbon Economy; The Focus for China's 12th Five Year Plan, " in John Kirton and Madeline Koch, eds. G20: *The Cannes Summit: A new Way Forward*, (Newsdesk: London), pp. 213-214.

[12] Zhang, Bin and P. Wu (2011), "Analysis of progress of the global economic rebalancing,"*DuiwaiJingmaoShiwu (Practice in Foreign Economic Relations and Trade)* 9.
[13] Zhang Boli (2009), "Economic globalization, financial crises and international cooperation and coordination" *Qiushi Journal (Journal of Seeking Truth)* November.
[14] Zhou, X. (2009), "Reform of international monetary system" http://www.pbc.gov.cn/English/detail. asp?col_6500&ID_178, 23 March.
[15] Zhu, Jeijin (2008), "China's Cautious Embrace of the G8 in 2008" unpublished paper.

## Appendix A  G20 Summit Performance

| | Domestic Political Management | | | Deliberation | | | Direction Setting | | | Decision Making | Delivery | Development of Global Governance | | | | |
|---|---|---|---|---|---|---|---|---|---|---|---|---|---|---|---|---|
| | | | | | | | | | | | | Internal | | External | |
| | Attendance | # compliments | % members complimented | # days | # documents | # words | Pol Openess | Rights | Total | # commitments | Compliance | # references | Spread | # references | Spread |
| 2008 Washington | 100% | 0 | 0% | 2 | 2 | 3567 | 10 | 2 | 12 | 95 | 0.53 | 0 | 0 | 40 | 11 |
| 2009 London | 100% | 1 | 5% | 2 | 3 | 6155 | 9 | 0 | 9 | 88 | 0.42 | 12 | 4 | 116 | 27 |
| 2009 Pittsburgh | 100% | 0 | 0% | 2 | 2 | 9257 | 28 | 1 | 29 | 128 | 0.28 | 47 | 4 | 117 | 26 |
| 2010 Toronto | 90% | 7 | 15% | 2 | 5 | 11078 | 11 | 1 | 12 | 61 | 0.28 | 71 | 4 | 171 | 27 |
| 2010 Seoul | 95% | 3 | 15% | 2 | 5 | 15776 | 18 | 4 | 22 | 153 | 0.5 | 99 | 4 | 237 | 31 |
| 2011 Cannes | 95% | 11 | 35% | 2 | 3 | 14107 | 22 | 0 | 22 | 282 | 0.54 | 59 | 4 | 251 | 29 |
| 2012 Los Cabos | 95% | 6 | 15% | 2 | 2 | 12682 | 31 | 3 | 34 | 180 | 0.47 | 65 | 4 | 143 | 22 |
| Total | N/A | 28 | N/A | 14 | 22 | 72622 | 129 | 11 | 140 | 987 | N/A | 353 | 28 | 1075 | 173 |
| Average | 96.42% | 4 | 12.14% | 2 | 3.14 | 10375 | 18.43 | 1.57 | 20 | 141 | 0.43 | 50.43 | 4 | 153.57 | 24.71 |

Notes:

N/A=Not Applicable

a. Domestic Political Management: 100% attendance includes all G20 members and at least one representative from the European Union, excludes those invited on a year-to-year basis. Number of compliments includes all explicit references by name to the full members that specifically express the gratitude of the institution to that member. The % of members complimented indicates how many of the 20 members received compliments in the official documents.

b. Direction Setting: the number of statements of fact, causation and rectitude relating directly to open democracy and individual liberty.

c. Decision Making: the number of commitments as identified from all official documents by the G20 Research Group in coordination with the Higher School of Economics.

d. Delivery: measured on a scale from −1 to +1, −1 indicating no compliance and +1 indicating full compliance. A commitment is fully complied with if a member succeeds in achieving the specific goal set out in the commitment. *2012 score is from the interim compliance report.

e. Development of Global Governance: internal refers to the number of references to G20 institutions in the official documents; the spread indicates how many different internal institutions were mentioned. The number of external references includes the number of references made to institutions outside the G20 and the spread indicates how many different institutions were mentioned.

## Appendix B  G20 Compliance Averages 2008—2012
### Caroline Bracht July 16, 2013
### N=90

| N=90 | Average | Argentina | Australia | Brazil | Canada | China | France | Germany | India | Indonesia | Italy | Japan | Korea | Mexico | Russia | Saudi Arabia | South Africa | Turkey | UK | USA | EU |
|---|---|---|---|---|---|---|---|---|---|---|---|---|---|---|---|---|---|---|---|---|---|
| Washington, 2008 (N=4) | 0.66 | 0.25 | 0.75 | 1.00 | 0.75 | 0.25 | 0.75 | 1.00 | 0.25 | 0.50 | 0.75 | 0.75 | 0.67 | 0.50 | 0.50 | 0.33 | 0.75 | 0.67 | 1.00 | 0.75 | 1.00 |
| London, 2009 (N=6) | 0.17 | -0.67 | 0.50 | 0.00 | 0.50 | -0.17 | 0.67 | 0.67 | -0.50 | -0.33 | 0.00 | 0.17 | 0.17 | 0.00 | 0.17 | 0.17 | 0.33 | 0.00 | 0.83 | 0.17 | 0.67 |
| Pittsburgh, 2009 (N=15) | 0.31 | -0.08 | 0.43 | -0.14 | 0.60 | 0.36 | 0.73 | 0.69 | -0.14 | -0.14 | 0.08 | 0.62 | 0.54 | 0.43 | 0.13 | -0.21 | 0.62 | 0.14 | 0.87 | 0.73 | 0.38 |
| Toronto, 2010 (N=14) | 0.40 | 0.27 | 0.69 | 0.45 | 0.69 | 0.50 | 0.54 | 0.50 | 0.09 | 0.00 | 0.69 | 0.50 | 0.62 | -0.09 | 0.18 | -0.10 | 0.00 | 0.22 | 0.69 | 0.38 | 0.73 |
| Seoul, 2010 (N=35) | 0.37 | -0.03 | 0.62 | 0.27 | 0.57 | 0.30 | 0.59 | 0.64 | 0.36 | 0.22 | 0.47 | 0.29 | 0.56 | 0.09 | 0.13 | 0.06 | 0.25 | 0.26 | 0.75 | 0.36 | 0.63 |
| Cannes, 2011 (N=16) | 0.54 | 0.00 | 0.67 | 0.60 | 0.73 | 0.53 | 0.60 | 0.67 | 0.60 | 0.14 | 0.80 | 0.47 | 0.60 | 0.67 | 0.60 | 0.21 | 0.47 | 0.20 | 0.67 | 0.73 | 0.85 |
| Overall Compliance Average | 0.40 | -0.02 | 0.60 | 0.29 | 0.63 | 0.35 | 0.62 | 0.65 | 0.22 | 0.09 | 0.49 | 0.42 | 0.55 | 0.24 | 0.24 | 0.04 | 0.35 | 0.22 | 0.76 | 0.50 | 0.66 |
| G8 Average Score | 0.53 | | | | | | | | | | | | | | | | | | | | |
| Non-G8 Average | 0.27 | | | China | | | | | | | | | | | | | | | | | |

Appendix C  20 Compliance Averages by Issue 2008—2012
Caroline Bracht July 16, 2013
N=90

| N=90 | Average | Argentina | Australia | Brazil | Canada | China | France | Germany | India | Indonesia | Italy | Japan | Korea | Mexico | Russia | Saudi Arabia | South Africa | Turkey | UK | USA | EU |
|---|---|---|---|---|---|---|---|---|---|---|---|---|---|---|---|---|---|---|---|---|---|
| Macro (12) | 0.60 | 0.63 | 0.90 | 0.14 | 1.00 | 0.63 | 0.60 | 0.90 | 0.57 | 0.38 | 0.50 | 0.30 | 0.67 | 0.38 | 0.88 | 0.50 | 0.43 | 0.57 | 0.90 | 0.30 | 0.71 |
| Trade (6) | 0.24 | -0.50 | 0.67 | -0.17 | 0.67 | 0.00 | 0.50 | 0.67 | -0.50 | -0.50 | 0.83 | 0.50 | 0.80 | 0.00 | -0.67 | 0.60 | 0.33 | 0.20 | 0.83 | -0.17 | 0.83 |
| Financial Regulation (12) | 0.50 | -0.17 | 0.75 | 0.45 | 0.67 | 0.50 | 0.92 | 0.92 | 0.42 | 0.18 | 0.67 | 0.73 | 0.50 | 0.36 | 0.33 | -0.08 | 0.33 | 0.00 | 0.92 | 0.58 | 0.92 |
| Development (33) | 0.32 | -0.16 | 0.52 | 0.16 | 0.61 | 0.23 | 0.56 | 0.70 | 0.13 | 0.00 | 0.32 | 0.35 | 0.41 | -0.03 | 0.10 | 0.06 | 0.23 | 0.20 | 0.83 | 0.52 | 0.62 |
| Climate Change (5) | 0.37 | 0.33 | 0.60 | 0.20 | 0.40 | 0.80 | 0.40 | 0.40 | 0.40 | 0.00 | 0.50 | 0.40 |  | 0.20 | 0.00 | -0.50 | 0.00 | 0.00 | 0.60 | 0.40 | 1.00 |
| Energy (9) | 0.54 | 0.22 | 0.67 | 0.67 | 0.44 | 0.56 | 0.89 | 0.50 | 0.44 | 0.33 | 0.75 | 0.78 | 0.89 | 0.78 | 0.33 | -0.13 | 0.67 | 0.13 | 0.78 | 0.67 | 0.25 |
| Corruption (4) | 0.19 | 0.00 | 0.25 | 0.50 | 0.50 | 0.25 | 0.25 | -0.25 | -0.50 | 0.25 | 0.00 | -0.50 | 0.25 | 0.50 | 0.25 | -0.75 | 0.75 | 0.25 | 0.75 | 0.50 | 0.50 |
| IFI reform (3) | 0.47 | -0.67 | 0.67 | 0.33 | 0.33 | 0.33 | 1.00 | 1.00 | 0.33 | 0.00 | 0.67 | 1.00 | 1.00 | 0.33 | 0.33 | 0.00 | 0.67 | 0.33 | 0.33 | 1.00 | 0.67 |
| Food and Agriculture (3) | 0.45 | 0.33 | 0.67 | 1.00 | 1.00 | -0.33 | 0.67 | 0.33 | 0.67 | 0.33 | 0.67 | 0.00 | 0.33 | 0.33 | 0.67 | 0.00 | 0.00 | 0.67 | 0.00 | 1.00 | 0.67 |
| International Cooperation (2) | 0.15 | 0.00 | 0.00 | 0.00 | 0.00 | 0.00 | 0.00 | 0.00 | 0.00 | 0.50 | 0.00 | 0.00 | 0.50 | 0.50 | 1.00 | 0.00 | 0.00 | 0.00 | 0.50 | 0.00 | 0.00 |
| Socioeconomic (1) | 0.70 | 1.00 | 0.00 | 1.00 | 1.00 | 1.00 | 0.00 | 1.00 | 1.00 | -1.00 | 1.00 | 1.00 | 0.00 | 1.00 | 1.00 | 0.00 | 1.00 | 1.00 | 1.00 | 1.00 | 1.00 |
| Overall Average | 0.40 | -0.02 | 0.60 | 0.29 | 0.63 | 0.35 | 0.62 | 0.65 | 0.22 | 0.09 | 0.49 | 0.42 | 0.55 | 0.24 | 0.24 | 0.04 | 0.35 | 0.22 | 0.78 | 0.49 | 0.66 |
| G8 Average | 0.53 |  |  |  |  |  |  |  |  |  |  |  |  |  |  |  |  |  |  |  |  |
| Non-G8 Average | 0.27 |  |  |  |  |  |  |  |  |  |  |  |  |  |  |  |  |  |  |  |  |

# Part 4
## G20 Think Tanks: *Joint Statement*

# "Great Finance, Great Cooperation, Great Governance" International Think Tank Conference: *Joint Statement*

1) We, leading experts from G20 members' Think Tanks, convened in Beijing on the 21st and 22nd of August, 2013, held the "Great Finance, Great Cooperation, Great Governance" International Think Tank Conference, and embarked on the establishment of an international network to deepen communication among G20 members and participants to contribute new ideas for the effective use of this important institution.
2) The global economy is recovering, but still faces several challenges. Economic growth remains weak and lacks new sources of strength. Increasing employment still faces great difficulties.
3) We call for G20 members to continue to strengthen research on international macroeconomic and financial policy reform, and to better include voices from developing countries.
4) We call on G20 members to pay close attention to financial markets and the international monetary system, to place the global economy on a path of sustainable growth and prosperity. This should be an important objective when coordinating economic policy and research among different economies.
5) We call on G20 member Think Tanks to strengthen their cooperation and research on the following issues.

a. International macro economic coordination.
b. International coordination to prevent excessive leveraging in financial markets and reduce the risk of financial crises.
c. Technologies for sustainable economic growth.
d. Causes and consequences of price fluctuations in financial and commodity markets.
e. Trade and investment liberalization.
f. Anti-money laundering mechanisms.
g. Measures to enhance transparency and competition between credit rating agencies.
h. International cooperation on financial education and a consumer protection agenda.
i. Access to financial services for impoverished populations.
j. Tax regime and tax evasion.
k. Anti-corruption measures.
l. International capital flows.
m. Interrelation of social, economic, and environment issues.

# Afterword:
# Think Tanks, Public Diplomacy and the Chinese Dream

*Wang Wen*

The essays published in this volume are a selection of the best research on the G20 submitted for the "Great Finance, Great Cooperation, Great Governance" international think tank conference, hosted by Renmin University of China and organized by Renmin University of China Chongyang Institute for Financial Studies. This conference received much attention from both the media and academia. The reviews included a lot of "firsts"; "the first G20 think tank conference in China"; "the first G20 think tank joint statement passed with China's leadership"; "Chinese think tanks show an international appeal". As the executive dean of the organizing institution for this conference, aside from expressing my deep gratitude for the enormous support we received from all of the participants, attendees and reviewers, it is important that I say a few words about the role think tanks play in public diplomacy and their relationship with the Chinese Dream.

While developing socialism with Chinese characteristics and pursuing the Chinese dream, we must be at all times grounded in our experience with reform, recognize reality and plan for development in the future. China needs to build a group of high-level think tanks to advance practical innovation for socialism with Chinese characteristics and to provide a knowledge base to support theoretical and institutional innovation. At the same time there is a need to utilize these think tanks as an effective platform for international communication. China can bring in knowledge from around the world to aid its own development and also influence other societies by diffusing Chinese ideas through public diplomacy.

From this perspective, the "Great Finance, Great Cooperation, Great Governance" G20 think tank conference is an extremely meaningful development. About two weeks before the G20 Leaders' Summit, representatives from think tanks from every G20 member were present and submitted research papers expressing their positions and ideas, providing much insight into the future development of the G20.

Within these papers submitted by world-class think tank scholars, we can feel the disagreement and worry they have over world governance, their concern and reflection over the G20 system and their assessments and suggestions for the role of emerging economies.

An important item to note is that we also clearly see the hope and desire of every G20 member for China to play a larger role in this forum. Without a doubt, the opinions presented here are an important survey of the contemporary world and an important evaluation of the international order.

The G20 is an important platform for leaders from developed and developing nations to consult and negotiate with each other on matters of international economic affairs. Underpinning the G20 platform there needs to be a track and two platforms for think tanks to communicate. As China and the world further integrate together, the role of public diplomacy through think tanks will need to grow, similar to the way the Shanghai Cooperation Organization, BRICS, and APEC should also establish more platforms for think tank communication. I hope that this G20 think tank conference has made a contribution to and provided more inspiration for building "new think tanks with Chinese characteristics" and realizing the "Chinese Dream".

(The author is the Executive Dean of Renmin University of China Chongyang Institute for Financial Studies)

***ibidem*-**Verlag

Melchiorstr. 15

D-70439 Stuttgart

info@ibidem-verlag.de

www.ibidem-verlag.de
www.ibidem.eu
www.edition-noema.de
www.autorenbetreuung.de